Contemporary Women's

Contemporary Women's Poetry

Reading/Writing/Practice

Edited by

Alison Mark
University of Luton

and

Deryn Rees-Jones
Liverpool Hope University College

First published in Great Britain 2000 by
MACMILLAN PRESS LTD
Houndmills, Basingstoke, Hampshire RG21 6XS and London
Companies and representatives throughout the world

A catalogue record for this book is available from the British Library.

ISBN 0–333–73437–8 hardcover
ISBN 0–333–73438–6 paperback

First published in the United States of America 2000 by
ST. MARTIN'S PRESS, LLC,
Scholarly and Reference Division,
175 Fifth Avenue, New York, N.Y. 10010

ISBN 0–312–23535–6

Library of Congress Cataloging-in-Publication Data
Contemporary women's poetry : reading, writing, practice / edited by Alison Mark
and Deryn Rees-Jones
p.   cm.
Includes bibliographical references and index.
ISBN 0–312–23535–6
1. English poetry—Women authors—History and criticism. 2. English poetry–
–20th century—History and criticism. 3. Poetry—Authorship. 4. Women and
literature—Great Britain—History—20th century. 5. Women poets, English—20th
century—Interviews. 6. American poetry—20th century—History and criticism. 7.
American poetry—Women authors—History and criticism. 8. Women and
literature—United States—History—20th century. 9. Women poets, American–
–20th century—Interviews. I. Mark, Alison, 1949– II. Rees-Jones, Deryn.

PR605.W6 C66   2000
821'.914099287—dc21

00–035394

Selection and editorial matter © Alison Mark and Deryn Rees-Jones 2000
Chapters 1–9 © the various contributors 2000
Chapter 10 © Deryn Rees-Jones 2000
Chapter 11 © Alison Mark 2000
Chapters 12–21 © Macmillan Press Ltd 2000

This book is printed on paper suitable for recycling and made from fully managed and sustained
forest sources.

10   9   8   7   6   5   4   3   2   1
09   08   07   06   05   04   03   02   01   00

Printed and bound in Great Britain by Antony Rowe Ltd, Chippenham, Wiltshire

for David, for Michael,
and
for our mothers, Mary and Angela

Contents

Acknowledgements

Our thanks to our institutions and colleagues, past and present, particularly Maureen Moran and Terry Phillips. Alison Mark is particularly grateful for the assistance received from Brunel University while she was working on this project. We would also like to thank Ian Gregson and Dave Smith for information and support at an early stage, and Charmian Hearne for her editorial enthusiasm for the book.

Copyright Permissions

The editors and contributors would like to thank the following for granting copyright permissions:

Anvil Press Poetry for permission to quote from Carol Ann Duffy's *Mean Time*, *The Other Country*, *Selling Manhattan* and *Standing Female Nude*.

Rachel Blau DuPlessis for kind permission to quote from *Tabula Rosa*, *Drafts 3–14* and *The Pink Guitar: Writing as Feminist Practice*.

Bloodaxe Books for permission to quote from Kathleen Jamie's *The Queen of Sheba* and Jackie Kay's *Off Colour*, *Other Lovers*, and *The Adoption Papers*.

Mei-Mei Berssenbrugge for kind permission to quote from *The Heat Bird*.

Nicole Brossard for kind permission to quote from *Lovhers*.

Carcanet Press for permission to quote from Eavan Boland's *The Lost Land*, *In a Time of Violence*, *Outside History* and *The Journey and Other Poems*.

Peter Fallon of Gallery Press for quotations from the work of Medbh McGuckian.

Fanny Howe for kind permission for all quotations from *O'Clock*.

Thanks also to Tim Kendall and *Thumbscrew*, where 'Defending the Freedom of the Poet' first appeared.

Methuen for permission to quote from Ntozake Shange's *for colored girls who have considered suicide when the rainbow is enuf*.

New Directions Publishing Corporation for permission to quote from 'On the Edge of Darkness' from *Light Up the Cave*, copyright © 1981 by Denise Levertov, and *New and Selected Essays*, copyright © 1992 by Denise Levertov.

Frances Presley for kind permission to quote from *Hula Hoop* and *Linocut*.

Reality Street Editions and the author for extracts from *Mop Mop Georgette*.

Denise Riley for permission to quote from her work.

Random House for permission to quote from Sharon Olds's *Sign of Saturn* (Secker and Warburg) and *The Father* (Secker and Warburg).

Routledge for permission to reproduce material from 'Postcolonialism in the Poetry and Essays of Eavan Boland', by Rose Atfield, which first appeared in *Women: A Cultural Review*.

Carol Rumens for kind permission to quote from *Best China Sky* and *Thinking of Skins*.

Thanks also to Peter Quartermain and *West Coast Line* where *riverrunning (realisations* first appeared.

Rosemarie Waldrop for kind permission to quote from *Lawn of Excluded Middle*.

The editors and contributors have made every effort to obtain permissions from all copyright holders. If any proper acknowledgement has not been made, or permission not received, we would ask you to inform us of this oversight, and we will do our best to remedy it swiftly.

Contributors

Moniza Alvi was born in Pakistan in 1954, and grew up in Hertfordshire. Her first collection, *The Country at My Shoulder* (1993), was shortlisted for the T.S. Eliot and Whitbread poetry prizes, and *A Bowl of Warm Air* was published in 1996.

Rose Atfield is a Lecturer at Brunel University, where she hopes shortly to establish a new MA in Creative Writing. Following her doctoral thesis on Seamus Heaney, she has worked on contemporary Irish women's poetry.

Helen Carr is a Reader in English at Goldsmiths College, University of London, and a co-editor of *Women: A Cultural Review*. Her books include *Inventing the American Primitive: Politics, Gender, and the Representation of Native American Literary Traditions, 1789–1936*, and *Jean Rhys*.

U.A. Fanthorpe, FRSL, was educated at Oxford, taught English at Cheltenham, and was a hospital receptionist in Bristol. She has been writer in residence at various universities, and has been a freelance poet since 1989. Her most recent works are the collection *Safe as Houses* (1995) and (with R.V. Bailey) the audiobook *Double Act* (1997).

Vicki Feaver's collections are *Close Relatives* (1981) and *The Handless Maiden* (1994). She is a Lecturer in English and Creative Writing at the West Sussex Institute, and was one of the judges of the New Generation in 1993.

Selima Hill's *Violet* (1998) was nominated for the Whitbread, T.S. Eliot, and Forward prizes; her eighth collection, *Bunny*, is forthcoming. She is currently working at Greenham Common and the Poetry Library, South Bank Centre.

Linda A. Kinnahan lives in Pittsburgh, Pennsylvania, USA. An Associate Professor of English at Duquesne University, she has published numerous articles on twentieth-century American and British poets and a book, *Poetics of the Feminine: Literary Tradition and Authority in William Carlos Williams, Mina Loy, Denise Levertov, and Kathleen Fraser*. She is currently exploring connections between language innovation, ideas of economics, and women's poetry in the modernist and contemporary periods.

Gwyneth Lewis was educated at Oxford, Cambridge and Harvard. She writes in both Welsh and English. Her collections in Welsh include *Sonedau Redsa* (Gwasg Gomer, 1990) and *Cyfrif Un ac Un yn Dri* (Cyhoeddiadau Barddas, 1996); and her first collection in English, *Parables and Faxes* (1995), was shortlisted for a Forward Prize and won the Aldeburgh Prize. *Zero Gravity* (1998) was again shortlisted for a Forward Prize, and is currently being filmed.

Marion Lomax is the pen-name of Robyn Bolam, Professor of Literature at St Mary's, Strawberry Hill. She is currently working on an anthology of three centuries of women poets. Publications include *Stage Images and Traditions* (1987), editions of plays by John Ford and Aphra Behn (1995), and two poetry collections, *The Peepshow Girl* (1989), and *Raiding the Borders* (1996).

Alison Mark has written on a range of literary and cultural subjects including the law, psychoanalysis, and poetry. *Veronica Forrest-Thomson and Language Poetry* and an afterword to the *Selected Poems of Veronica Forrest-Thomson* are forthcoming, and future projects include a book on psychoanalytic criticism. She is a Lecturer in English at the University of Luton, and assistant editor of *Women: A Cultural Review*.

Janet Montefiore is the author of *Feminism and Poetry*, *Men and Women Writers of the 1930s: The Dangerous Flood of History*, and numerous essays on twentieth-century literature and critical theory. She lectures on English and Women's Studies at the University of Kent.

Maggie O'Sullivan, whose collections of poetry include *In the House of the Shaman* and *Unofficial Word*, is the editor of the anthology *Out of Everywhere: Linguistically Innovative Poetry by Women in North America & the UK*.

Ruth Padel has published four collections of poetry, most recently *Rembrandt Would Have Loved You*, and won the 1996 National Poetry Competition. She reviews for the *New York Times*, writes the *Independent on Sunday* 'Sunday Poem' column, has written two books on ancient Greece, and is finishing one on rock music and Greek myth.

Deryn Rees-Jones had her first collection, *The Memory Tray*, shortlisted for a Forward prize in 1995, and received an Arts Council Writer's award in 1996. *Signs Round a Dead Body* was published in 1998. She is Reader in Poetry at Liverpool Hope University College. Her monograph, *Carol Ann Duffy*, was published in 1999, and *Consorting with Angels: Modern Women Poets* is forthcoming.

Jo Shapcott is the only person to have won the National Poetry Competition twice. Her books include *Electroplating the Baby* (1988), *Phrase Book* (1992) and *My Life Asleep* (1998). She is the editor, with Matthew Sweeney, of *Emergency Kit: Poems for Strange Times* (1997).

Anne Stevenson's ten collections of poetry include *Correspondences*, *The Fiction Makers*, *Four and a Half Dancing Men*, and *Collected Poems* (1996). The author of *Bitter Fame: A Life of Sylvia Plath* (1989) and she has recently brought out *Five Looks at Elizabeth Bishop* (1998) and *Between the Iceberg and the Ship: Selected Essays*. One of the founding editors of *Other Poetry* and recipient of the University of Michigan's Athena Award (1990), she now lives in Durham, England, and in North Wales.

Harriet Tarlo lectures at Bretton Hall College, University of Leeds. Her essays on modernist and contemporary poetry have appeared in *Fragmente*, *Gramma*, *Sagetrieb*, *Feminist Review*, and *Kicking Daffodils: Twentieth-Century Women Poets* (1997). Her poetry appears in publications by The Other Press, Reality Street Editions, and Etruscan Books.

Carol Watts is a Lecturer in English at Birkbeck College, University of London. She has published on a wide range of literary, film and philosophical subjects, and is the author of *Dorothy Richardson*.

Susan Wicks's most recent collection, *The Clever Daughter* (1997) was a Poetry Book Society Choice and shortlisted for both Forward and T.S. Eliot prizes. She is also the author of *Driving My Father* (1996), and of two novels.

Clair Wills is a Lecturer in English at Queen Mary and Westfield College, University of London. She has written widely on contemporary Irish, English and American poetry. Her most recent book is *Reading Paul Muldoon* (1998).

Joanne Winning is a Lecturer in Twentieth-Century Literature at Middlesex University. Her interests centre on the relations between writing, gender, sexuality and race in the twentieth century. Her publications include *The Crazy Jig: Lesbian and Gay Writing from Scotland* (1992), *Archive of the Self: Reading Lesbian Modernism Through Dorothy Richardson's 'Pilgrimage'* (forthcoming), and articles on Richardson, Bryher and Radclyffe Hall.

Preface

This collection can be thought of as a collage of voices. The voices of women poets, speaking about the way they write, are juxtaposed with those of critics writing about women's poetry. Though the poets' meditations begin this volume, the editors have deliberately refused to break up the sequence of essays according to the distinct categories of poet and critic: 'writing poems is a way of knowing about knowing', a form in symbiotic relation to critical activity, Deryn Rees-Jones insists (p. 61). A collage respects but relates different materials, refusing to classify them – poetry, criticism.

I also find the oxymoronic notion of a sound collage apposite because contemporary poetry persuades us to listen with the eye, see with the ear. It engages with the aural and the visual. The form and shape of words, heard as well as seen on the page, is paramount for very different poets, from Maggie O'Sullivan, whose haunting experiments with verbal installations make words into particles of sound as well as blocks of material we have to see from all angles, as if walking round them, to Anne Stevenson, who is preoccupied with the potential of rhythm and metre to structure speech rhythms.

Enquiries into poetic language among the poets, enquiries about what language can do, how words are to be used, are sometimes anxious and sometimes celebratory. But such enquiries are nearly all connected with what it means to write as a woman today. These questions are just as intensely shared by the critics writing here. Concern with language and its possibilities is linked with a desire to complicate what have become some of the orthodoxies of feminist identity politics without losing sight of the connections between writing and gender in our culture. It is no longer tenable to hold that there is a specifically 'feminine' language, and with the disappearance of this essentialism has also come a sense that the politics of gender have become progressively more complex. The idiom of confrontation has long since lapsed. Nevertheless, what it means to write as a female lyric poet, explored problematically rather than polemically, is the concern of poets and critics alike.

Poets are 'always suspects', Gwyneth Lewis writes (p. 24), and perhaps a woman poet more than others, but what authorises the woman poet? 'You have to grant yourself the authority to do it,' is

Selima Hill's answer. '[Y]ou need to be obsessed' (p. 26) and to be willing to be responsive to linguistic promptings, entering into what Maggie O'Sullivan calls a 'Tonguescape' (p. 52). Poets speak constantly of this willingness to be led and connect it with their deepest creativity. Perhaps this porousness is more characteristic of women than men in our culture today. They describe themselves, for instance, as being led by a rhythm: 'I think I start with a rhythm ... I'm not one of those A–B sort of poets' (Hill, p. 27); 'We are born rhythmic' (Stevenson, p. 4); 'A scrap of a phrase or rhythm and image, maybe just a word' (Ruth Padel, p. 12). For Susan Wicks the core of poetic language is syntax and the jolt across the threshold that line-breaks produce for the reader (p. 19). Rhythm and syntax are both about words felt viscerally, heard and seen.

For some poets, writing as a woman means thinking about what makes their work different from that of male poets. Freeing the tongue from male traditions is one of O'Sullivan's projects, and avoiding a 'taboo' on tenderness preoccupies Hill (p. 30). Padel, Wicks and Hill all speculate on the subtle forms that women's writing takes. Padel struggles with what it is to be a woman writing but knows that some women may be made 'cross' by the themes of her work (p. 17). Wicks refuses to have subject-matter and language 'proscribed' for her: her subjects may seem superficially women's subjects, yet the point is not the subject but the way she questions the subject (24). Hill speculates that men's poetry may be 'more about words' (p. 28) than the affective 'colours' she works with in her poems (p. 27).

Yet for other poets writing as a woman means not so much differentiating oneself from male poets as breaking with linguistic norms. Jo Shapcott's frustration with the unvaried 'vowel meadows' (p. 41) of Hemel Hempstead new town, where she grew up, prompted her to write that 'Language is impossible/in a country like this' (p. 44). A search for a voice other than the flattened tones of her young womanhood sent her to North America. She did not see why she should conform to some quintessential norm of the Englishwoman's language, and sought out the Canadian-North American poet Elizabeth Bishop in order to explore new idioms in shifting territories. Just as Shapcott questions the category of the *English* woman, so Moniza Alvi craves 'different voices' (p. 39). Her ambiguous status as a British Asian, intensely British when returning to Pakistan but almost an 'imposter', she felt, as a 'Black writer' in Britain (p. 37), has led her to explore models of writing that are multicultural and 'vibrant' in their *diverse* exploration of mixed race experience. For her the woman poet is characterised by multiple voices. The same is strue of U. A. Fanthorpe, who 'tipped over into poetry' (p. 33) in the attempt to represent the multiple registers of language in the little world of the hospital. The doctor's technical language ('the predictable, bloodless, polysyllabic sounds' (p. 34)), so easy to wield as the agent of mystification, and yet oddly beautiful, and the patient's local vernacular, made her a 'jackdaw' of languages, not a univocal writer of lyric.

Above all, this self-conscious concern with the multiple forms of language arises from a need not to be trapped inside the expressive self of the female subject but the obligation, *as a female subject*, to release the lyric 'I' from the trap of a narrow identity politics. The result is that one refuses one's own subjectivity as the central theme of the poem. At one extreme of this refusal of self are Maggie O'Sullivan's lapidary poems, where the potentials in sound and language are sought in the tonguescape not simply of human but of animal and other sounds. Hers is an ecopoetics, an open field of sound, aware that the human self is not at the world's centre. At the other pole of the refusal of ego is Deryn Rees-Jones's search for a non-dyadic lyric that will dramatise the lived-with public world of the self.

Perhaps it is this repudiation of the central lyric 'I' that makes the poets represented here very catholic in their response to other poets, male and female. Influence is neither a matter of egocentric seizure nor a sense of being dominated. Keats and Shakespeare are freely acknowledged by Wicks and by Stevenson as creators of poetic traditions to which they belong, though for Anne Stevenson this affiliation becomes an affirmation of cultural centrality that avoids the restrictive label of woman poet. Chaucer, Shakespeare and Wordsworth are for Fanthorpe her natural models. Paul Muldoon is important for Rees-Jones and for Padel. And most poets name female contemporaries, often Carol Anne Duffy, as a vital influence.

To turn to the critics, there is a remarkable continuity between the preoccupations of poets and critics. Alison Mark begins the critical debate by imagining the poetry of 'many different voices' (p. 68) that linguistically investigative poets can achive. Her theme is the significance of the Language poets, whose aesthetic depends on a writing that 'deliberately leaves the subject out of sight' (p. 66). Though Charles Bernstein is Language poetry's best-known exponent, the poetics of Gertrude Stein (who believed in 'knowing and feeling a name') and Veronica Forrest-Thomson (who was fascinated by the power of the non-signifying elements of language) lie behind Language poetry. The book concludes with Harriet Tarlo's meticulous analysis of the virtuosic way a group of American women poets, Rachel Blau Du Plessis and others, handle 'the sexed pronoun' (p. 262) or 'female shifter', 'she'. This essay is an index of the distance critical debate has moved since the early days of gender politics. Tarlo shows how a sophisticated experiment with subtle reconfigurations of pronouns – to name an obvious strategy that dramatises the process, expressing the subject as I and i, for instance – avoids essentialism and remakes these tiny particles as vehicles that can represent women as subjects. The subject here is less left 'out of sight', in Marks's phrase, than radically repositioned, a move that accomplishes the same work by refusing the sovereign status of the self.

Carol Watts's discussion of Denise Riley's work is another demonstration of the remaking of language that goes on in the attempt to circumvent identity politics and escape from the 'prison house of language' that structures the female subject (p. 60). When Riley revolutionises pronouns by writing of a 'she-husband' or of 'her wife' (p. 159), she is offering not representation but syntax as a way of organising a new subjectivity. In her later work she explores the 'grammar of power' (p. 165) to identify, not a power struggle between sovereign female self over and against a hostile world, but a 'phenomenological drama' in which female interiority is itself part of a field of cultural meaning, leading to a profound sense of disjunction between lived body and the perceived world. Clair Wills also rejects the opposition of lyrical against 'anti-subjectivist' poetry (p. 119) as too simple for the work of Fanny Howe and Medbh McGuckian. Yet Howe's solution to such polarisation is not the materialist drama adopted by Riley. It is to explore the possibility of transcendence in a world ruled by syntax, which is for her the linguistic manifestation of a teleology of time. Words, whose order cannot be disrupted without the breakdown of sense, are 'an image of the pressure of temporality' (p. 121). Language as prison house or liberation becomes the dilemma experienced by very different poets.

How far it is ever possible or even appropriate to avoid the defining traditions of patriarchal language and culture is an issue for many writers. In an essay that offers a dissenting voice in the sensitive area of lesbian aesthetics, Jan Montefiore argues that Adrienne Rich's quest for a self-sustaining female culture is a flawed project. The beauty of a lesbian poetics that slips the noose of masculine culture can never be the pure enterprise it purports to be. The very need to define lesbian experience against patriarchal values reintroduces masculine culture and shows it to be *constitutive* of this form of lesbian poetics. Implicitly

Montefiore argues against reifying masculine culture and then throwing it out. And she is right to the extent that many of the essays in this volume show female poets as constantly testing themselves against masculine traditions and texts, redefining these for themselves. Marion Lomax's lovely analysis of Carol Rumens's 'Thirst for Green', a poem that tests itself against Philip Larkin's 'The Trees', shows how productive such intertextual conversation can be. Rumens defines thirst, 'a desperate, basic need' (p. 177), against Larkin's understanding of the narrow Irish republicanism signified by the colour green. Though doomed elms, in the grip of 'an old disease', come to represent the state of Ireland, Rumens's poem refuses the sectarianism that is at the centre of Larkins's critique of Irish politics.

For both Carol Rumens and Denise Levertov, Lomax says, political poetry, as represented by poets like Neruda, 'is more emotional than any other'. For most writers in this book political poetry means not confrontation but analysis that stems from both mind and emotions. Political poetry prompts a deep questioning of identity and affiliation. Rumens finds that she can be neither British nor European nor English. The dispossessed, the figure of the immigrant or the refugee, becomes an insistent subject for women's poetry. Women poets adopt multiple identities and selfhoods, and many voices and registers, in the effort to escape from a single national identity, become stateless, even alien, in order to record a history of oppression. Interestingly, this is not a narcissistic 'herstory' but an analysis of forgotten or invisible socal exclusion. Rose Atfield shows how Eavan Boland negotiates the double difficulty of coming in 'at an angle' (p. 189) to both the English language and Irish poetic tradition. A rigorous mapping of colonisation in the marks on a landscape – the forgotten, unfinished famine roads built by unemployed labourers in the nineteenth century – or in the origins of material objects such as the silver heirloom that resulted from 'wounding an artery of rock' (196) is Bolan's response to the violence of history. Joanne Winning explores the way two poets outside Scottish national identity, Kathleen Jamie and Jackie Kay, adopt multiple voices and the comedy of dialect in order to deconstruct Scottish masculinity, the black Scottish girl (Kay), for instance, or a harriden's dialect (Jamie). Exiles and outsiders belong to their poetic landscapes. The questions, 'Where do you come from? Where's home?' (p. 235), with their implicit accusation of racial difference as a failure to belong, dominate both poets' work. A similar dramatisation of the language of exile is the theme of Linda Kinnahan's essay on Carol Ann Duffy. She shows up the deeply sombre elements, often overlooked, of Duffy's work as critique of 'the discourse of nation' (p. 209) for which the test case is the immigrant. The words 'home', 'alien', 'foreigner' point up the inherently 'restrictive definition of citizenship' (p. 209) at work in postwar British society. It is drama and the dramatic monologue that enables Duffy to analyse such language from the inside, as it affects psychic life at the level of everyday experience. The immigrant who is forced to think in one language and talk in another, or the woman of 'Mrs Skinner, North Street', whose racist bitterness has misrecognised 'the discursive construction of the foreigner' (p. 217) as an explanation for her own dispossession, are brought to us through Duffy's finely self-effacing dramatisations.

Finally, the idea of the contemporary woman's poem as a healing force or a form of reparation is strongly present in this collection. For Deryn Rees-Jones the poem is both a loss (because experience is externalised) and the attempt to repair it. Wills thinks of metaphor as a healing process for McGuckian. Vicky Feaver explores the 'metaphorical transformation' of pain (p. 140) – here the suffering of sexual abuse in the poetry of Sharon Olds – that can be achieved when the distancing of metaphor allows for an impersonal release into the body instead of a hysterical or violent response to the physical. Helen Carr writes of the importance for women's writing of Native American oral poetry. Outside the western tradition, this 'sub-literary poetry' (p. 79) by women claims a value for individual subjectivity and desire without making their identity as women a priority. This is because these Shamanic oral texts drawn on traditional discourses that have found communal forms and idioms for exploring the liminal subject, for describing extremities of experience, going to the depths and back, and above all for using the power of ritual to transform those who participate in it. Ritual in this oral poetry is an intensely social, *performative* process, in which words actually bring about transformation through narratives of change. Poetry is a collaborative act between poet and listener.

At the conclusion of her essay Rose Atfield reminds us of Mary Robinson's punning aphorism about feminist politics. The hand that rocks the cradle can rock the system (p. 206). Contemporary women's poetry today negotiates and questions both meanings of this pun rather than choosing a single way of 'rocking' the world.

Isobel Armstrong

Introduction:
Looking On, Looking Back

In its examination of the relationship between women and poetry in the 1990s, this book attempts the difficult balancing act of seeking to emphasise the significance of poetry by women while also trying to interrogate rigid demarcations of gender and genre. At all stages we have been confronted by a range of questions which the essays, rather than answer bring into sharper focus. These questions include: the nature and importance of women's poetry; its diversity; the recurrent themes which preoccupy women poets writing today; and in particular the ways in which women's poetry is read by women critics. The contributions are arranged in two successive sequences of essays: poets on their writing process, and critics on poetry and poetics. These categories are by no means mutually exclusive, as is evident from the fact that several of the poets, while writing here predominantly on the subject of writing, are also academics and literary critics, and a number of the critics are themselves recognised as poets. The problematic bifurcation of 'creative' and 'critical' writing has long been challenged by the work of many of the women writing here.

Not all of our contributors would identify themselves as feminist, although inevitably their work is informed by the results of feminist activism, debate about the role and nature of women, and definitions of the feminine. Nor would all accept the designation 'woman poet'. Certain of the poets included are highly valued by what might be called the 'mainstream' (predominantly male) tradition and are anthologised within it; sometimes, and occasionally surprisingly, others are not. This tradition is not by any means as homogeneous or monolithic as the term might suggest, but all the same – and however it is described – it is a powerful discursive institution. Confronting the question of the importance of, or the need for, a collection of essays exclusively on women's poetry at this juncture was inevitably central to the enterprise.

Resistance to the constraints of a gendered positioning has led some poets, like Elizabeth Bishop and Sheenagh Pugh, to refuse or restrict their inclusion in women-only anthologies, or to argue that the very promotion of a collective identity inevitably creates a situation out of which it is difficult for the individual poets, with their diverse aesthetics and wide range of interests and work, to emerge. Recent anxieties regarding the gender, class, and sexuality of prospective poet laureates demonstrate that it is still impossible for poets to rely on the quality of their work – by whomever this is to be assessed – to ensure their representation. However, there is a considerable difference between the situations obtaining in poetry itself and in its criticism.

Currently, within the field of contemporary poetry, women's work tends to be far less prolifically interpreted, mediated, and analysed than that of men. It is worth the evident risks of reinscribing gender divisions or perpetuating the category of 'woman poet', in order to provide a critical perspective on the work of a range of women whose work is in the main critically neglected. And not just so that this work is represented, but as part of a wider project to promulgate a more diverse range of critical engagements than exist at present: the reading and writing of poetry by women solely in gender terms may give us a prescription but not a remedy. Poetry by women needs to be read not only in relation to wider poetic traditions and resistances, but also in conjunction with the work of male poets, and by critics who take account of these issues in all their complexities. Unless poetry by women is read seriously in all these ways, it is hard to envisage how contemporary poetry can develop beyond the current inherited paradigms and imagined parameters.

The varieties of poetry considered here are diverse, and the range of approaches to those poetries and the poetics which inform them are correspondingly diverse. Many of the writers challenge established categories, some drawing on philosophy, others working more self-reflexively. In discussing American, English, Irish, Scottish and Welsh poets here, we do not underestimate cultural differences, but many of the poets represented here defy and challenge simplistic demarcations, both cultural and textual. Anne Stevenson, American by birth, now lives between North Wales and the North East of England. Fanny Howe is an American poet of Irish descent, whose heritage informs her work. The late Denise Levertov, born in England, spent most of her adult life in the United States. Eavan Boland, discussed by Rose Atfield, although born in Dublin of Irish parents, was educated in England and in the States, and Carol Rumens, who together with Levertov is the subject of Marion Lomax's essay, is an English poet who lives part of the year in Belfast.

An English poet, Vicki Feaver, reads Sharon Olds, an American poet who – together with Stevie Smith – has been an important influence on Feaver's own poetry. And the American critic Linda Kinnahan offers an interesting perspective on British racial and ethnic relations and politics in her reading of Carol Ann Duffy's work. Critic (and poet) Janet Montefiore analyses her changing relationship to the work of Adrienne Rich. Two very different poets, Kathleen Jamie and Jackie Kay, are discussed by Joanne Winning in relation to their negotiations of Scottish identity. Gwyneth Lewis, who publishes in both Welsh and English, writes a detective story as a parable for her bilingual poetic position and its discontents. In contrast to this exploration of identity through national language, Jo Shapcott discusses the potential of a nomadic sense of poetic self. Geography and its influences also appear in Moniza Alvi's essay, together with an unpicking of some of the complexities frequently elided by easy ascriptions of 'the multi-cultural' to a poet's work. Helen Carr interrogates 'the relation between lyric poetry and subjectivity, between poetic and personal identity' through her readings of oral poetry, particularly Native American, and the very different work of Boland and Amy Clampitt.

Most of the poets, like Lewis, find metaphor irresistible in delineating their own processes. Ruth Padel's analogy between writing poetry and sculpture explores the materiality of language from a different perspective than Maggie O'Sullivan's performative contribution. Susan Wicks draws attention to her need to separate the two functions of poet and critic, but revels in the exploration of the possibilities of poetic language and form: 'manipulating words successfully is for me an almost sexual experience'. U.A. Fanthorpe, on the other hand, contemplates the resonances of different registers of language in an institutional context. Poets as diverse as Stevenson and Selima Hill emphasise the centrality of rhythm to their writing practice, and Stevenson particularly talks of the dance, the march, and the body's relationship to the word. This is a connection also made by Clair Wills in her readings of Fanny Howe, a poet more frequently discussed in terms of the linguistically innovative or avant-garde, while gender, subjectivity and the avant-garde are discussed by both Harriet Tarlo and Carol Watts.

A division which many of the critics – and the poets – seek to interrogate is that between the expressive and the discursive constructions of the poetic subject, articulating the fictionality of the poetic 'I', even at its most biographical, while closely examining contextual material which attests to the historical, social, and political specificity of that 'I'.

The essays here show the diversity of two generations of women's thinking about the reading, writing and practice of poetry. The contributors have written about the work of composition, its difficulties and its rewards. They have articulated the context – background, fore-ground, cultural diversity – which informs the work under consideration, and have attempted to situate their own work, and that of others, with critical intelligence and generosity. Inevitably there are omissions, certain of which are a particular source of regret. Sometimes these have occurred through circumstances beyond our control, some-times through an understandable reluctance on the part of those who earn their living by writing to contribute to that financially under-rewarded medium, the academic book. Inclusiveness, currently in danger of becoming a fetishised concept, is always difficult to achieve.

We are delighted to be able to bring together so many kinds of writing from poets and critics who represent an important stage in the – thus far erratically read – history of poetry by women. Rather than elaborating our own particular concerns more fully here, we have placed these at the junction of the two aspects of the book where they can engage in dialogue with the other contributions, theoretical and practical. The end of the twentieth century seems a fitting moment not only to register both contemporary accomplishment and its diffi-culty, but also at least to attempt to circumvent the necessity for the next generation to 'recover' work by women. We look on as well as back.

Alison Mark and Deryn Rees-Jones

1
Defending the Freedom of the Poet/Music Under the Skin

Anne Stevenson

Defending the freedom of the poet

I sometimes suspect that I am drawn to poetry because it nurtures contradiction. Unlike the arguments from conviction that characterise the language of politics and philosophy, poetic language is essentially oxymoronic, a coinage stamped on two sides with logically irreconcilable messages. Yeats famously distinguished between rhetoric that quarrels with the world and poetry in which the poet quarrels with himself. Walt Whitman boasted that his self-contradictions contained multitudes. As served by Shakespeare and his Metaphysical successors, poetry became a legitimate, highly sophisticated form of punning. No emotion, secular or religious, was too sacred to be flipped from one side to another in the ongoing wordgame. It is precisely the lightness of George Herbert's dialogue with his God that, for me, tinges his poetry with pathos. John Donne thundered from the pulpit, 'Ask not for whom the bell tolls, it tolls for thee', but were his listeners more frightened or thrilled by the ring of his cadences? Surely they were both. The serious import of his language was at odds with the theatricality of his performance.

Four hundred years after Donne, performances still attract rapt audiences. We live, I would say, in a difficult age for creative arts but in a great era for the performing ones. Though we have spawned no Shakespeare, thanks to technologies such as video and television, Shakespeare's plays have never been more widely available or effectively staged. Mozart would have been dumbfounded by the perfectionism we take for granted when we listen to music on our CDs or gaze at his operas on the ubiquitous screen. Our precision brains that have brought about near miracles in science serve the arts mainly

1

in a secondary capacity. And our Globe Theatre, catering to all tastes, is the television, an hypnotic form of *trompe l'œil* that creates wonders of visual illusion while reducing language to sound bytes.

The degradation of language seems to be the price the gods have exacted for our hubristic presumption. Overwhelmed by a deluge of information, dumbed down by computer technology that paralyses our naked minds, our human sensibilities have been numbed and desensitised on a massive scale. It is not, as Yeats and T.S. Eliot feared might happen, that democracy and increased accessibility of the arts have corrupted the general taste. It is more that our attentiveness and capacity to judge for ourselves suffer constantly under a vast barrage of artificially created dazzle and noise. Worse, I suspect it is all but impossible today for a writer of the first magnitude to sustain success in the competitive, commercially sponsored world of the media, or even academia, without compromising that rare ability to reveal the deepest, hidden sources of human self-knowledge, the springs of wisdom of all great art. The rewards of fame, of a personality cult and, above all, of money, are just too great.

Nonsense, you protest, what about poetry? We are living witnesses today of a huge boom in poetry throughout the world! I have to disagree. In these late, decadent days of Western civilisation it is easy to pass off as poetry almost anything that labels and markets itself as such. And while contemporary genius for labelling and marketing has begotten the punning wit of advertising, it has not pulled off the Metaphysical trick of selling contemporary poetry to the common reader. What it does successfully sell are personalities or life-stories of particular poets. The media, which infiltrates every cranny of our lives, doses us all the time with biographies, opinions and emotionally charged issues while, at the same time, providing us with a set of conceptual categories in which to file them. Poetry, along with other creative arts, has become for many of its adherents an issue-linked category associated with the rectification of social evils. Poetry is rated, for example, on the basis of its attitude to cultural imperialism, or to racial persecution – and of course, very conspicuously in its attitude to women.

Without wishing to dissociate myself from the politics of feminism or from any anger at social injustice that has pricked the consciences of many people in the post-war years, as a poet I have to question the wisdom of linking poetry with political movements of any kind. In theoretical chains, poetry tends to yield up its integrity and sell out to rhetoric or journalism. Such a point of view obliges me, too, to question the literary value of any course or category that defines itself as Women's Poetry. How can a multiplicity of jostling, incongruous, historically produced texts be bundled up under a gendered and , especially in our time, emotively pressured appellation? To talk or even to think of women's writing as a category distinct and separated from the rich, multilayered traditions of literature in English is, to my mind, reductionist. Reductionism may be useful in political argument, even valid in cases when a complex reality has to be sacrificed to the greater importance of implementing a just or juster social policy, but it ought never to be taken seriously as a measure of value by any artist in a free society.

John Berryman, defining 'The Freedom of the Poet' in a collection of essays published posthumously in 1976, quoted that supremely insightful novelist Joseph Conrad: 'All the great creations of literature have been symbolic, and in that way have gained in complexity, in power, in depth and in beauty.' Symbolism, as Conrad and Berryman understood the word, is the writer's answer to the challenges of political reductionism. Instead of treating issues and categories as realities in the charged political arena of literary criticism, symbolical language can be found in, for instance, the poetry of Marlowe, Blake, Dickinson, Yeats, Bishop, Plath. Symbolism, as I am well aware, can be twisted into a term of derision. Today's postmodernist, politically correct academics tend to brand it as elitist. For a poet, however, symbolic, paradoxical, figurative language is instinctive as it is rhythmic. As Keats and Yeats, in their different times, so well understood, poetry that lasts, whatever the labour or anguish of its making, always sounds as if it came as naturally as the leaves, bole and blossom to that famous chestnut tree. The sound of poetry naturally fits the ear; and a real poem's universality, associated always with its music, can be recognised long after the issue – political or personal – that originally inspired it has been forgotten.

What we are living with to day is an undefined, unrecognised confusion between two types of speech that cannot, I'm afraid, be reconciled by the paradoxes inherent in the language of poetry. The set terms of theoretical-cum-political language simply kill off their more delicate rival. And when excessive self-consciousness as to the methods and uses of poetry is promulgated by critical dogmatists, or when students of 'creative writing' are taught that writing poetry is no more than a self-evolved route to self-expression, or when literary doctrines or manifestos become pawns in politically motivated power-games, then poetry is forced to yield up its essentially symbolical, apolitical nature and even, under the protection of its most loving and fervent promoters, limp along instead as a worthy branch of journalism.

Music under the skin

> In poetry, speech rhythm continues permanently to be part of much wider (and almost certainly much finer and unobservable) systems of bodily movement.
>
> D.W. Harding

People sometimes ask me why I write poetry and not prose; generally I give them a short answer: rhythm – rhythm, the unconscious engine of poetry, the pulse or muscle that governs it and has its physical source in walking, breathing and heartbeat. For, though rhythm is really more kinaesthetic than aesthetic, it is felt and shared like an emotion. Together with speech-sounds and their relationship within the lines, rhythm keeps poetry alive. I may be saying no more than that when sounds 'belong' to each other and recur in a recitable rhythm people remember them. Rhythms also matter in prose. But where in prose the controlling unit is the thought-phrase, the lift and fall of the language in sentences and paragraphs, the energy that drives poetry is the beat, as in the drum beat (heartbeat) of primitive ritual and dance.

Even ignoring the social or cultural origins of poetry, we know how impossible it is for any human being, at any time, to learn a language without engaging in rhythmic activity. We are born rhythmic. Listen to the tiny baby's cry as it issues in pulses of breath: Waa. Waa. Waa. Listen to common nursery rhymes and clapping games: 'Pease porridge HOT (pause) / Pease porridge COLD (pause) / Pease porridge in the Pot / NINE DAYS OLD (pause).' The clapped words fall into a pattern of four beats to a phrase, the voice rising to a sharp emphasis on 'hot' and 'cold' in the first two lines, forcing the voice to break off for a rest, as it were, before repeating the pattern. In the third line, an extra accented syllable (IN the POT) pushes the voice more quickly into the three strong beats, followed by a rest again, of 'NINE DAYS OLD (pause)' – and I think one naturally drags out that o-sound at the end to point up the rhyme.

In verse, at more complicated levels, something in us wants to establish a beat at the same time it wants to spike its monotonous regularity with variation. Take the bass line in rock music: thump, thump, thump, thump. For people like myself who suffer from deafness and can't hear the 'tune' in a higher register over that basic beat, the playing of a jukebox in a pub, for example, can be a form of torture. In jazz drumming, as in African and Indian drum music, a regular beat is counterpointed by variations that run against it. Syncopation's rapid rolls of sound, dramatic pauses – through which we still feel the beat – stir up physical, no doubt sexual, urges in us, or at least make us want to dance. Or march. When I was a small girl growing up in Connecticut, I used to watch army recruits being drilled in a nearby park. The fall of the men's feet had to be synchronised: Left right, Left right, Left right, Left right, and the marching rhythm was beaten out in a nonsense line:

I LEFT my wife and twenty-four children all alone in starving condition with nothing but gingerbread LEFT

If you march correctly to this rhythm, your left foot comes down on the first and last syllable, LEFT. The rhythm, irregardless of syllable count and meaning, proceeds from natural speech-stresses for the left foot to stresses for the right foot: I LEFT my WIFE and TWENty four CHILdren ALL aLONE in STARving conDITION with NOTHing but GINgerbread LEFT.

Although the dancing and marching chants most of us remember from childhood are not poetry and often not even verses that make sense, they laid down for me, I'm pretty sure, a number of rhythms common both to music and language, the accentual English sound-pattern that Gerard Hopkins identified as 'sprung rhythm', and that, for me at least, is usually overheard, in one form or another, before I write a single word of a poem.

Finer and more dedicated writers than I am have done the same: T.S. Eliot, Hopkins, Yeats, Housman, Valery, even Virginia Woolf, who had this to say about her own writing:

Now this is very profound what rhythm is, and goes far deeper than words. A sight, an emotion, creates this wave in the mind, long before it makes words to find it; and in writing ... one has to recapture this, and set this working (which has nothing apparently to do with words) and then, as it breaks and tumbles in the mind, it makes words to fit it.[1]

So for Virginia Woolf, even expressive prose had its beginnings in the natural physicality of rhythm. Today, as we know, the absorption of prose rhythms by poetry has become commonplace – so much so that a definite line between poetry and prose is difficult to draw. As the psychologist D.W. Harding wrote more than twenty years ago in a fine little book, *Words into Rhythm* (1976), 'It is from rhythms inherent in the natural speaking of a language that all rhythmic writing begins'[2] – a dictum that takes us one step further towards civilisation than Virginia Woolf's experience of waves in the mind before words. These days, few poets adhere to strict metrical patterns, and even when they do, they usually allow the rhythms of spoken English to take precedence over mechanical regularity.

Like my contemporaries, when I'm working on a poem – that is, once I've got started and found a line of words to put on paper – I try to be as faithful as I can to the speech-rhythms of English. Yet I rarely write entirely 'free verse' , and never syllabic verse; and this must be because I have always associated poetry with music. My earliest attempts at poetry were songs or ballads. 'Who is she there / with golden hair / Picking the gold of the meadow' – I remember writing that in arithmetic class and getting my knuckles rapped for not paying attention to what Miss Marritz was saying. Much later, in the 1950s, when I was a music student at the University of Michigan, I was captivated by the folksongs that were popular in that Joan Baez era. An older girl, named Adèle Hager, who was living in Ann Arbor at the time, sang and accompanied herself on the guitar, very beautifully as I recall. She was from Kentucky or West Virginia, and from her I learned not only how to thrum on the guitar a little myself, but how to sing in a tuneful drone some of those haunting Allegheny lyrics:

> Black, black, black
> Is the colour of my truelove's hair.
> His ruby lips are wondrous fair
> So sweet his arms and so strong his hands
> I love the ground on where he stands.

Lines like these, though they rhyme, are not particularly rhythmical I suppose one might conduct them roughly in a 2/4 time, but they don't urge us to clap or dance or march. They only ask to be sung. If you learn words and tune together, they become inseparable, difficult as it is to notate either. The three long vowels of 'Black, black, black' rise slowly in a minor triad, but the third 'black' topples over into a quick phrase 'black is the colour of my', followed by the three long syllables of 'true love's hair'. In the next line, the melody of 'His ruby lips are wondrous fair' insists that the singer draws out the long u in ruby and pass swiftly over the short I in 'lips' before rising to an emphasis on 'fair'. Again, in the third line, 'sweet' and 'strong' stress their long vowels – 'strong' in fact is dragged out to cover a descending triplet, drawing attention to 'hands' and anticipating a rhyme with 'stands' at the end of the stanza. In the last line, 'love' gets a long, drawn-out o and 'ground' a shorter one, rather swallowed by the quick triplet 'on where he' before 'stands' fades away on *la* in the *sol-fa* scale.

A descriptive analysis such as I have attempted is, of course, wholly superfluous to enjoyment of the song. The words are quaint, but nothing in themselves; and the tune, while affecting in its almost Lydian mode, sounds thin without a voice to sing it. Only in combination, words with music, does it strike the heart. Notice too, how when words are set to music, musical rhythms predominate over speech rhythms. In prose we would never repeat that first 'black'. In a lyrical poem, one might conceivably write 'Black is the colour of my truelove's hair', only slightly accenting love in truelove. Both the rhythm and the tune of the song, however, override the natural speech sounds, so that, remembering the musical phrase, even when we say the lines, we linger over 'true love's hair'.

Ted Hughes, in an invigorating essay on metre and rhythm,[3] makes a case for just such a musical reading of Sir Thomas Wyatt's lyric that begins, 'they fle from me, that sometyme did me seke' a poem that almost everybody loves, though to a dogmatic ear it sounds, in places, metrically incorrect. Hear it as if Wyatt were singing to his lute, Hughes advises, and don't try to force an iambic scansion on the lines. Hughes goes on to castigate the Elizabethan song-compiler, Tottel, for imposing, in his *Miscellany,* smooth-sounding Italian metres on the strong, rough rhythms of Anglo-Saxon speech. But to my ear, Shakespeare's lyrics, and Ben Jonson's too, are hardly tied down to strict metres:

> Come away, come away, death,
>   And in sad cypress let me be laid.
> Fly away, fly away, breath;
>   I am slain by a fair cruel maid.
> My shroud of white, stuck all with yew,
>   O! prepare it.
> My part in death, no one so true
>   Did share it.

One summer, it must have been in 1950, my sister and I undertook to paint the interior of a derelict farmhouse my parents had bought in Vermont. While we were painting, we sang straight through an Elizabethan songbook we'd brought with us in our enthusiasm for singing with guitars. (My sister later became a fine guitarist.) I still remember all those songs; their words and tunes are inseparable in my memory from the swaying to and fro of paintbrushes on dilapidated walls.

The strong physical ties that bind natural speech-rhythms to poetry do not relax their hold over it once syllables cease mainly to be sounds (as in songs) and join together to form chains of meaning. 'Meaning', in the sense of saying things, simply makes poetry more difficult to write. For once a stress-pattern is established – whether in iambics or in freer rhythmic units – speech accents and metrical accents have to coincide; or even more interestingly, fail to coincide in an arresting way. Hopkins constructed his prosody around a principle of reversed feet, 'counterpointing' one set of expected rhythms against another. Actually, a great deal of so-called metred poetry breaks with its metrical set pretty often. Otherwise it gets far too boring. How can you possibly scan the ten syllables of 'Tomorrow, and tomorrow, and tomorrow / Creeps in this petty pace from day to day', in iambic pentameter? The actor who plays Macbeth is given a number of options, one of which is to put a heavy stress on the second syllable of tomórrow each time it appears; that produces only three stresses in what should be a five stress line. Another option is to emphasise the hopeless futility of time by putting stresses on 'and' , i.e. 'Tomorrow,# AND tomorrow,# AND tomorrow.' Here we get five stresses, all right, but at the expense of the heavy stresses on that lugubrious groan, to MORrow. Whatever the actor chooses to do, he will probably for interpretative reasons lengthen the line beyond the requirements of the metrical set. 'Creéps ĭn thĭs pétty páce' in the next line reverses the iamb at the beginning, and though 'frŏm dáy tŏ dáy' is regular, it is only a brief interlude of normality before the irregular rise and fall of 'Tŏ thĕ lást sýllăblĕ#ŏf rĕcórdĕd tíme'.

Meaning, then, in metrical poetry is everything so long as it both confirms and (sometimes) deliberately conflicts with the pulse beat that gives it life. Meaning also seems to be the attribute of imaginative language that sets it apart from the other arts. This is not to say that music and painting affect us without meaning anything! On the contrary, for approximating the 'truth' of experience, without interference from ideas or theories, wordlessness can be a positive advantage. As I think Isadora Duncan remarked, when she was asked to explain the 'philosophy' behind her dancing, 'If I could say what it means I wouldn't have to dance it.' Poets – Yeats, Housman, Elizabeth Bishop – have likewise defended themselves against too much intellectual investigation with the argument, 'If I could say it in prose I wouldn't have gone to the trouble of putting it into verse.' The fact remains, though, that words do have meanings in different contexts. The enormous flexibility of language, iridescent with possibilities and capable of expressing innumerable shades of feeling, mood, innuendo, is its irresistible attraction. At the same time, it puts power into the hands of people (politicians, media advertisers) who cunningly use or abuse its immense resources for exploitative ends.

For language, when it draws on its deep, kinaesthetic, sources of rhythm and tone, whether in poetry, rhetoric or propaganda, is the most powerful art (tool, weapon) that we human animals possess; and with it, for good or evil, we surely govern and manipulate the world. Luckily (because skill with language can be as dangerous as it is exhilarating) most people – even many who call themselves poets – are not up to wielding language effectively enough to make a mark on society. Most literature – I think this is true of all times, not just of our own – is imitative and time-bound by fashion, written for entertainment, or in hopes of achieving fame, or indulged in therapeutically: poetry as socially justified self-seeking.

Any of these motives, or all of them together, can bring about writing that lasts, at least for a time. But I can't believe any poetry will survive if its makers don't naturally love – adore, worship, strive ceaselessly to create – what Peter Levi has called the wonderful noises poems make. The Elizabethans, and seventeenth-century Metaphysicals were exemplary in this respect, and despite the fact that they were all men! They were my earliest inspirators. Later on came Blake and the Romantics, Yeats, Hopkins, Frost, Eliot, Auden, Bishop – hosts innumerable! Yet looking back at the poems I've written over the years, and watching myself write today (though I don't think self-consciousness helps the writing much), I realise that my dependence on music and rhythm has been exceptionally great. Perhaps too great. Certainly the poems I will stand by (though I never will completely renounce 'Willow Song') combine strong rhythmic components with natural speech-flow; they also, like 'Swifts', 'Poem for a Daughter' and 'The Fiction-Makers' have something to say.

One poem I think of as being typically 'me' is called 'Trinity at Low Tide', from *Four-and-a-Half Dancing Men* (1993), in which a repeated falling cadence – 'whisperings', 'doubling you', 'under you', 'feature-less', 'copies you', 'cancels you' – threatens, somehow, the free-moving rhythms and word-chimings within the stanzas. The 'idea' expressed is not really translatable into prose; it has , I think, to do with a strange phenomenon of evolution, with a man's body, spirit, life-span and environment rising, so to speak, out of the sea. I couldn't possibly say how I came to write it, except that I did, one day, observe my husband walking, reflected by the wet sand on Harlech beach, with his black shadow beside him.

> Sole to sole with your reflection
>   on the glassy beach,
> your shadow gliding beside you,
>   you stride in triplicate across the sand.
> Waves, withdrawn to limits on their leash,
>   are distant, repetitious whisperings,
> while doubling you, the rippling tideland
>   deepens you.
>
> Under you, transparent yet exact,
>   your downward ghost keeps pace –
> pure image, cleansed of human overtones:
>   a travelling sun your face;
> your breast, a field of sparkling shells and stones.
>   All blame is packed into that black, featureless
> third trick of light that copies you
>   and cancels you.

Note on Scansion Marks

´ = stressed syllable
˘ = slack syllable
˘ = lightly stressed syllable, spoken quickly
= pause; // above the line = heavily stressed syllable

Notes

1. Quoted in D.W. Harding, *Words into Rhythm: English Speech Rhythm in Verse and Prose* (Cambridge, 1996), 87.
2. Ibid., p. 97. Harding also comments, aptly, 'It is not "rhythm" or "metre" that matters, but the unique rhythm of the unique poem' (p. 86).
3. Ted Hughes, 'Myths, Metres, Rhythms', in William Scammell (ed.), *Winter Pollen* (London, 1994), 310–72.

2
How and Why

Ruth Padel

Back-up

I never know I'm going to write a poem.

I live by journalism – regular reviews, interviews sometimes, and at present a discussion column on poems in the *Independent on Sunday* – plus readings and radio work. These things have a sort of scrambly priority. But there's always a prose book on the go. At the moment it's a book for Faber called *I'm a Man*, on maleness in rock music. The last, *Whom Gods Destroy*, was on madness. The prose book I'm writing affects what I'm thinking about, the way I react to the world, so of course it affects poems when they come along. My second collection, *Angel*, is full of mad voices, and those poems got written while I was working on *Whom Gods Destroy*. They got in its way and held it up. The two next collections, *Fusewire* and *Rembrandt Would Have Loved You*, were written while I was planning the maleness in rock book (which started out as a book about female desire in song), so they are a sort of askance look at maleness. Plus *Rembrandt* is also full of song. Both held the Faber book up terribly.

It helps to think and speak of poems as having an urgency and purpose of their own; as if they come from somewhere not yourself. I don't want to know why.

All the time

There are three stages to writing an actual poem, anyway to me doing it. But before, there's an ongoing thing, keeping the soil prepared. This means letting things come at you all the time and being open to them. A scrap of a phrase or rhythm and image, maybe just a word, or an idea, which feels important and imperious. If it's at night, I have to turn the light on, find a biro, write it down somewhere. If I'm driving or walking, it gets done on the steering-wheel, a wall, the back of a cheque book. Then whatever-it-is gets transferred to a 'quarry' file on the computer. Other things get there too, things that catch at me: something I read or hear, in the paper, on TV, on the bus, which feels important. A late-night programme on tornado tourism or okapis; a dream, something a child says; a slogan on a van. Like last night I learnt that when you go through the Panama Canal east to west, because of the way the land is you actually move west to east. That sort of thing.

I suppose I vaguely assume that because all these different things feel important to me, they belong with each other somewhere and will cohere, in the end, in things I make, simply because it's me making it and my interest in them is what they have in common. There's a coherence it's not my business to see, though I'll have to work it out in action, for the movement of each poem. They work through images, these things.

My job at this stage is to be open, but not too watchfully. To let things come. Like being in a forest not looking round, busy on something of your own, letting animals make their own way to you.

This goes on all the time, but some times more than others. After a book is finished, there's a blank period, a winter, when nothing seems to happen. This can be very uncomfortable, and it's good to have other work to be getting on with so you don't notice it too much.

Beginning

The first stage of a poem is when a phrase or rhythm, a feeling or thought or image, turns up and says: drop everything, work at me now. I'll have to do the review, or whatever else, in the night, because if you lose that moment you lose the poem. Then the first draft comes. A morning goes by and you don't notice; following through some thought till the whole arc is on paper in some form.

This stage may take a day or several weeks, depending on the poem and the material.

When it's there, I'll turn to the quarry and begin finding things there that belong to this poem. I suppose the rationale for this is, that I put in the quarry things I'm currently reacting to at a level where the poem comes from, so they're part of each other and it's my job to recognize how.

Some of the quarry material may go into the poem and out of it again, but leave a trace behind. What you leave out of a poem is as important as what's in. Maybe more.

At this stage the poem may or may not have found the shape it wants. I'll go with what it seems to want, for the moment. What's certain, whether it's ten pages or just twenty lines, is there'll be three times too much. I know, now, that's what happens. But it's all got to stick around together for the moment.

That's the first stage: quarrying and rough-modelling, fetching up the raw material and slapping it down on the board all together. Then I leave it to breathe, pick up the pieces of life, phone editors to say copy's coming in a minute.

The leaving to breathe may take quite a time, several weeks if it's a long poem; or I might go almost inmediately onto the next stage, the second. Or I may think, God, this is a mess, and leave it around a while. Maybe even not come back to it.

The main bit

The second stage is freeing the image from the stone.

There are two ways of making a sculpture – building up a model or moulding, and cutting away the stone to reach the image inside. Gathering material is just being open, listening to what's important; getting down the first draft is just a kind of automatic dictation. This stage is writing.

I read a novel about Michelangelo, the way he'd approach a block of stone. It's expensive material, you can't afford to waste it, you're lucky to have it in front of you to work on. You have to see where the shape will be inside it: your work is freeing it. A sculptor told me you look at a block of stone and think where the furthest-out points and the most recessed parts, 'the blacks', will be. Because you're working with light and shadow. So you reach a rough idea of the shape, how you're going to tackle this stone, not waste this beautiful raw stuff, because once you start cutting, that's it. I don't think I'm as clear as that about it, but it's something like.

If you go wrong, at this stage, don't think you're going to be able to use this material again in another poem. It's all part of the same thing. This is its chance to reach the light.

This cutting shaping stage typically takes two or three obsessed days – well, for a longer poem maybe a week – when I only think about that, run it through lots of drafts, think of it all the time while I'm doing other things like fetching a child from school, cleaning up dogshit, writing a review or having a meal with someone and I suddenly see 'Oh, I could put that word there'. Or a new word occurs that would fuse two of the themes, or bring two sounds into relationship in a new way.

After this stage I let it alone again, to dry. Get on with other things. It's taken me up in its claws for a while, till it doesn't need feeding with that sort of obsession, then it lets me go. It wants to be alone a bit.

Going back

The third stage. Some poems hardly need it, others depend on it. I go back to it when it's dried, and look at it much more critically. This process may take months, and may mean radical surgery, taking whole chunks out. Or the whole process from stage one to three may have taken a day. The poem decides.

This is when I might run it past someone else. There are two or three friends I might read it to on the phone, or fax it to, or show it to over a drink. To see if it works, where they think things go wrong. I don't do this with poems I'm sure of, just poems I'm uneasy with for some reason.

Influences

Everything is an influence. Poets I did for 'O' and 'A' level, Tennyson, Gerard Manley Hopkins, Keats. I used to know the whole of *The Wreck of the Deutschland* and *The Eve of St Agnes* by heart. When I'm at the dentist or in hospital I say Tennyson, or maybe Shakespeare, to myself, to not be frightened. There's something so firm about the music and the thought going through it. You always hear new things in it.

But I did classics at college, and the Greek poets are an enormous influence, particularly choral lyrics in tragedy. The way the words curl in images over each other, the way a song is built up through images, and the delicate language, acidly sensuous but probing moral questions of belief and fear and the fragility of life all the time. The way one word can turn the whole feel of a poem over on itself – I learnt all that from the Greek poets. The lyric poets, Sappho, Alcaeus, Pindar, but mainly the tragic poets and Homer. Structure, movement through, and images.

So my reading in English classics is accidental and poem-led. Wyatt – I had a big Wyatt obsession; Auden got me for a long time; so did

Browning. Eliot and Donne I did at school; Yeats exploded on me by himself and took me over for years. The modern Greek poets, especially Seferis and Cavafy: I like the wryness of Cavafy, the way he can leave everything out and say so much by silence; but still be so sensual, in just a few words. Seferis addresses big things more explicitly; but in his masterpiece, *Thrush*, he's more oblique and I like that best.

Bishop and Plath: when I discovered each of them it was through a large *Collected*, a hardback. Each time I remember lashing out on this expensive book and carrying it round with me everywhere till it was in me. They are the foundation of where I think from now.

Of Americans, I love Sharon Olds, Anne Carson (well, she's Canadian) and C. K. Williams particularly. They have all turned their own voice and writing persona into unique form; as Paul Durcan has. He's a central influence too. Heaney always: different people have a different favourite and mine's *Station Island*. Geoffrey Hill, early work – I carried *Mercian Hymns* round with me for a year when I lived in Crete. Basil Bunting too: I met *The Spoils* when I was living in Greece and it seemed to matter more out there than *Briggflats*. Something about the glint of landscape and history came out there. History, the present in the past, always gets me.

Muldoon is the core. It isn't the cleverness, but the way he can make words do absolutely anything he wants; like a hairdresser who the minute she gets her hands on your hair it behaves the way it never does for you. Muldoon does that with words; and with thought-connections. But there's always a deep sea of feeling underneath. The passion under the wordplay, the fuck-you erudition plus a clear current of feeling – the way these two meet in his poems; the way his poems are always about art and history as well as feeling, politics and thought – there is a whole world of reaching out in every word-connection.

Carol Ann Duffy, Jo Shapcott, Mike Donaghy, Selima Hill, Matthew Sweeney, Ian Duhig and Don Paterson are people whose new work I rush to when it comes out. Apart from the pleasure, there's seeing where they are going. All of their work is in me, I think.

There are so many good poets writing at the moment and I'm very grateful for it – the climate of listening and reading around. The fact that you can show a poem, get shown one, make a suggestion, see how someone else is doing new things – I love all that. Everybody going a different way, finding and growing new things but sharing it.

Working on my Faber book I've been listening non-stop to rock and pop music. What a lot of women's rock has been doing since the

Eighties, is like what Eavann Boland in the last essay in *Object Lessons* says women poets are doing. Your starting-point is your sense of what it is to be a woman writing, of the struggle to be aware, behind and in your voice.

I don't want to think about this hard; I've written a lot of academic things and don't want that note in my voice. It doesn't help me. But having written two books of love poems in a row, *Fusewire* and *Rembrandt Would Have Loved You*, I can see I thought more carefully in the second about what I was doing; one of the themes really was 'what it is for a woman to write a love poem'. What a dicey, slippery project that is. I chucked a lot of poems out.

I get to see a run of poems as the beginning of a collection when I can see several themes, or angles, or obsessions if you like, moving through them in a similar way. In *Fusewire* it was history – Britain brutalizing Ireland – and how it gets in the way of a relationship between people from the two countries now. Writing *Rembrandt*, I felt I'd always hidden behind history and it was time to stop that. There's a lot in that instead about ways of seeing, who's seeing whom, how you see yourself. John Berger stuff maybe. Or its fall-out. But some women may feel uncomfortable and cross with some poems in that book.

There was a lot about death in it too, and I think that's going to come in more, the end of a book looks forward to whatever's coming next. I suspect.

Or maybe not. I don't know where I'll go now. When a book's gone to press, I think, What is a poem? What are poems for? Where do they come from? Will I ever write one again?

Why

I can't imagine living without it. I know people manage. I'd go mad.

3
Home Fires

Susan Wicks

I don't think anyone has ever seriously denied that writing poetry takes time. But for me the conventional model of the poet writing a first quick draft and then taking weeks, months, or even years to polish it, is a distortion, or only a part of the story. For me the first problem is a problem of 'access': how to get myself into that frame of mind where poetry becomes possible.

By now I know from experience that it will usually take me about three days.

Sometimes, of course, that work has been done for me. There are moments when you feel naturally as if your body has an electric charge in it, moments when the poems just come. But I've always regarded poetry as something both more and less mysterious than that. What comes can also be provoked. With three days of work and concentration I can begin to silence some of my more functional modes of thinking and make space for the tentative beginnings of something that in the end interests me more.

It's the reverse of what gods are supposed to do, the reverse of what happens to Adam and Pandora and Galatea. It's not a matter of counting ten perfect fingers and ten perfect toes and then breathing the life in. It's a matter of recognising and trying to safeguard the first small pulse of life while coaxing fingers and toes into a first rudimentary existence. Even when I've worked extensively on my poems at the editorial stage, that work has been less a matter of tinkering with unsatisfactory words or line-breaks than of regaining access to the original feeling that, finally, authenticates the language. At times, that emotional agility has felt almost impossibly hard.

My poems often start life as fragments of prose. After a school diet of Shakespeare and Keats, the first poetry I studied seriously was French.

It was obvious to me then that an extraordinary image like Éluard's 'The earth is blue as an orange' didn't come to him through ordinary discursive channels, and a belief in the possibilities of automatic writing and the privileged status of childhood hasn't entirely left me. Many of my poems have sprung from unlikely images or conjunctions of material that have surprised me with a smell of truth; sometimes I've explored the image further, digging until it gave up its secret – or until my spade rang on stone. This, just as much as what some poets call 'craft', feels to me like the real work.

This is how – whether I'm theoretically engaged in writing fiction, autobiography or poetry – I spend much of my writing time. Thousands of hours apparently wasted. Perhaps actually wasted. But this apparently aimless, unfocused verbal dreaming feels necessary. When I stop doing it my writing soon starts to veer towards the cerebral and self-conscious. It seems I need this instrument to abstract myself from the busy supply-and-demand economics of everyday living. It's highly impractical: in this state I could walk into town for a book of stamps and come back with a pound of haddock. A friend rings me and when I answer the phone I realise my answers must be inappropriate by the way she's starting to laugh. At times I find it frightening.

Concentrating on my work is so easy compared to concentrating on the graceless mechanics of my life. Given their initial shape on the page, it's not surprising that my poems are sparked less by the heard rhythms of groups of words than by a strong visual image. I'm more concerned with what the poem is than with some isolable conception of the sound it makes; for me, line-breaks have at least as much to do with the possibility for tonal shifts, emphasis and dramatic deferral as with metrical satisfactions. I'm not writing a lullaby. I think what I'm trying to write is a kind of ideal speech, a voice intimate enough to use the gaps between words and give the reader the freedom to fall through. In these circumstances, line-breaks are crucially important. Many of my 'prose' drafts come, in fact, with a few critical line-breaks already indicated. I think of that tiny, almost imperceptible hesitation while the eye or the reader's voice moves across white paper from one line to the next as a part of the poet's raw materials, a part of the necessary relationship between words. It's a slight irregularity, an unseen three-inch threshold that puts your body momentarily off-balance as you walk between two familiar rooms. Sometimes it's convenient to see the line of poetry as an entity and line-breaks as a kind of quiet underlining of a poem's most explicit meaning. But sometimes the building-block analogy is less helpful. Deciding where and how and how discreetly to fracture something is an artistic prerogative too.

Every first draft is different. Some come with a kind of confidence, and some are initially unpromising. Some are set out as verse right from the beginning; others are in prose with a few lines already distinct and cohering, like pieces of jigsaw. But in virtually every case, what I have is a feeling that I half-know where this might be going, an intuition of overall shape and colour, of where I might expect to have to put the reds and where the greys. The task is sometimes to link what I sense are finished fragments with something that will not undercut them.

Sometimes that involves conveying necessary information economically. More often the challenge is almost purely syntactical. The poet's first and most important tool is syntax: the challenge is to make it do what you want it to invisibly, to get things in the best possible order without a sense of strain.

It sounds easy, but it isn't. At times it feels almost as difficult as trying to write conventionally formal poetry in a natural, unpretentious, contemporary voice. The danger at this stage is one of impatience, or laziness: it's the danger of reaching your destination too soon. It's so easy to be caught up in the premature urge to tidy, to polish and prettify and generally smooth over, something that could only have benefited from the chance to grow. On good days I have the beginnings of one or several pieces that I sense have real possibilities. On average days, nothing at all. On bad days I can find myself with three or four neat little poems, often rhyming, mostly in spare, clipped, un-self-indulgent language, divided into more or less equal stanzas, formally almost watertight – and all worthless. On those days I have to remind myself that writing poetry is uncomfortable! The state appropriate to the writing of poetry is a state of non-resolution. It's the very opposite of what our ordinary lives demand. And most of us are unwilling or unable to lead our lives in that condition for very long.

I write, as I imagine most of us do, for two reasons: to create something that delights me, and to communicate. There's a tension between the two that sometimes threatens to turn the poem into something else, pulling towards obscurity on the one hand and journalism on the other. And both impulses are in their way important. Form is what gives me pleasure. It's the gratification, the reward. Manipulating words successfully is for me an almost sexual experience, and I'll chase it as long as I can. But somewhere in the relationship, there's also the child, perpetually reaching out, trying to make contact, frustrated by a world which doesn't match any of the templates she holds up to it. In my own experience, the self that writes and the self that lives her day-to-day life are, as they were for Proust, rather far apart. I sense that in my case the self that writes is almost irresponsibly uncompromising. There's an irony there: allowing that part of me expression, I may in fact be risking a kind of artistic autism. If the world is not remotely as I see it, then why should anyone hear me? And yet I go on. We go on. For years now I've found it helpful to think of my poems as messages in bottles. The message is crucial to its sender. If it's discovered it means possibility, perhaps even life: the recipient is in a position of great power. But for every bottle found, there are ten more still float-ing or destroyed. And even when the message is unfolded there is still the knotty question of provenance and native language. And you are never to be definitively rescued. You don't actually want to be rescued in any final way. If you were, the messages would become formalities. Or you would stop writing them. The island would be untenanted. You'd have to give yourself some sort of flesh-wound and get some obliging person to cast you away again.

My gender is a basic part of my writing identity: I can hardly imagine writing from a position in which I were sexually unaware of myself. For me, it's still where the energy is. Some of the most excit-ing or shaming events in my life have been events that it would be difficult or impossible for many men to share directly. It shouldn't matter. The endeavour is larger and more serious than that. Proscribing certain areas of subject-matter is as absurd as proscribing present participles or adjectives or dashes. Language is usage, what we hear spoken around us; why should the material of poetry be restricted to the preoccupations of a single group? The more people speak their mother-tongue and are heard, the more the common language expands to accommodate them. 'Crowds, nebulae, oceans, nations,' as Apollinaire had it, as far back as 1917 – 'a hand feeling in a pocket, a match being struck on a wall, animal noises, the way the garden smells after rain, a flame curling upwards in a hearth ...' Women drinking coffee and sewing, he could have said. Jesus Christ, cham-pion aviator. All your body's doors.

I'm not surprised at certain uneasy reactions to my work which have come predominantly from male critics. I think many of my poems do offer an implicit challenge to certain fond male assumptions, and do it obliquely enough to look almost innocent.

In the end, it's not the fact that I write about 'women's subjects' – about parenting and illness, birth and death and yearning and interiors – it's the way I write about them. I think it's the way I question my own relationship with them, the way I still can't take them for granted but see them as paradoxical and treacherous, as belonging to an area of experience which is essentially troubling, even, at times, slightly grotesque. I am still *troubled* by child-rearing and repetitive domestic chores and elderly relatives – I am torn, still at some level unprepared for and perhaps angry about the unlikely part they've somehow come to play in my life.

Talking in rational terms about my own poems isn't easy. It's not playful, in the way writing a poem or story – even one's own story – is playful. It doesn't seem to me to contain its own justification in the way a poem or story does. The most you can hope for is perhaps to be honest, and serious – not to be defensive, or self-promoting, or coy.

I was a graduate student in the early seventies, at a time when literary criticism was laying claim to a creative status equal to that of more traditionally imaginative genres. It seems to me now that poetry and critical writing, however inventive, are very far apart. Criticism is a public arena, a common ground in which arguments and counter-arguments jostle for prestige and credence. The natural critic is an intellectual fighter. And a poet needs to be just the opposite. There's a parallel search for meaning, but there's also a kind of acquired passivity, a sustained 'refusal to conclude' that allows the more interesting things to happen. The poet needs the critic, perhaps, to fight her battles, and she's fortunate if at times she can find that critic in herself. And the critic surely also needs the home fires, the solid-fuel boilers, oil-filled radiators, electric convector-heaters – the smoking embers where a family's been bombed out, or simply packed its few things and moved on?

4

The Poet's Dilemma: A Murder Mystery

Gwyneth Lewis

Chapter One

In a cottage in West Wales a body lies on a flagstone floor. The kettle's boiling its belly out, and the horses in the adjacent field have gravitated to the hedge, impatient for carrots and apples that won't now come. What's died in the cottage is a mother tongue. Or was it murder? If so, by whom? Its poets? An incomer? Or a frustrated elder of the church? The kettle boils dry and its aluminium bottom starts to glow.

Chapter Two

The Inspector arrives, opens his book, begins with the facts. In his notes he records the Welsh language is dead and was killed, after centuries, by a stab in the back. Its remaining speakers are no longer in touch with the soul of the language, but use a debased patois of Cymric words strung, like laundry, on an English sentence washing-line. It's far too late for a life support machine. The language had substantial hidden assets, all tied up in land and grazing rights. Who stands to gain from the inheritance? The neighbouring farmer brings molasses up the mountain for his sheep, stops to watch the cop cars at the gate, but doesn't come in.

Chapter Three

The first to be questioned is the victim's daughter. She's a poet, acts suspiciously, writes in both languages. She denies all knowledge of events at the cottage, but fails to look the Inspector in the eye. A neighbour (who gives the Inspector Welsh cakes) tells him with glee that the daughter's been involved with the incomer doctor and that the mother, a cultural purist, strongly disapproved. Confronted with this, the daughter admits a severe case of divided loyalties. 'Respect thy Father and Mother' is the text of the sermon in the church that night. The air is heavy with accusation. The Inspector lights a candle to remember the dead.

Chapter Four

The Inspector heads for Aberystwyth to do some research in the library. There was more to the victim than met the eye. Though she presented herself as a respectable matriarch, there was evidence of cruelty: a narrow life, others controlled rigidly, shady investments, clues about illegitimate children. The Inspector begins to look further afield, beyond the daughter. After all, poets make nothing happen of themselves, but they're always suspects. Unbeknownst to him, a Land Rover follows the Inspector home. Ancient eyes watch him from behind the steering-wheel.

Chapter Five

The local doctor turns himself in, confesses to murder. The wise Inspector packs tobacco into his pipe, decides he's protecting the daughter. The doctor comes clean and blurts out a story of emotional blackmail and hidden shame. The old woman, ill, had been ready to die, but had framed the poet so she'd never forget. After all, mothers and languages of a certain age won't take the blame for anything. The funeral service, the place is black with mourners. The police force mingles, straining to hear the post-burial chat.

Chapter Six

The Inspector takes a mountain walk, looks down on the village. It's a place at the mercy of two opposing forces – passing clouds and rooted fields, with cows like lightning rods in between. Translators are murderers, the Inspector recalls, turns his back to the wind, attempts to light his sputtering pipe. The question is: Who has been translating whom? If you see a Language along the way, kill it, before it ruins your life, robs you of silence. Once speech is an icon poets have a dirty job as propagandists. By now the Inspector knows he's being watched. Sheep gather for their molasses, which fails to appear.

Chapter Seven

'All men kill the thing they love,' blubs the farmer, once the Inspector catches him with his crowbar at the policeman's tyres. 'She'd never let me say what I meant,' he said of his mother (how long had he known?). He'd loved the poet all his life, never had the words to tell her so. He'd hoped that the mother would be able to help, but she knew of the incest and, besides, wanted more than a sheep farmer for a son-in-law. On a desperate visit, had been mocked by the mother he wanted as his advocate. Things had got ugly and then out of hand. The tragedy was he never knew his own strength. He does time for the poet he adores while another marries her. When the daughter sweats and procreates with the doctor, she'll know which words to give the rhythmic air between her and her children, colour and its code.

5

God's Velvet Cushions

Selima Hill

First of all you need to be obsessed. There's no good reason to do it, nobody wants you to do it, or gives you the time or the space. You have to do that yourself. (Try putting a sticker saying I'D RATHER BE WRITING POEMS on your car window.) Being a poet is like having an invisible partner. It isn't easy. But you can't live without it either. Talent is only 10 per cent. The rest is obsession.

But it's subtle. You have to grant yourself the authority to do it, and make no compromises, and be bloody-minded, and implicate your whole being – but not impose yourself on it either.

So the obsession is invisible: unless you count, in my case, note-books everywhere. My house is a mess, but inside my notebooks all is order. They are like aviaries or laboratories or haberdashery depart-ments. I have one in the pocket of my dog-walking coat, one in my bag, one by the fire, one in the kitchen (male journalists always respond to that one!), two by my bed (one a sort of journal that I make it a rule never to reread, the other a scribbling one I can tear pages out of), and about eight by my desk.

One is a hardback I write as detailed an entry as I can in, on the same day (my birthday) every year. One is a book I collect quotations in, what used to be called, I can't think why, a 'commonplace book'. (I used to have one called W, with extracts from writers, and one called S with uplifting or provocative or more spiritual kinds of teaching, but over the years I've realised these can't be divided.) One is an exercise book I collect words or phrases in for poems I haven't the time to work on straightaway. One is a list of books I want to read, with notes about who recommended them and why. One is a book of ideas for work-shops that I add to as I think of them, with lists of relevant texts, and samples of complicated verse-forms in various languages. One is my notebook for notes on current projects – at the moment, riddles for the Science Museum. (I also have a little book I hate where I herd together facts and figures and dates and anything to do with numbers. Medbh McGuckian said women terrify her: numbers are what terrifies me!)

Obsession. Notebooks. Thirdly, it's my desk that helps me write, my calm companionable desk. (I remember a friend saying her goat was a better companion than her husband. I thought, for me it's my desk.) The last time I moved I took with me my shoes, my rabbit and my desk. I remember working for my 'O' levels on it (*at* it?) in an upstairs room in Hampstead with two pianos and a xylophone in it. I remember getting up and checking in the mirror, checking my fringe, my bra, my smile, then going back to my books – and my dreams of marriage ... And here I am, 30 years later, still sitting at it, married now, and separated, in a house of my own by the sea, 'being a poet'. To quote from a paper that interviewed me the other day: *No car, no word-processor, no lover, no problem.* ('No lover' was a bit presumptuous, but they got the general idea.)

So, having got the members of my family where I want them, and made it to my desk, I set to. It's no good making one more cup of coffee, as my teacher used to say. I think I start with a rhythm. Once I've got that, it begins to take shape, like water. I'm not one of those A-to-B sort of poets. I've no idea where I'm off to. Poetry is a big space, and I see if I can launch myself into it with as little baggage as possible. It's like undoing congestion. Being naked. I like to think the poem I'm writing is much better than the poem I ought to be writing. It's no good worrying or judging or asking questions. It's no good whinging. If you're not happy, you're not really writing. You get to a place where nothing can hurt you. Time stops. Which is not to say it's not scary. If you don't make mistakes, you're not trying!

But to get there, you need hard work. Obsession, a bit of talent if you're lucky, lots of notebooks, a big sound secret *safe* desk, time, these you will need. So far so good. The next thing's the hard work. Flannery O'Connor has said that writing a book is like 'giving birth to a piano sideways'. Isn't that brilliant? To add a male voice, Yeats's: 'All that is personal soon rots. It must be packed in ice.' Or T.S. Eliot: 'It's not the expression of personality but the escape from it.' Or Flaubert: 'Art is not interested in the personality of the artist.' So true. It is not self-indulgent, it's sane. It may be subversive – that is precisely its power – but it's basically sane. In the words of C.E. Moore: 'It may hang out any number of wild-looking flags of fantasy, but it hangs them out from the battlements of the fortress of reason.'

After that brief foray into my afore-mentioned (funny how one says 'afore') common-place book, let's add, for ourselves, bloody mindedness. *Art is what you can get away with.* It's an attitude of perception – even a mode of being. It's no good writing about rain (it's pouring down with rain as I type this) by talking to someone else who has been out in it, with an umbrella. That would be like someone who just writes poems.

And there is a difference between 'I write poems' and 'I am a poet'. a big difference. Would I be write in saying 'men are poets: women write poems'? Certainly this has been true in the past. Think, if you can bear to, of Theodore Roethke referring to women who write as 'stamping their little feet against God'! I don't want to make a big thing about the gender issue, but I remember Michael Donaghy saying 'They don't want to know how you're feeling', and thinking to myself, but not liking to say so, 'Of course they do. It's just that they don't know they do.' It's the poet's job to tell them without them realising it. Tricky. Without them realising in fact that it is 'poetry' they're reading. As if poetry is something you put on like party clothes. Maybe there is a gender difference here; I don't know. Men's poetry seems to be more about words. As intimate as crosswords or lectures. I don't like to feel I'm being converted, do you? But then I know I can be paranoid and defensive. I sometimes feel I'm working in enemy territory.

But don't get me wrong. I certainly don't think it's clever to be confessional for the sake of it. I remember a dream I once had, before a reading in Belfast. I was about to begin my reading but nothing happened. I opened my mouth: silence. A doctor in a white coat came up onto the stage and thrust his fingers down my throat and pulled out miles and miles of long slimy tubes like spaghetti. I was terrified that if it didn't stop there wouldn't be any of me left. The theatre would be full of bloodstained string. (My voice?)

Anyhow, heartened by Rose Macauly saying 'a house unkempt can never be as distressing as a life unlived' (write that on your kitchen wall!), I carry on, although I don't know why. Maybe the poems themselves are the houses. So we are doing house-work after all? 'Unkempt' means uncombed. The fine-toothed comb of poetry. Why not?

I often remember Jeni Couzyn, at the launch of her anthology of women poets, saying a married woman poet has three choices: she can either give up her writing, give up her marriage, or commit suicide. I remember thinking – this was ages ago – that she was being sensational and silly and unhelpful. Perpetuating the myth of the impossibly hysterical self-centred female poetess (I am always trying to disassociate myself from Sylvia Plath who, it seems to me, failed 'as a woman') and made their work unreliable. In fact, although I was 'happily married' then, and intended to remain so, I am now, along with every other female poet I can think of I knew then, separated. Maybe it's nothing to do with being women, or poets. All I know is we're human. Poetry is here to answer the question: how do we know we exist? We're God's spies. Married or not. Grist to the mill. Just be there. I don't understand it either.

So, after 'loosening with looseness', I 'tighten with tightness'. After cruising along as expansively, lightly, freshly as I can, I leave it, and do something different – take the dog for a walk or go swimming. Then I come back, maybe days later, and try to get the whole thing to stand up. I usually put something in front of me on my desk to hold it, keep it on track – a shell, or a piece of material or a packet of something. It's the colour that's important, or the texture of the colour. It gives the poem body and integrity.

You ask what my interests are. The single thing that interests me most, that gives me most pleasure, most provocation, most consolation, is colour – as if Love itself were made present for us by light. I suppose it would make more sense if I were a painter. Then you can say what you want. And no one gets hurt; or asks what you mean. You can be as abstract as you like – in the sense, I mean, of 'not figurative'. Sometimes people and stories aren't enough. I envy the language of silence.

Be that as it may, my poems, for me, are colours. They begin, end, and are grounded in, and informed by, and unified by, a particular colour, or colours, or relationship of colours: each poem is an exploration of a colour.

It's hard to explain but I'll try – at the risk of seeming pretentious. For instance the line, taken more or less at random, from THE ACCUMULATION OF SMALL ACTS OF KINDNESS: 'Bluebells, Bovril, somebody's blind spaniel.'

That may sound like a completely random set of objects. In fact it took me many walks and warm baths and lonely meditations to get them completely right – that is, so they suggested a particular soft but rather sinister violet colour. Why I had to do this, why I had to have no peace of mind until I had described a particular colour, I've no idea. It is the colour of the mood I am getting the energy from; I am trying to identify my prevailing mood. To put myself on the line. To testify to myself. And somehow, by so doing, to celebrate others, the ten thousand things. As Virginia Woolf puts it: 'I think it is true that one gains a certain hold on sausage or haddock by writing them down.'

When I am writing, I'm moving through fields of light.

Other examples might be, say, the poems 'How To Be Happy' (brown), 'Marguerite' (crimson), 'My Sister's Kitten' (yellow), 'Please Can I Have A Man' (pink); or, more obviously in VIOLET, a whole character – or the ugly and shameful emotions that character gives rise to, the bitterness, the jealousy – is turquoise: 'Her Little Turquoise Scarf', 'Her Little Turquoise Dress', 'Her Turquoise Breasts'. The unforgiving turquoise of cold silk. (Not the same colour as the green of the parrot, like lettuce or glass, in the next poem, 'Green Glass Arms'.)

Talking about texture, how about: 'male poets – or men poets – are God's spies (suggesting they have some kind of agenda), women poets are God's velvet cushions'? (I am afraid I don't remember whose phrase that is, 'God's velvet cushions', or quite who it referred to. I know that the word 'velvet' is not allowed in my workshops, or only if you think you're advanced enough. Other dodgy words are 'woodsmoke', 'dolphin', 'defiant', 'rainbow' and 'soul'. You can use them , but you've really got to earn them!)

This is not to say we can't go for what's beautiful. On the contrary, poets have the privilege of being allowed to be – subversive, yes – but above all, beautiful. I think a lot of poets are forgetting that, or are scared of it. I certainly am. There's still this taboo on tenderness. Let's address it.

What, for other people, is their religion, for me, and other artists, is our art. It's a way of making sense of things. And to be there doing that we need a stock of tenderness. Sometimes it works and sometimes it doesn't. To go naked into the shower of truth with tenderness. Or Shower of Truth. Or Life. Whatever it is, I'm obsessed by it. You don't have to like it; but if you're a writer I think you do have to love it.

My other interests (which I share with Flannery O'Connor and Nina Cassian) are thinking my face is ugly; and rare poultry. Flannery O'Connor even made dresses for hers, and trained them to walk backwards.

6
Hospitalspeak:
The Neuro-psychiatric Unit

U. A. Fanthorpe

Poetry for me has been a refuge from two ways of life, two forms of speech that were otherwise intolerable.

The first way was teaching. I did this for sixteen years, with as much verve as I could find. No question of writing poetry; I was busy teaching it, explaining it, probably making it fly out of the window. My business was to get pupils through exams, and a major way of doing this is talking. So I talked.

Ultimately I came to feel that I didn't want to be the sort of person I was becoming, so I dropped out into a world of brief holidays, low pay, but, I hoped, freedom of mind. This was the world of the hospital receptionist. The change was beneficial in many ways. Essentially, it was a move forward, from talking to listening. No one had the least interest in what I thought. No one consulted me, except of course the patients, and they don't count. I grew fond of the patients, who tended to come regularly. I knew about them from their notes, I heard their conversations while they were waiting, I answered their questions when I could, I met their relatives. Opposed to this talk, warm, lively, affectionate, loyal, humane (nothing brings out humanity like hospitals), was the clinical language of the doctors. Some of it I enjoyed. Splendid words, if you detach them from their meaning, like *glossolalia, pulsus paradoxus, ataxic*. But the words of discovery can degenerate into an arcane vocabulary for a clique. A particularly nasty trick was a way of depriving patients of their dignity by allowing them only weasel verbs. For one doctor, patients never *said* anything: they *claimed, admitted, denied*. Poor things, they didn't even know this was what they did.

Such a narrow glossary became intolerable for me. I decided to reclaim the English language. This was of course a purely private affair

31

(hospitals fret endlessly about confidentiality), but I could let the rascal words, imagery, rhythm, all the things that were waiting to be let out, run free in my head, and later on scrap paper. The sad thing is that, in retrospect, I can see that what helped me most to escape from hospitalspeak was the fact that many of the patients had suffered various kinds of brain damage. The gaps and repetitions of their speech, their sallies into and out of sense, had a kind of wild poetry. This mad language figured in medical literature in a purely descriptive way. I began to tinker with it myself. Then it became clear that Shakespeare had heard people talk like that, and so had Wordsworth. This was a comfort. There were precedents. It also meant that I no longer need bore my friends with a recital of what-happened-today, which had previously discouraged all conversation. Now I had a different use for it. From my glass dugout I could feel that I was doing something to redress the way patients are spoken of in case notes, and also to celebrate the tremendous energy and resourcefulness of their ways with words. Rhyme, it quickly became clear, was out; in my hands it was altogether too jaunty and confident for the circumstances. I worked hard at silence, being surrounded sometimes by the mute; but there are limits to the uses of silence, I found. If 'everything must go' was overdoing it, I could still scrap a lot of things like punctuation. The important thing was to make what I wrote as unlike the official, the authoritative, the rational, as I could. No doubt the ex-English teacher in me was having a ball. All the things my pupils couldn't do, I was now allowing myself.

When I settled down and became less angry, I began to notice not so obvious sorts of coding at work. My boss, for instance, intimidatingly efficient at everything, including noticing when I wasn't concentrating, had unnerving speeds at shorthand and was much given to a game in which she pretended to forget I couldn't do it, sending me urgent messages in hieroglyphics. Then the neurological case-histories were written in an interesting medical cypher. Some of the patients could read this upside down, and would let me know after the consultation about their real, as distinct from their apparent, progress. 'Not what he tells me, but what he writes down. That's what matters' was their (absolutely correct) formula.

Yet another kind of communication was shown me by my doctor boss. She was the only woman doctor, and as she wryly remarked, got all the bread-and-butter cases, showing them how to make charts of fits so that she could pinpoint their most vulnerable time of day. She also showed me, with great delicacy, that I was making cruel distinctions when, on the list of the day's clinics, I referred to Mr Samuel Coleridge and then (clearly something missing) Billy Wordsworth. I hope I learned from her something of her anxious care for people. At any rate, Billy became Mr William.

In all this hurly-burly of codes and languages, I discovered I had my own. As doctors are trained to protect themselves from feeling too acutely for patients, and need some inner sanctuary to which they can retreat, I found that I'd brought my own sanctuary with me. When the moppers and mowers, the endless weepers, the helpless sad relatives became too much, I could take refuge in the world of deep language that I'd grown up with. Great surges of Shakespeare would wash over me, and interfere with the typing. Sometimes I became characters from literature, whom I hoped no one would recognise. Cerberus is suitable for a receptionist, and Jeeves was useful for talking to doctors with insincere servility. 'All professions are conspiracies against the laity,' says Shaw. I was, for my own amusement, asserting my own profession against the doctors'.

Quite early on, after a month, I tipped over into poetry. I could think of no other way of responding to this babel of voices, this jumble of codes, everyone wanting something and most of them held back, by illness or etiquette, from achieving the effective spark of communication. I was the translator in my job, and I tried to translate when I wrote. At first it was the patients, because they were so present and persistent, and I had every opportunity to learn their speech patterns and their distresses. (*Confabulation*, detestable word, is hospitalspeak for this. (It was no use writing about them; to write about was to distance them. It was necessary to give them their own chance to speak, and sometimes only their own words would do. At this point the great god Confidentiality must have flown out of the window, but I didn't notice. The writing was more important. Indeed, some of the patients asked me to write them a poem about themselves, but most had forgotten by the time I'd produced one. The patients were mostly harmless, friendly, brain-damaged, baffled. They often didn't know where they were, or why. It was hard not to be drawn to them. As a lay person, there was nothing useful I could do, except listen. As a poet, I wanted to testify to the way they went on being human in the midst of such confusion. They seemed like World War I casualties, staggering through No Man's Land, while I watched from the safety of my dugout.

The most useful to me of the great poets at this time were not medical ones (William Carlos Williams, Dannie Abse, etc.) but the ones who understood the strategy of folly: Chaucer, Shakespeare, Wordsworth. It's clearest in Wordsworth. The poet confronts someone marginalised by society – an idiot boy, a small, poor girl, a leech-gatherer, Basil (of 'Anecdote for Fathers') – and manages the story or encounter in such a way as to subvert the values of society, including, presumably, those of the poet. The marginal one comes out on top, like (though with qualifications) the fool in Shakespeare. I came across this strategy in my own work by accident, trying to write about Patience Strong. You can't use this trick too often, but once in a while it may fit what wants to be said.

These were some of the elements in the equation. But I found that I needed also to include official administrative language. The language of the damaged, being damaged often itself in syntax, vocabulary and rhythm, quite often had to be set off against other more confident voices. I already had the strong sound of English poetry in my head, but I found I needed the predictable, bloodless, polysyllabic sounds of administration too. In spite of my rejection of medical style because of its manipulative nature, there were ways in which it was beautiful. It could be hieratic, esoteric, learned. One might have reservations, but there were qualities to be used. There was also the interesting way in which neurologists are trained to set down their observations; a pattern that became very familiar, and began to acquire characteristics in common with liturgy. The final element in this Berlitz school of languages was the local vernacular, spoken by most patients and their relatives, and some nurses. This started me off on another tack, which is hardly relevant here.

I recognise that this account of a rebellion is as fractured and confusing as some of the speech-patterns I've been describing. For one thing, it's been impossible to keep myself out of it. The process of learning was so extraordinary, the things I learned so bizarre and unexpected, that I can only relate this as the story of me, and possibly another example of the poet-as-fool. I worry about having written unfairly about doctors, all of whom went out of their way to be kind. It was their language I resented, not them. And anyway, I used – and still use – fragments of their language like the jackdaw I am. But my greatest gratitude goes to the cleaners, who spoke plainly and from the heart, and the patients, whose gurgles, silences, wild language gave me a nudge forward.

7

The Least International Shop in the World

Moniza Alvi

There used to be a shop in Hatfield, where I grew up, called The International Stores. It was the subject of a recent poem, inspired by something my mother said – that there didn't seem to be anything international about it at all. I remember that it was rather a posh shop for Hatfield, with a dignified atmosphere. There were impressive pyramids of tins, well-swept floors, and the cheddar and ham loomed large, presided over by the solemn shopkeeper. As words have connotations for us before we really think about their meanings, I probably gained the impression that 'international' was something to do with being more English than the English!

As I grew up in this Hertfordshire town in the fifties and sixties as a child with a mixed race background, there were few children in my situation. I was aware of one family of our acquaintance who seemed rather like us. This family also became the subject of a recent poem. I marvelled at how dark the Ceylonese father was and how extremely pale his English wife appeared in comparison. I didn't consciously think that my parents might appear like this to observers. I envied the children because they had English names! It was startling to me, and in my poem 'The Other Family' the children carried 'their English names like snowballs'. I imagined my life would have been much more straightforward if I'd been called Mandy, for example.

There was a great deal of racial invisibility at that time. The term 'multicultural' was unknown to me and different backgrounds were not given focus at school or celebrated as they may well be now. I felt roughly the same as my classmates, but different – it was all very vague, and all the more so because I had an English mother and in many ways my family was very anglicised. Children do not like to be considered different and do their best to fit in, so on one level I was quite happy to consider myself *just the same as everybody else*. I would have half-accepted what some well-meaning teachers still say now-adays – 'I just teach children.' That is, *their origins are not important to me.*

I didn't begin to write poetry so as to explore my background. I had been writing seriously for several years before I started writing anything of my fantasies of Pakistan, and how the country made its impact on my early life. I read the poem 'The Bowl' by Mimi Khalvati and delighted in the richness of its imagery. It was soon after this that it occurred to me that I too had something to say about another culture. I didn't envisage a group of poems at first. I wrote 'Indian Cooking' and, shortly afterwards, 'Presents from my Aunts in Pakistan' thinking that was all, but very soon further poems were pressing to be written, even when I had decided that I really wanted to write about something else. I suppose this is what's invigorating and risky about poetry – it's not entirely in the poet's control. I was very excited because I'd chanced upon an area of writing that was my own – un-explored territory. There was relief in at last making the invisible visible, and in creating something positive about what was, in child-hood and adolescence, rather unsettling and difficult to think about.

The writing gave me the confidence to make my first return visit to Pakistan, which features in *A Bowl of Warm Air*. I felt that the oppor-tunity to write would give me a way absorbing the experience – the extremity of the culture, and the alienation of meeting relatives who didn't speak English while I was unable to speak Urdu. Unsurprisingly, though disconcertingly, I have never felt so English as on that return trip to Pakistan. An overwhelming experience in many ways, the visit helped me to understand many aspects of my growing up, for instance, the family stress on education. Although many Pakistanis looked towards America rather than Britain for progress and the widening of their sphere, a British education was still regarded as supreme. It was commonplace to someone to be introduced as 'this is Mr — who received his Masters from Imperial College.'

When I entitled my first collection *The Country at My Shoulder* I thought of this country not necessarily as a geographic location, but as a reference to the hidden worlds that can be entered through poetry. There is a danger in my being pigeon holed as a writer whose main concern is 'Asian themes', though I do want that major aspect of my work to be valued. What concerns me is what is at the edge of the mind and can be brought to light and viewed form unusual angles. Fantasy interests me strongly – its obliquely subversive power, and its links with the dream world and the unconscious. I have been impressed by the prose of Angela Carter, J.G. Ballard, and Italo Calvino. Partly, what was compelling about Pakistan was that I had no actual memories of it. Pakistan was a fantasy, nourished by vivid family stories, extraordinary gifts, letters, news items and anecdotes.

Thus I wouldn't describe myself exactly as a poet of place, as I am sometimes considered. I write about my experiences as broadly as I can, and my birthplace has been significant. I am aware that poetry I've written about my background has sometimes been rather different in style, even in mood from my other poems. I must confess I haven't fathomed the reason for this! Perhaps it's because Pakistan and my connection with the country strikes me as so surreal and fantastical in itself that I haven't quite got over it. Perhaps the country of my birth has become a symbol for other losses.

Initially I was alarmed and disorientated to find myself almost metamorphosed overnight into a Black writer. I felt a real impostor, and it also seemed as if other parts of me were being eclipsed. At a recent conference on Black writing, however, where I thought I would be very out of place, I found that other writers present, such as Bernadine Evaristo, were also of mixed race and in the verse-novel or novel form had some comparable concerns to myself, although their voices were very different. It was a great relief not to feel as misplaced as anticipated. Writing which portrayed growing up in London, and explored issues of race, was vibrant and very contemporary – essential reading. I hoped that their work would be widely appreciated, in schools and colleges, for example.

Poetry that reflects multicultural Britain is badly represented in the mainstream, particularly aspects of the Asian culture. I was delighted to read Meera Syals's novel *Anita and Me* about a girl growing up as the daughter of the only Punjabi family in a mining village near Wolverhampton in the sixties. Here was much with which I could identify, but I also want to read poetry by someone from such a background, not necessarily writing specifically on 'Asian themes'. I don't mean that I want to read one poet's work, I mean I want to read several, and to be inspired!

Recently I head that one of my poems is to be included in a forthcoming GCSE examination anthology under the section 'Poems from Other Cultures and Traditions'. This at once made me feel like an inhabitant of a distant corner of an empire. Surely the heading should be an inclusive 'Literature from Our Cultures'. It is excellent that school students are now studying a range of poetry, but it is important they don't receive messages that could reinforce a sense of their own lives as being 'other', and marginalised.

II

As a teenager I wanted to be a writer, though I had no clear idea about what kind of writer I could be. I didn't view poetry as connected to any kind of profession or role in life. I grew up with poetry, though. First there was a book of nursery rhymes, *Lavender's Blue* (published by Oxford and still in print), which I savoured, as much for the graceful, detailed illustration as for the rhymes themselves. I inherited from my mother *A Joyful Book of Verse for Children* (dated by its title!). I don't know the actual publication date, but it was given as a school prize in 1941. There were poems by Blake, Tennyson, Robert Louis Stevenson and Eleanor Farjeon and others. All the poems from greater and lesser poets merged to form one alluring world, often more sinister than joyful. There was no Jackie Kay or John Agard writing for children in the early 1960s! I was given *The Puffin Book of Verse,* which, on recent perusal, I was surprised to find covered very similar ground to *A Joyful Book of Verse.* I also had de la Mare's *Poems* – a selection for children, which charmed me with its mystery and melancholy. When I realise how much I valued this early reading, though limited in comparison with what is available to day, it is clear that the power of poetry written or published for children shouldn't be underestimated.

An enthusiastic teacher introduced us to a wide range of poetry at secondary school. We read Adrian Mitchell's 'Stufferation', and this was one poem which opened my eyes (and ears) to the possibilities of modern poetry. We were encouraged to write ourselves, and to experiment with different styles and voices. For GCE we studied *Ten Twentieth Century Poets.* The book could have been entitled *Ten Twentieth Century White Male Poets,* but this did introduce me to Edward Thomas. I quickly fell in love with his poetry and still value it enormously. I admire his exploration of difficult emotions, and the delicacy of expression which is so haunting in such lines as these from 'Tall Nettles':

> I like the dust on nettles, never lost
> except to prove the sweetness of a shower.

I encountered some women poets when, as an older teenager, I started to collect the attractive Penguin Modern Poets series, and became absorbed in Denise Levertov, Stevie Smith and Elizabeth Jennings. The idea that my own life could be material for poetry didn't strike me, however. I think that is partly why I didn't start writing seriously until I was about 30 and was made aware of the unconscious and the symbolic richness of a dreamlife. Writing became an act of discovery on the border where inner and outer worlds meet, an attempt to extend myself and transform that which was constantly being taken in.

The reading of other poets' work and writing my own poetry belong together. I'm often inspired to write by what I read, by energy, freshness and inventiveness. Contemporary poets who've fired me recently are Vicki Feaver, Sujata Bhatt, and Susan Wicks, and I've been drawn to the work of Mark Strand and James Tate. I greatly admire poems by Louise Gluck and Raymond Carver. The list is thankfully endless. I like poems where the excitement of their creation shows through. If I couldn't read other poets' work, I wonder, would I continue?

When writing from personal experience I try to avoid heaviness and instead indulge in my own form of serious play. Currently, I have been working on a series of poems from a male or husband viewpoint. It has been a valuable way of distancing myself and then zooming in closely. I've found that surreal aspects of relationships emerged through this slightly new, strange-seeming voice, as well as the humour that can be buried or overlooked in a more direct approach. Poets, not just novelists and playwrights, may crave different voices. Shakespeare had men playing women playing men, as well as men playing lions. I've found it very satisfying and playful being a woman depicting a man, depicting a woman. This 'bisexual' activity didn't *feel* at all artificial!

In many respects it is a good time to be writing – this period at the end of the twentieth century when so much fine poetry is being written and published. But I must also look to the future for a greater variety of poets from diverse ethnic backgrounds, poets who may well be writing, but have not yet been published, or have not yet been widely read.

8
Confounding Geography

Jo Shapcott

> we are driving to the interior
>
> Elizabeth Bishop, 'Arrival at Santos'

In autumn 1979, my first week at Harvard, I took the street car down to Boston University to hear Elizabeth Bishop read her poems. I had been reading and studying her work for the previous two years, and to hear her deep rich voice and the strange, precise, profound poems emerging from this small, plump, well-dressed woman (she dressed like the sort of woman who lunches) was sheer pleasure and the fulfilment of a private excitement. At that time, her work wasn't widely known or appreciated at home in England; I had felt pretty much a lone fan. I was far too shy to approach her after the reading and stole off back to Cambridge full of the poems.

I was taking a poetry class taught by Seamus Heaney, who offered to intercede for me with the notoriously private Bishop, and pretty soon I received a charming letter from her in reply to my own, offering to meet me. But I was to miss her. On 7 October I crossed the quads to hear her read at Harvard. The hall was packed; everyone else there seemed to know what I didn't know, that she had died suddenly the day before, at her apartment overlooking Boston Harbor. I was slow to grasp what was going on, still expecting her to appear, as a collection of her friends and fellow-poets – including luminaries like Heaney – came to the microphone in turn to read her poems as a tribute. The understanding and sorrow hit me like a wave.

I had lost two things: not only the possibility of direct connection with one of very few major women poets writing at that time, but also the possibility of direct connection with the contemporary poet (of either sex) whose work I admired most. I was also haunted by the idea that I was part of the first generation of poets for whom both these statements could be true at once – given that the door had only just started to open beyond a crack to women poets – which compounded my sense of loss.

All poets will tell you of the importance of their predecessors. The poets who have gone before are the ones who teach us our business, help us refine our craft, and carve out our territories. We quarrel with them, rebel against them, restate their positions, assert our own. We have imaginary conversations and arguments with them; we write (but do not send them) letters in which we arrogantly try to correct the mistakes in their writing and their lives. In this way, Elizabeth Bishop has been my teacher. More particularly she has been my geography teacher, or perhaps even my anti-geography teacher.

When I wrote the poem 'Phrase Book' in 1991, I had just tripped over the following sentences in an old Collins Italian/English Phrase Book dating from 1963. 'Let me pass please. I am an Englishwoman.' I was stunned and amused. I couldn't think where in the world that order would actually work now. Pulled this way into the phrase book, I combined its world and language with language of the technology of warfare and so the poem was born. The encounter with the Englishwoman of the phrase book also caused me to pause and think about her. Who was, or is she? The word even sounds colonial. It carries far more connotations than simple gender and place of habitation, making it almost too difficult, too uncomfortable to use, to the point where it has died as a word in common currency. There are layers of meaning which make the designation of her original country just as much an evocation of time and political context as of place.

Any poet has to think hard about her origins. When I was first trying my wings as a writer, the tyro poet was always told, first, to write about what you know and, second, to 'Dig where you stand', to delve into the language and landscape of your own territory. In a writer like Seamus Heaney the landscapes and place-names of his home could become, in the poem 'Anahorish', 'soft gradient / of consonant, vowel meadow'. As a young writer I felt at a disadvantage. I grew up in a new town, Hemel Hempstead, where there were absolutely no vowel meadows and where the spoken language was flat, a version of London watered down by a mild accumulation of the various modes of speech of the many people who had moved there from all over the place. My own parents, from England's West Country, were a case in point. Over the years I heard their rich Forest of Dean accents and phraseology fade. To my ear the speech mixture around us was milk and water rather than, say, the tang of language you hear on London streets today. In addition, and if it was true then, it is even more true now, the best poetry in English was by writers from other countries or, at least, with strong links back to other countries, cultures and languages.

Since then, my quest has been to discover how to be a different kind of writer, for whom place and language are less certain, and for whom shifting territories are the norm. It's no wonder that from the start I found a model in the reluctantly American poet Elizabeth Bishop; her travels through geography and poetry led my own steps. I am not the only writer to feel this way about her. Robert Lowell famously said that 're-reading her suggested a way of breaking through the shell of my old manner. Her rhythms, idiom, images, and stanza structure seemed to belong to a later century.' I suspect there is a hint of early post-modernism in her work which speaks to writers who want to make an aesthetic of the fragmentary and rootless experience which now seems the norm. Julia Kristeva spoke of the theorist as 'an impertinent traveller' passing across 'whole geographic and discursive continents'. It is in this context that Englishness, the meaning of being English – and yes, an Englishwoman, because gender certainly has something to do with it – has nagged at me, and has cropped in many of my poems. Who is this Englishwoman?

Part of the answer to the question of how to engage with the material of my own country came from Bishop. Born in Nova Scotia, she was a reluctant American, describing herself as 'kidnapped' from Canada when, as a small child, she was taken by her grandparents to the United States. In her moving essay, 'The Country Mouse', she gives an account of the move, and at one point describes the wrench from the language of her old home. This early dislocation would ensure that she could never be a poet of the 'vowel meadow' and would have to find another way.

> I had been brought back unconsulted and against my wishes to the house my father had been born in, to be saved from a life of poverty and provincialism, bare feet, suet puddings, unsanitary school slates, perhaps even from the inverted *r's* of my mother's family. With this surprising set of extra grandparents, until a few weeks ago no more than names, a new life was about to begin. It was a day that seemed to include months in it, or even years, a whole unknown past I was made to feel I should have known about, and a strange, unpredictable future.[1]

Most interestingly, she decided at once that she did not want to be American and her relationship with her second country remained ambivalent for the rest of her life, large parts of which were spent living abroad:

> The War was on. At recess we were marched into the central hall, class by class, to the music of an upright piano, a clumping march that has haunted me all my life and I have never yet placed. There we pledged allegiance to the flag and sang war songs: 'Joan of Arc, they are ca-alllll-ing you.' I hated the songs, and most of all I hated saluting the flag. I would have refused if I had dared. In my Canadian schooling, the year before, we had started every day with 'God Save the King' and 'The Maple Leaf Forever.' Now I felt like a traitor. I wanted us to win the War, of course, *but I didn't want to be an American.* When I went home to lunch, I said so. Grandma was horrified; she almost wept. Shortly after, I was presented with a white card with an American flag in colour at the top. All the stanzas of 'Oh, say, can you see' were printed on it in dark blue letters. Every day I sat at Grandma's feet and attempted to recite this endless poem. We didn't sing because she couldn't stay in tune, she said. Most of the words made no sense at all. (*CP* 26–7)

A life spent travelling, living for long periods in other countries, a distaste and longing, for political or emotional reasons for one's homeland. These aspects of Bishop's life felt familiar to me and, as I came to understand, more typical of western contemporary experience than rootedness. Imagine my glee, on first opening *The Complete Poems* to find the names of Bishop's books – *North & South; Questions of Travel; Geography III* and then, turning to the first page, an exquisite poem called 'The Map', which read to me like formal permission to put travel, rootlessness, even lost identity, at the centre.

When, in 1993, I was commissioned to write a version of Marina Tsvetaeva's poem 'Motherland' I surprised myself by starting to explore some of these issues. For Tsvetaeva, the motherland is Mother Russia. Her poem movingly evokes its landscapes and its history with nostalgia and passion from the perspective of her exile in Paris in the 1920s. My Motherland is England, and I found my version evoking quite a different emotional tone:

Motherland
after Tsvetaeva

Language is impossible
in a country like this. Even
the dictionary laughs when I look up
'England', 'Motherland', 'Home'.

It insists on falling open instead
three times out of the nine I try it
at the word Distance: 'Degree
of remoteness, interval of space.'

Distance: the word is ingrained like pain.
So much for England and so much
for my future to walk into the horizon
carrying distance in a broken suitcase.

The dictionary is the only one
who talks to me now. Says, laughing,
'Come back HOME!' but takes me
further and further away into the cold stars.

I am blue, bluer than water
I am nothing, for all I do
is pour syllables over aching brows.

England. It hurts my lips to shape
the word. This country makes me say
too many things I can't say. Home
of me, myself, my motherland.

Such a viewpoint need not always be tragic. In her essay on Elizabeth
Bishop, Anne Shifrer quotes from a letter Bishop wrote to Anny
Baumann in 1952: 'It seems to be mid-winter, and yet it is time to
plant things – but my Anglo-Saxon blood is gradually relinquishing its
seasonal cycle and I'm quite content to live in complete confusion,
about seasons, fruits, language, geography, everything.' Shifrer finds
Bishop sounding

refreshingly postmodern and not like Crusoe, moribund with lost meaning and collapsed symbolic systems. At this moment in her life, she finds vitality in cultural relativity. Rather than hungering for the anchored and absolute systems, she seems content with occasionally numinous secular objects and events that may well be disconnected or connected only by 'and' and 'and.' Perhaps this attitude of nonmastery, of accepting bafflement is less imperial.

The reference here is to *Crusoe in England*, Bishop's most ambitious poem of travel. The poem is spoken by the old Crusoe, reflecting on his life on the desert island from the safety – and prison – of England. The question now is what is left after travel, what is memory, what is loss, what is home. Crusoe's – and Bishop's – worst nightmare changes during the course of the poem from the dream of infinities of islands, all to be described in detail, to its opposite: the nightmare of exile – in England, the so-called motherland – exile from travelling, and a subsequent shrivelling of the imagination.

Changes in the outer world have been as just as important to what is left of the Englishwoman as changes in her inner world. Cicely Hamilton comments on what happened 'when the first aeroplane rose from the ground' and the subsequent effect on warfare, on the lives of civilians and especially women. Gillian Beer has written on the effect of the coming of the aeroplane on the essentially island story of England looking, in particular, at the writing of Virginia Woolf:

> Woolf's quarrel with patriarchy and imperialism gave a particular complexity to her appropriations of the island story. At the same time her symbolising imagination played upon its multiple significations – land and water margins, home, body, individualism, literary canon – and set them in shifting relations to air and aeroplane.

The wars of this century, the end of empire, the aeroplane, the channel tunnel, the World Wide Web, the role of women, the power of multinational conglomerates, the preponderance of great literature in English from elsewhere, our many changed viewpoints as we enter the new century, all these unite to tell us that the island story of England, little England, is finished. Borders and edges of territory and language, home and body, land and water have always offered some of the most attractive hide-outs for women writers who have long understood that the secret might be simply to let the other in or to sift through whatever flotsam washes up.

Note

1. Elizabeth Bishop, *Collected Prose* (London: Chatto & Windus, 1994), 17 (hereafter *CP*).

9

riverrunning (realisations
For Charles Bernstein

Maggie O'Sullivan

TALK.
Tell-Tale.
Heard-Tell.
Tell-Tales.
Heard-Tell-Of
Uttering – Tell-Tale.

'WELL YOU KNOW OR DON'T YOU KENNET OR HAVEN'T I TOLD
YOU EVERY TELLING HAS A TALING AND THAT'S THE HE AND THE
SHE OF IT'

A Crack   A Rip   A Spin   Minding a Spin

SPIN CLACKY SABLE

In Irish, AMHRAIN: COEL:
A Song, A Song Said Otherwise, half-sung/half-said,
SINGS – Speaking the Self/whom sang/ Singing over/ --
The Irish again – ABAIR AMHRAIN – Say us a Song –
ASBUIR – Say, Speak / Words Spoken /Give us Your
Tongue It to See – dark blades how sang crows
disquieting the auditorium's fabular harmonics –
Worlds by Words / Telling Alive Mirrors to the
stream affrighted Speaker & Listener – turn by turn
between, & the moon late in rising – Live Blood/Its
Rise with the Other/ A Wilder Air Chancing toPoetry's
Music (Amplified) Edgewise –

                    Then. Now. There. Here.

So with the lamp's tiny farces whimpering

THE SOILS OF
SPELLING,
SCRYED
SMUDGED
STREELED

LILTING

CAVORT &
SULT
SLIDE OF –

CONSTELLATIONS –

A Blessing.   A Curse.   A Spell.

A Riddle winding Prayer.

A Retort.
(Include a Nightmare – i am in the house i grew in my family
abound me   Charles Bernstein & 2 aides alarm the fading door they
have bicycled in the rain   i know this because when i move my air
in greeting his hand drips all & of none   clanging back the waters
so nervous & so tore my tongue frets & webbing Bided   the 3 settee
& ask me every piling upofme my talk   i cannot speak my family
hover in multiple & little spits of outness gentle   danny flexes the
sun   stenches & figures hectories gang   he hands me the glacial
surge & maps me how he nearly lost himself in the glisten of ears
still i cannot speak   i battle to say swans, lizards into the nerve's
woke since in the south such as silver sleet over cost oaks   because
coax you use seem

hug fall as snow on the larynx   he damsons phlegm adieu like all
pantomimic wildbrother   still i cannot speak)   i scant, dwindled
stammering before speech, i

TREMORING BUSTLE & MUTE
(-- WRENS CROSS MY PATH --)
DO PLAY, DO SIGN,

THE BEADS & LIGHT RECITING –
ON ICYCLES WE LIVED.

Spirally & Counter. (Include Scene-Shifts – The Painter with head
in birdcage draws with rope herstory hymn emerald primates,
frogs' far-spread of the dipthong attired, powdered it erupts laking
the floor). (Include guiDance from Beuys: 'FIRST I USED RUBBER
IT DID NOT SATISFY ME BECAUSE IT WAS TOO DIRECT, TOO
DIDACTIC AND THEREFORE QUICKLY REDUNDANT').

THE 2 CIRCLES/ECLIPSE/& BEYOND THE MIRROR, BEYOND
DIALECTICS, HIGH UP AT THE BACK OF THE PALATE, TOUCHING
BROOMS IN DUST CLOUD-POUR CAPED INTO FLOOD

> (FISH
> DALLY
> IN THESE GREEN DEPTHS –
> THEY SHEEN & CROSS
> &
> WHISPER
> FORRESTS
> OF ANIMAL
> AT EACH CURVE IN THE WATER
> THERE IS A CREATURE
> THERE IS A DANCE
> OF CREATURES
> IN DANCE OF
> WANDERING
> DANCING
> INTO
> THE SUN --)

Frames of Seizure, Frame as Threshold, as Interpretation, as
Ambience, as Refuge, Outside the Frame – skin wines go indoors
or be, a cluster of moth steps The Pale Moon Rising forming,
breaking up, plundering, blundering, sounding: voicing:

'HITHERANDTHITHERING'

fanning out to

'REPEAT, REPEAT ...BLED, BLED ON A SUDDEN AT A SOUND'

What happens in the telling?
A Blackbird, its gouged throb unscripted ---
Marigold's plush & Boiling sheer
geranium Tang.
A Chirp. Braided, attended misbehaves
animated by extension, lips drove I eared/Listen out for
the light –
Ear-Loads I Sing!

'WRING OUT THE CLOTHES!
WRING IN THE DEW!'

Sounded by Un – I DENT/if/EYE/where, to, to towards the far end
– far away from: at fault: breach: in error: at a loss: outlying: ruled
out: caesarian: exiled: unknown: outCRY july I

    I THE SHADOWED SIDE –
    COLDER & SORRYING'S CURTAIN WOULD HAVE –

    DISPARATE HARMINGS

    DAY.D. DAILY-NESS.

    ABDICATOR, INCENDIARIST, RELINQUISHER,
    TATTERER, BATTERER, MENACER, HERETIC
    HOOLIGAN

'ANNA LIVIA'

say SO / dill/dash/ --
        say so LESS

turning & returning & stirring the phrases in the plate of
promise, what promise of I can't for you?
           for me?
           for whom?

Poetry finds my life – Poetry as she has Arisen 'AS SHE
ARRIVES OUT OF THE FUTURE, WORDS LIVING', moving

m eye out among the ribbed & swimmish places
Uncoiled,Endowed among us
in the arrival of
remembrancing   responding   realising   journeying
the moment by
moment
anchor out of her
depth that is
LANGUAGE
DANCE
DREAM
'COLLIDERINGS' –

*

Moving Up in the Spring & Down in the Autumn –
Collaborations / Liberations /
VISION / MYTH / RITUAL /
Words, Breath,
Divergence & Multiplicity, my tend sees errant, Vulnerable
Chanceways –
BECOMING
Strains of Lament & Desire
& Perpetual Strong SONG –
physical fictions, vertiginous & angular swole divulgements,
resistances, unwisdoms, dither-sickings, Earsick tongue–
spew – Displacement – Pluralities – Diversity – Convergence,
Flux of Utterance, Mistakes, Da-mage, Duncan's 'MISUSE,

MISUNDERSTANDING, THE WHOLE SPIRITUALISED UNIVERSE'
Activated, closely, broadly, introspectively – Charting ambiguity,
tending the possibilities in language. In Saying this I am Telescoping /
have you witness I am Sing Lingered, Indeterminate:

IN PLACES/RECALLED ASSERTIONS/ SWEEP/SINISTER BURNETS FROM
DISTANCE/LARCENOUS/REFLECTIVE/ MARL & CHALK PREPONDE-
RANT/
ELONGATIONS/VARIANT GALLONS/CHANTING PERPENDICULAR.

The works I make Celebrate Origins/Entrances – the
Materiality of Language: its actual contractions &

expansions, potentialities, prolongments, assemblages –
the acoustic, visual, oral & sculptural qualities
within the physical: intervals between; in & beside.
Also the jubilant seep In So of Spirit – Entanglement
with vegetations, thronged weathers, puppy-web we agreed
animals.   Articulations of the Earth of Language   that is
Minglement, Ceasura, Illumination.

Heart
At once several times TUMULT & Beak-Sup Dusting/
Believing/Convulsions break out in the next line. SILENCE

introduction of
sound:
introduction of
sight:
introduction of
texture:

*

What 'Making' -- 'Unmaking is / a Mattering of
Materials (motivations and practise) – Living to live in
that Learning – Uncertain, Uncurtained Tonguescape
SUNG. SHUNTS. ARM WE. Living Earth Kinships on the
vast-lunged Shores of the Multiple Body imbued with
wide-wake slumberings & cavortings. Constructions.
Intuitions. Transmissions. Radiations. Thinking.
ATTENDING. Feeling. Will –
Digressions
Pauses.
Came to my hands. A play's acres & category in the
sheltering characteristics of tea & there being no sugar,
no milk, no whole glazes of the symphony we search
among.
Divination. Location. Is it the Thorn & Curse &
Gap & Gone of my ancestors? Is it their thong &
Plight & flood of which i still   EM Embark & fall
through – the first ones to say a whole body of
'A RAINDROP WINKING ON A THORN' – Excavation /
Exploration /

Experiment –
EXCLA
&
collaboration / incomplete / inexact / <u>ENACTING</u>
her own speech & even outside it?
'Twinedom to a Tent... The Wing of stitchy / Sermons...
Our Theatre has Loud of the Skull... I'm.very.often. dimmed.
is. that?   Challenging/ Transpiring/ Provoking/
Engaging with the OUT, the UNDER – the UN—the OTHER-THAN,
The NON & the LESS – transgressions; trespass; disparity;
Subversion: Milton's 'UNTWISTING THE CHAINS THAT TIE'

*

It's easy to loss here.

<u>Numerology</u>:

1.   Vermeer's wife had 11 children.
2.   My grandfather Michael O' Sullivan was a skilled mower. The
     skill was in the sharpening & smoothing of the blade. Using the
     stones, he mowed for 50 pence an acre. (A mower is now a
     machine with revolving blades).
3.   One of the MacBrodins, poets of Clare, was cast over a cliff by
     a Cromwellian soldier who cried after him as he fell: 'Sing now,
     little man'.
4.   Electricity didn't come to Skibbereen until 1962.
5.   Under Cromwell it became the law that any man would earn £5 by
     producing the head of a wolf or a priest – it didn't matter
     which.

*

In 1984, I began my assemblages or visual constructions – (I do not
know why they began but they needed to begin) – ASSEMBLAGES,
after Kurt Schwitters who made superb use of the UN – the NON
and the LESS – THE UNREGARDED, the found, the cast-offs, the
dismembered materials of culture. His work shows me to look away
from, beyond the given. In this concern for the retrieval of potentials
within material his influence and teeming upon how I work is
closely akin to that of Joseph Beuys.

*

In 1988, after having been involved in the transformative experience
of working on a television film on Beuys, I stepped out, away from
the city to the moorland impress of tongue
In celebration of this, I praised trees & hugged & planted them
– to make a wood – a spirit of the woods in Celtic imagination
where the whole world was alive – oak, alder, birch, willow,
cherry, mountain ash –

'THE BLACKTHORN IS A JAGGY CREEL
STIPPLED WIT DARK SLOES'

LITERGICAL / THE CLIMB FORM BARK TO BRAIN

'THE ASPEN PALES
AND WHISPERS, HESITATES'

GREAT PLAIN / TEMPERAMENT / WHILE / WHITE THE NECK'S
GIRTH / HEART & LUNG / STEEPENING / HOURGLASS COUGHING
UPWARD /

*

'In the House of the Shaman' is borrowed from the title of one of
Beuys' drawings. In naming my work after his I am tributing his
work: fluid, changing, inviting new material, urging new responses.
His urge to begin with mistakes, to show frailty...is at once starfish
abdominal nuance   its moorings unsuspected – rescued starlight.

*

Jerome Rothenberg and the exemplary work he makes wide is a key,
too in my workings. A richness of difference: Disparity: Difficulties:
Dismemberment/Reconstituion: Sickness: Contradiction:
Improvising Upon: INTENT. ADJUSTING TEETH / WITHIN WORDS
/ WOUNDS OF CHANCE / CARESSER OF CHAOS LEAPING HABIT /
Counter to the inert everydom that breathes the slave.

THE FOLD INTRODUCES ANOTHER MOVEMENT, IN CONTRAST
TO THE STRAIGHTFORWARD PILING OF FELT.

It dusks & throws. Plucked, plucked, Unsteady Drifting perspectives
Beyond the materialist world: 'THE HARDSHIPS & DELIGHTS OF

THE SEASONS', (stance in streams hurl their pieces in kinship):
DANCING THE STAND OF ROOTS / A LUTE IN THE IDDLING AIR
interspeciel/interrealmic Joy:stone of light water, flaxfield,
scrub of juniper, shifting in the life of trees: SMALL PERPETUAL
REDS OF HEAD & YELLOW SCARLETS / HURLING CLAW STUT
PIGMENT (BE IT FISH MAMMAL OR BIRD).

In words, other rooming for what is at RISK inside out in language.
Oppositional dialogues, realities, cartwheels, sway substances,
Language Undeniably, Ably drowsed, dowsed even.
THE WAY YOU'D BE BUILDING A WALL & YOU'D KNOW WHERE
TO PUT THE STONES.

*

Drifting, Shape-Shifting thinner stringed 8 leaning Loanded Ebb –
Like all dredger sepulchral – hold it/don't lose your expression –

RAW IT SWIMS / THE PACE THE LIPS / TWISTING (t'woud twist,
Twist, twist) / THE BRITTLE / CRACKLY DRAWINGS OF /

VULNERARY
SNAPTIC EQUILIBRIUMS –

THEY CAME TO ME
MAMMALS PLOUGHING SKULL –

               (WILLOW
                I DO
               TO IT –

DOG
VIXEN
BOAR
SOW

SHE-FOXES

&

SHE-BADGERS
IN MY EYE ISLET OF

SADDLE VALENCES
ILKES COMETAL, ILKES OF THE COMPASS –

& then maybe you go to another place –
2ND LESSON FROM THE COKEREL

RIVERCRAFT, CAREY NEON, DOVE-WEBBING FATIGUES. THE
SASHED, SILENT ONE WHO HEARS, THEN AS ONE WHO.
CONJURING SPAT LIGHTS ON THE PALATE. MUSEY TIGHT SADDED
HAWDY KERDY'S, RAGE RUGGING JET, PORTAGE THICKENS
          (NEVERINE SPARROWS IN THE MOUTH
          BLISTER). RED STROUDERS DEW-BUCKLING
RIGHT-HAND   WINTER, TONGUE-A-SAD-OF-ALL-BIRDS
PASSAGEWORK   WHEN THE WAVES COME BONED, BLEED
          LICKS THE SWIRE-HEAD, THE DONE-SKIRT.
          THE SCALDING. THE SHOT-OVER BELLIES
          READ WITH JASPER, MINCE, THE MASSIVE
          SHIVERS, LOOF, SWOLE   J U T T I N G
          MULTIPLICATION.

Sources

Bruce Andrews, Maggie O'Sullivan, *EXCLA* (London: Writers Forum, 1993).

Charles Bernstein, *A Poetics* (Cambridge, Mass.: Harvard UP, 1992)

Basil Bunting, *Collected Poems* (Oxford: Oxford UP, 1978).

Robin Flower, *The Irish Tradition* (Oxford: Clarendon Press, 1947).

N. Kershaw Chadwick, *Poetry and Prophesy* (Cambridge: Cambridge UP, 1942).

James Joyce, *Finnegans Wake* (London: Penguin, 1969).

Velimir Klebnikov, *The King of Time: Poems, Fictions, Visions of the Future*, trans. Paul Schmidt, ed. Charlotte Douglas (Cambridge, Mass.: Harvard UP, 1985).

Seamus Mac Reamoinn (ed.), *The Pleasures of Gaelic Poetry* (London: Allen Lane, 1982)

Sean O'Faolain, *The Irish* (London: Penguin, 1969).

Jerome Rothenberg, 'Ethnopoetics & Politics/The Politics of Ethno-poetics', in *The Politics of Poetic Form*, ed. Charles Bernstein (New York: Roof Books, 1990).

Caroline Tisdall, *Joseph Beuys* (London: Thames and Hudson, 1979)

This text is based on a talk I gave at the State University of New York at Buffalo on Tuesday 26 October 1993 and also at the Kootenay School of Writing, Vancouver, on Wednesday 3 November, 1993.

10
'Nothing That Is Not There and the Nothing That Is'

Deryn Rees-Jones

> For the listener, who listens in the snow
> And, nothing, himself, beholds
> Nothing that is not there and the nothing that is.
>
> Wallace Stevens

Writing poems is always a negotiation of loss, a way of capturing time in the moment of writing. In that sense I like to think of all poems as elegies to experience or the experience of imagination – gateways or lintels under which both poet and reader stand, looking both forwards and back. And yet here, too, is the point at which memory meets imagination, for poetry is loss as much as it is a resistance to loss. The mouth's own elegy, as Adam Phillips beautifully describes the kiss. For if the kiss is something we desire it is also something we can never give our own lips: we are, in a sense, the kiss, but we can never experience it except through another.

It's the same with the relationship between poem, experience, poet and reader. There's a sense as a poet that one can ever really know something through the writing of it, and yet, in the act of writing you transform and also lose part of the experience you needed to communicate. The lyric poem demands an engagement between the you and the I, the self and the other, and nowhere is this more obvious than in the love lyric. Many of the poems that I write end up being love poems of one sort or another: that leaves me with a very easy option when looking for a muse, a figure of otherness: the desired other. But it would be wrong to assume that that other is or exists. Often I find when writing that people coalesce into the figure of the desired other; and again the charge of the poem revolves around the fact that the other can never be possessed. Another way of exploring otherness in a less dyadic relationship than the I-you relationship of the lyric, is of course, the dramatic poem. I started exploring the dramatic monologue through my readings of Carol Ann Duffy, and then a return to Browning, because I found it a liberating form; it's hard to describe, but it did just give me a license I didn't have at the time, a sense of authority over experience in the imagination which I didn't feel poetically belonged to my own voice. Of course, there's a sense in which the poem never is your voice, an echo of voices: I'm very interested in the way intertextuality works in poems: like to consciously haunt my poems with fragments or rhythms of other writers: a postmodern project in some sense, I suppose, but not one which is only postmodern in its reach. In my poem 'Song for Winter' I try to capture some of the rhythms of Rilke's first ode:

> These days, even love is terrible,
> Like a plane, taking off inside the heart.
> And now there's nowhere left to go.
> For you've brought me to the edges of hell
> With your soft ways and your gardener's hands;
> You, who'd turn your hand, your eye, to anything,
> Filling the house with the smell of bread and roasting lamb,
> Bringing in wood for the fire from the yard
> As if it were a task of love, or something to be guilty of ...
> And if I cried out in the night, if you cried too,
> To the buildings and the lightless houses,
> To truck, to retail parks, to helicopters, taxis,
> The digital, the car alarms, who is there to answer?
> Who amidst the landscape that I almost recognise,
> The rest homes and the hospitals, the pubs,
> The restaurants, the neoned clubs, the bric-à-brac
> Of roof and trees, a mutilated statue in the park,
> Wh laughing, who retching, who weeping,
> Who is there to tell how sorrow puts a name to sorrow –
> With language or the body? T.V., the radio,
> The little gods of noise? For we carry love
> Like a kind of pain, desire like terror,
> A sticklebacked wave.... And who, looking down,
> Would offer more than this, a shrug, a look of pity, or a smile?
> Who, seeing us now, our gaze upturned, the knowing stars
> Like a litter of rice, confetti of fractured bone, of broken glass,
> Could pluck us, unhurt from the universe,

Rechart the stars, make everything strange?
Wht's more, who'd even ask, or have the right to ask
Why nothing comes of nothing, still?
I play back voices on the ansaphone, a prayer

Tree-twist   feather   tangle-hair

In this poem I'm trying to deal with loss, and in particular, loss in a secular age. The poem is almost about the disintegration of the self through an acknowledgment of such loss; and in it I'm questioning how one recognises the familiar. It also celebrates the urban song of voices, car alarms, ansaphones – all devices which in this context testify to the absence of the self. As well as the Rilke, there are references to Shakespeare's *Lear*, to Yeats's 'Leda and the Swan': ones which I hadn't consciously planned on putting in there, but which somehow appeared.

As John Hollander says in the introduction to his recent book, *The Work of Poetry*, what's amazing about writing a poem is that in order to write it you have to get into a state where it looks from the outside as if you are doing nothing. The more I write the more I realise that there is no one way in which a poem may come. Poetry allows a sense of a rich inner life which in everyday life becomes numbed. So much of the world we experience in a capitalist society is concerned with numbing one's responses to things, to feelings, and I love the surprise and potential radicalism of revisiting the familiar, the unseen, as the new. As the Russian formalist Shklovsky wrote: 'art exists that one may recover the sensation of life; it exists to make one feel things, to make the stone stony. Art is a way of experiencing the artfulness of an object, the object is not important.' Our outer life is such a bombardment of images and sounds. The late romantic me wants to run screaming from that bombardment in search of some ideal and idealised expressive self, while the postmodern me loves the fragmentation, the multiple levels on which I can experience my self in the urban world or even disappear. I'm aware of the strange dichotomy that sets up but I don't think it's that unusual a response to the world.

Like many poets, I write criticism and poetry at the same time – or perhaps it's something I've needed to learn to do as way of earning a living. But at this stage the relationship between writing poetry and reading poetry creatively is one which I would describe as a symbiotic relationship. Criticism is a way of making oneself think about poems in a certain way and I'm aware that I have a tendency, sometimes, to be a lazy or inattentive reader. But thinking about it as objectively as I can, I also think that one validates the other for me, too. When I had more time as a student I'd sit and flip between computer screens – one criticism, one poetry. There'd be a sense that one idea could feed into another. At the moment, though, I use criticism as a way of 'blocking out' periods of creative time for myself. Times when I have to be, or feel I have to be, writing other things which clutter up my head and draw on my energies to such a degree that I can't write poetry. Perhaps times when I feel I'm not ready to write, but when I know I can be doing a diverting but necessary groundwork. That means that I have to get to grips with ideas and that I don't have always to work on an emotional level. That isn't of course to say that one precludes the other: it's just that one becomes a silent but vital partner. For me, writing poems is a way of knowing without knowing, a way of exploring things I can't adequately express in their fullness in the words of daily-ness, or even the words of the critic. It's also something very hard to talk about because at all levels it resists explanation. The poem says what it means to, with and without the poet's help. And yet it has always seemed necessary to be a close reader of poems in order to be able to write them. When you read as a critic you are always analysing. It's not that you're starving yourself of the pleasure of a poem but multiplying its complexity in a conscious way, and battling to make an argument coherent. The most dismal failures of poems seem to be the ones that originate from ideas. Not that poems shouldn't be concerned with ideas – on the contrary – but my sense is that the ideas have to surface in a poem in a non-rational way. The way in which these things take hold is magical. But only in the way that many ordinary things are magical. *Birth, copulation and death!* Criticism, at its best, gives you an idea of the ability of a poem to explore multitudes, gives you an idea of what a really good poem can be.

When I'm not writing a poem it's a mystery how I ever managed to write at all. Those periods of silence when one is not writing anything one could call a finished poem can be long, but they are also useful and it's comforting to see them as periods of transition. It's the time I allow myself to give my unconscious time to stew and bubble. But it's also a time of anxiety in which I try not to allow the fretfulness take over. When I read other things as a way of finding material for poems, I like to read in a way which is not analytic. If one can make such reductive distinctions it would be fair to say that I like to read as a poet not a critic, not for sense but for the images and the ideas: not necessarily in a formal or coherent way. Pieces of criticism or philosophy capture the imagination: Wittgenstein's *Remarks on Colour*; Freud's essay 'The Mystic Writing Pad', an essay in which you can hear the crinkle of the waxy paper, feel the textures; newspapers, the internet; popular books on gardening, astrology, feng shui. As a poet I think I need to read and play off writers who both remedy and consolidate my own writing. Often what one needs as a writer is not what one needs as a reader – it's curious that I feel I don't write the kind of poems I need to read. One of my favourite poems at the moment is Muldoon's 'Incantata' – because it allows a kind of intellectual dizziness. It's an amazing song of memorialisation and an attempt at recovery through an acknowledgment of loss. Another poem I love is Thom Gunn's 'Ode to the Great Dejection'. I can't quite understand it as a poem, where it's coming from, its ironies, its terror, but as a reader who writes poems I read it as a poem which shows how you can travel great distances, but still manage to make the most subtle of shift of feeling without apparently doing anything.

As I've continued writing, I've realised that it's just as important to be obsessed with aspects of the world that can be used 'objectively' as it is to be interested and engaged with the work of other poets. The idea of a contained, confessional self is one which in the moment of writing gets written away. A poem has to engage with the times in which it lives; there is a way in which it cannot escape it. In the current climate there is, I think a responsibility to think about science, gender, love, war, identity. And yet you can't *make* a poem do anything. Sometimes you can be thinking about these things and they never work themselves explicitly into a poem. The worst and the best thing about writing a poem is that you can't force it. It has the will of your own unconscious and its battle is with your own creative consciousness. Sometimes you're doing battle with the force of ideas, sometimes it's a case of trying to overcome your own technical limitations. And all the time you can be thinking – it can't be that hard. It's just a question of shifting a few words around on the page. And yet the imaginative process can be exhilarating and totally exhausting. But it is different to when one is writing criticism, however creative that criticism may be; it exhausts you in a different way – you perhaps falsely feel you're grasping always for the known. Poem are, as Bishop describes Joseph Cornell's boxes: 'Monuments to every moment, / refuse of every moment, used: / cages for infinity.' Writing a poem you're not even sure you know what you're looking for – just that something is out there wild and running and for some reason you're not quite sure of you have to run after it, in the hope you might just catch sight of it, catch up.

11
Writing About Writing About Writing (About Writing)
Alison Mark

> Poetry is doing nothing but using losing refusing and pleasing and betraying and caressing nouns. That is what poetry does, that is what poetry has to do no matter what kind of poetry it is. And there are a great many kinds of poetry.[1] (Gertrude Stein)

I am a reader, and not a poet. I rarely even identify myself as a writer. But of course I do write, and I have chosen for the most part to write about those who write, and in particular, those who write poetry. Just why is a question I've pondered at different times, but never before addressed myself to in writing. I have often thought of myself as an accidental writer about poems. On a relatively late return to academic life I was fortunate enough to be captured by a poet taught on my part-time MA course in modern literature, in the very first term of my return.[2] The extraordinary linguistic manoeuvrings, intellectual enquiries, and piercing emotional acuteness of the poems of Veronica Forrest-Thomson demanded attention, and a wider attention than they had received – although a small number of people, mostly poets, had kept her work alive both in Britain and America since her tragically early death in 1975. Since then I have worked intensively on her poetry and poetics, and on the work of other poets and theorists whose work, like hers, is written in what she called – with a nice eye for an oxymoron – 'the tradition of innovation'.[3]

Why poetry? The simplest answer, is: for its intensity. And this is by no means simple. The compression of language, thought and affect possible in poetry is possible in no other form of discourse. Part of the intensity is the effect of that compression itself, and the capacity that often miraculous compression has for overdetermination; for a plurality of significations. And this it exercises not just through the multiple

meanings of the words themselves, or the metonymic chain of language
– connotative as well as denotative – but through the power of poetic
artifice to manipulate syntax so as to allow many readings, many natu-
ralisations, narrativisations, and often with little or no certainty of
which is to be 'preferred'; for there is no ultimate authority. There are
only readers – who are also writers – and a writer who is inevitably, as
Helen Carr notes in 'Poetic License',[4] her or his own first reader.

When in the lecture which provides my epigraph, 'Poetry and
Grammar', Gertrude Stein defines poetry as 'caressing nouns', she cites
as an example her brilliant defamiliarisation of the red rose of romance
and lyric:[5]

> When I said.
> A rose is a rose is a rose is a rose.
> And then later made that into a ring I made poetry and what did
> I do I caressed completely caressed and addressed a noun.
> (Stein 138)

Stein goes on to unite the cognitive and affective aspects of poetry,
knowing and feeling, with the issue of names and naming which lies
at the core of 'a great many kinds' of poems – naming which includes,
she says, 'emotions as well as things' (Stein 141). 'That is what poetry
is', Stein says; 'it is a state of knowing and feeling a name. I know that
now but I have only come to that by long writing' (Stein 140). It is
even the core – though by negation – of the kind of poetry which articulates what she carefully called 'a way of naming things that would
not invent names, but mean names without naming them' (Stein 141).
Much, if not all, of Stein's own work presses against the borderlines
between poetry and prose in ways that prefigure the writing of those
who came to be called 'Language' writers (American poets from the
West and East coasts, many of whom were associated with the journal
L=A=N=G=U=A=G=E),[6] writing which American poet and theorist Ron
Silliman attempted to theorise in 'The New Sentence'.[7]

That Stein was writing new sentences in 1934, if not quite 'the new
sentence', Silliman clearly knows. In his essay – originally a talk, like
Stein's lecture – Silliman cites as his favourite sentence from *How to
Write*, and which Stein herself quotes in 'Poetry and Grammar': 'A dog
which you have never had before has sighed' (*NS* 87).[8] He invokes this
just prior to quoting Stein's discussion of prose, and in particular how
'prose can be the essential balance that is made inside something that
combines the sentence and the paragraph' (Stein 137) which can

capture the tension between the two. In the prose poetry he goes on to discuss,[9] in which, he says, 'the paragraph organizes the sentences in fundamentally the same way a stanza does lines of verse' (*NS* 89), Silliman's 'new sentence' not only sustains the grammatical form of the sentence but internalises, usually through what he calls 'torquing' the syntax, the effects produced more overtly by conventional devices of poetic artifice like line breaks. For me the torquing – to borrow Silliman's phrase – of Stein's sentence creates a melancholy that the separate elements fused in any other way could not achieve. A dog has sighed. You have never had a dog before. It is a torquing similar to, and creates an effect of immediacy much like that which is also set up by the narrative technique of free indirect discourse. In Stein's sentence the double coding (which in free indirect speech is often inflected with irony) makes for the impression of melancholy.[10]

Silliman also remarks of Stein's work how at times 'her use of ellip-tical sentences – 'Not to be. Not to be narrowly.' – deliberately leaves the subject out of sight' (*NS* 85), much, it seems to me, in the way that the so-called Language poets, and other – variously called linguistically innovative, formally active, or linguistically investigative – contem-porary poets writing in English attempt to interrogate and reposition the construction of subjectivity in language.[11] Fragmentation and discontinuity, double coding, torquing sentences, and a certain occlu-sion of the subject: these are all properties of what is considered to be postmodern poetry. And while this is not the place for a detailed exploration of the continuities and discontinuities between the modernist project and postmodernism, it is worth remarking how close Stein's technique is to the latter, particularly in her concern – which is also mine here – with the *activity* of writing as much as writing as product.[12]

From the very beginning of his remarkable long poem of poetics, *Artifice of Absorption*, which in a thoroughly postmodern fashion breaks down the distinction between poetry and theory, as well as challenging that between poetry and prose, Language poet Charles Bernstein asks in what poetic meaning consists (*AA* 6). In a much earlier critical era, A. C. Bradley's inaugural lecture at Oxford (first printed in 1901) considers the same question: 'it is, in strictness, impossible to express the meaning in any but its own words, or to change the words without changing the meaning.'[13] In the history of the attempt to shift the emphasis in reading – and writing – poetry from the primacy of meaning (which views meaning as an extractable 'essence' of the poem), Forrest-Thomson has an important place for her emphasis – in her poetry and theoretical work – on the significance of what she called the non-meaningful (or, less intransigently, semi-meaningful) levels of poetic language, which include 'phonetic and prosodic patterns, and spatial organisation' (*PA* xi), in discussing the question of poetic meaning. Bernstein takes her poetics one step further by refusing to designate any aspect of language unmeaningful, observing that 'Content never equals meaning' (*AA* 7), and that 'the poem said in any / other way is not the poem' (*AA* 11).

Bernstein offers a solution to the long-standing problem of what a poem might be by invoking the poetic as a possible attribute of reading rather than of writing. And as Silliman reminds us, 'as Jonathan Culler cautions in *Structuralist Poetics*, literary criticism is the study of reading, not writing' (*NS* 72).[14] Or so at least it has been – *pace* Barthes's distinction between the readerly and the writerly text[15] – for the most part, even with regard to contemporary poetry (it is of course the reader who completes, however presumptively, the hermeneutic circle). At the same time Bernstein maintains the significance of the writer, but not precisely in terms of her or his intentionality – their intention to write a poem – but in terms of their practice of what Forrest-Thomson capitalised as 'Artifice': their specific design for the reading of the piece *as* poem, with what Bernstein calls 'proactive – rather than reactive – styles of / reading' (*AA* 6).

What that first writer, the poet, may have meant is by no means negligible or of little interest, either from Bernstein's or from a more traditional perspective. Nor can we, if we really want to understand both the communicative and the aesthetic aspects of a work of verbal art, automatically despise biographical elements, in spite of the demolition by contemporary theory of the 'biographical fallacy'. It is clear that some references, significations, intertextualities, cannot be discerned except by the availability of some privileged information. However, like Wittgenstein (an important influence for Forrest-Thomson and subsequent 'innovative' poets), I am dubious about how 'private' language can ever be. Certainly in the case of poetry there will always be nuances of rhythm, juxtapositions, recognisable registers of languages with all their associations which offer indicators for interpretation. A reader interested in poetry at all might be expected to be sensitive to these movements in language (through which meaning itself can become part of the technical apparatus of the poem), even if not primarily concerned with their analysis. And this is true even of the work of a poet who utilises the language and epistemology of another discourse, science, say, or philosophy, in their poems, or similarly invokes an intertextual relationship through a postmodern employment of parody – not simply to burlesque or satirise, but as a structural and semantic tool of artifice. Postmodern parody does not of necessity always involve either denigration or amusement, but at one and the same time allows homage, interrogation and appropriation, conservation and transgression, tradition and resistance, free play. And this element of play in poetry is another of its remarkable attributes. Again, not just the play of language, but also of thought and feeling, and not of the poet alone, but also of the readers. Poems offer a transitional space, the possibilities for many identifications, and are of their nature liminal. Their construction can offer what Forrest-Thomson described in the Note following the poetry text of her collection, *Language-Games*, as 'the record of a series of individual thresholds of the experience of being conscious; they form the definitions, or affirmation, in time and in language, of human identity.'[16]

Poetry, and not just in this century, demonstrates – indeed enacts – what contemporary theory suggests about 'the postmodern': that identity is not unproblematic, given, or unified. Part of the performativity of poetry – performativity being a large part of its charm as a speech act – devolves upon the possibility of speaking with many different voices, and not one. From its earliest incarnations in epic, in all the languages I know of, poetry has been plurivocal, ventriloquising a range of figures including all genders, sexes, sexualities, races, ethnicities, classes and conditions, the non-human, and immortals, gods and demons. Identification is the very condition of possibility of having an identity, however provisional, and I am particularly drawn to write about those forms of poetry which problematise and disturb the kinds of identification that readers inevitably make with the subjects of their reading. And of course I write about them because I wish to understand what I, very dimly at first, perceive or experience – emotionally as well as intellectually – without yet knowing quite why or how it happens. So it is not just a pursuit of the meaning of poetry that engages, not just what a poem means (not that one could satisfactorily delimit the meaning of any poem), but how it means; how that meaning is constructed. This was, too, a passion for Forrest-Thomson, who says in her posthumously published *Poetic Artifice*, 'The question always is: how do poems work?' (*PA* x) And of course, this leads (back) into a consideration of what it is that makes poetry different from prose.

The fascination with poetry which sets out to destabilise the very notions of self (expressive), of identity (descriptive/definitive) and subjectivity (discursive) is itself far from being solely an intellectual pursuit.[17] The sense of self is of intimate concern to an individual, and to those in their close vicinity. Identity shifts with identifications (including the identifications made by/of others), some of which definitions or descriptions are persistent; and of course when one speaks of identification, one is inevitably already inscribed within the discourse of psychoanalysis of which it is so central a concept. Subjectivity, on the other hand, is constructed through the various interconnected discourses that situate the subject, such as language, ideology, and culture. And that subject can always only be, as Julia Kristeva remarks, a subject-in-process, never completed or established, and always itself subject to the range of discursive practices that operate upon all subjects. The disturbance of the categories is precisely what permits me to think about them at all, rather than taking them for granted. 'Freud's most basic insight', as Jacqueline Rose says in *States of Fantasy*, is that sight – or insight – really begins 'when you know that your vision is troubled, fallible, offkey.'[18] Hence Rose's own insight that 'the only viable way of reading is not to find, but to disorient, oneself'.

Disorientation is certainly an effect of reading some contemporary linguistically investigative poets – at least at first. One of the arresting features of reading poetry is the way in which readers naturalise, narrativise these complex forms of words, whether they be canonical or innovative; indeed, poetry relies on this for its intelligibility. The most semantically and syntactically intransigent material is also rendered at least sufficiently assimilable, particularly with some exposure to the conventions of this form of discourse, or it is doubtful that anyone would continue to read it for very long. As Bernstein suggests, 'The unreadable text is an outer limit for poetry' (*AA* 47).

Poets, like other writers, may expend enormous amounts of energy and time attempting to control the reception of their work, within the poems themselves and in discussions of them, but once that work is in the public domain, its readers (who are also writers, as reading inevitably involves a form of rewriting, or more precisely translation) are not easily restrained from making their own narrative assimilations. It is, of course, poetic artifice – which in a phrase sums up the difference between poetic and other forms of language – which offers some control over this inevitable process of naturalisation. Forrest-Thomson, recognising this in her theoretical as well as poetic work, wrote that 'whoever is powerful outside a poem, only the poet is powerful within it' (*PA* 9). Through her poetry and writing on poetics,

Forrest-Thomson tried to extend this absolute power, which ends with the poem's transmission or translation, whether vocal or written, beyond that moment. That this is not a rare phenomenon Fredric Jameson confirms, remarking in a similar context that 'no small part of the art of writing, indeed, is absorbed by this (impossible) attempt to devise a foolproof mechanism for the automatic exclusion of undesirable responses to a given literary utterance'.[19] In Forrest-Thomson's case, the attempt, verging on the obsessional, to control the reception of her poetry from without, as well as from within – by the use of the 'rhythmic, phonetic, verbal and logical devices which make poetry different from prose' (*PA* ix) – is mirrored within her poems in terms of the search for identity, while fiercely controlling what of identity is allowed to be perceived: the status of the 'I' set up by the poems is deliberately problematic.

Writers of criticism and theory often write to find out what they think, to explore the process of thinking in a more material medium than that of the internal world. Putting my thinking down on paper shows up its limitations (some of them, anyway), prevents some of the notorious slipperiness of language from deluding me about the clarity of this thought, in its capacity as argument. But when saying 'thought' I do not exclude feeling (rather than sensation) which is inevitably part of the thinking process: certainly it is when thinking about a poem. Reactions to language are never purely cerebral. In fact like writing and reading, real thinking and feeling (and this distinction between them conveniently engineered the possibility of a gendered assignment of masculine and feminine respectively) are indivisible. In the case of Forrest-Thomson it was particularly the capacity of her poems – acutely cerebral at first sight – to deliver an extraordinary affective impact, which convinced me to engage with her work.

Anthony Rudolf, who in *Poems for Shakespeare* also suggests that 'reading and writing are a palimpsest or a continuum rather than two separate acts',[20] and that 'Reading/writing is an act of translation', says of Forrest-Thomson's work that 'her poems have been described as "cerebral" ... but only by addlepates, folk who do not live ideas physically, who are blind to a dialectically articulated presence of lived abstractions'.[21] It is, as Rudolph suggests, impossible to be concerned only with the cerebral aspect of her work, the intellectual context, which includes the articulation of important theoretical and philosophical intuitions and ideas, without also engaging with affect. And not only in Forrest-Thomson's poems. Without the affective dimension, poetic language would be impoverished indeed, as

Forrest-Thomson herself remarks in *Poetic Artifice*, with reference to Shakespeare's Sonnet 94 (while dismissing the biographical fallacy):

> while it is easy to refute the notion that Shakespeare is talking directly about his love life or any specific person or persons, it is not so easy to do away with the idea that there is emotion in that poem, that there are attitudes which emerge from that arrangement of words, and that these attitudes and emotions are not entirely explicable as the result of the words' meaning as part of technique. In point of fact it is not entirely clear why we should want to do away with the notion that there is feeling in poetry, for we should find ourselves very quickly arguing that poetry is of no interest at all. (*PA* 18–19)

This is a conclusion with which I sympathise, although there are likely to be more than a few contemporary poets who might disagree. It is precisely that which escapes definition, slips between the links of the chain of signification, with which my own interpretations tend to be concerned – after taking into account, as Forrest-Thomson also prescribed, the significance of those words as part of technique. This proceeding is sited on the borderlines between poetry and psychoanalysis: 'in poetry as in psychoanalysis, language is pushed to its limits, and becomes a struggle with the inexpressible.'[22] Forrest-Thomson's technique creates a structure which enables the suspension – a splitting off – of the affective component of the poem until the final working through of the system of images is complete. In her later poems she increasingly found a further way to express the apparently inarticulable, through her use of structures of parodic juxtaposition. And by her use of the white space on the page and the manipulations of that space which typographical techniques allow, from the conventional wide margins and division into stanzas, to splitting and displacing elements of text, a technique developed with great subtlety by Susan Howe.[23] Other poets, of course, also negotiate the interfaces between consciousness and the unconscious, and the cognitive and the affective, in these and different ways.

In her doctoral thesis Forrest-Thomson explores in some detail the relationship between the cognitive and emotional aspects of knowledge as they appear in different forms of discourse, and her own resolution of the division between them there is in terms of the structure of the poem, rather than through the system of reference to an external context.[24] Poetry is a means to knowledge, but not primarily to knowledge about the external world; it is a means to knowledge *of* language, as well as *in* language. 'Language', as Stein said, 'as a real thing is not imitation either of sounds or colours or emotions it is an intellectual recreation and there is no possible doubt about it' (Stein 142). Forrest-Thomson's position is clear: any emotional or other relationship to experience is mediated by the poem:

> What is clear is that we cannot locate the emotion in either our minds or the poet's mind as situations outside the poem. If this were the case then T.E. Hulme would be right to claim that poetry was shorthand for a language of feeling that would hand over sensations bodily, and we should all be dying to get rid of the poetry to enter empathetic, kinaesthetic and inarticulate rapture. (*PA* 19)

No doubt there are such readers, but they are unlikely to be as interested in radically innovative poetry as in more accessible forms of lyric poetry which – sometimes misleadingly – apparently offer more readily assimilable, what Bernstein in *Artifice of Absorption* calls absorptive, material. 'Where, then', Forrest-Thomson asks, 'can we safely situate these troublesome emotions? Where else but in the language of the poem itself'; and we are held there by poetic artifice (*PA* 19).

What interests me in poetry is largely created by poetry's potential for the reimagination of language; language is intimately connected to, constructs even, our relationship with the world. Reimagining language involves an active participation in changing perception: 'The world is not something static, irredeemably given by a natural language. When language is re-imagined the world expands with it.' (*PA* 20) That expansion of the world includes the capacity for forming new, as yet unthought or even presently unthinkable connections, and not only between lexical units: it facilitates an enlargement not only of our understanding, but also of our potential identifications, and even, therefore the possibility of alternative forms of life, at present unimaginable. From poetry as incantation – and contemporary versions include Maggie O'Sullivan's extraordinary and powerful work with sound and signification in *In the House of the Shaman* and other collections – to Susan Howe's carefully crafted, meticulously researched palimpsests,[25] and the range of contemporary women's 'linguistically innovative' poetry as it appears in O'Sullivan's invaluable collection *Out of Everywhere*, the work that interests me fulfils the requirements set out by Forrest-Thomson in her poem 'S/Z':

Poems teach one that much:
to expect no answer.
But keep on asking questions;
that is important.[26]

Notes

1. Gertrude Stein, 'Poetry and Grammar', in *Look at Me Now and Here I Am: Writings and Lectures 1909–45*, ed. Patricia Meyerowitz (Harmondsworth: Penguin, 1990), p. 138 (hereafter cited as 'Stein').
2. By Isobel Armstrong, at Birkbeck College, London, to whom many thanks.
3. Veronica Forrest-Thomson, *Poetic Artifice: A Theory of Twentieth-Century Poetry* (Manchester: Manchester University Press, 1978), p. 125; hereafter *PA*.
4. See Chapter 12 of this collection, p. 95.
5. And of which, according to the Editor's Foreword, she apparently said: 'I think that in that line the rose is red for the first time in English poetry for a hundred years.' Stein p. 7, n.1, reads: 'Quoted by Thornton Wilder in his introduction to *Four in America*'.
6. This term is heavily contested, and seems to sustain its life permanently within at least implied scare quotes. Bruce Andrews and Charles Bernstein (eds), *The L=A=N=G=U=A=G=E Book* (Carbondale and Edwardsville: Southern Illinois University Press, 1984) is a collection of pieces from the journal. An earlier journal, *This* (Iowa City, 1971), edited by (initially) Robert Grenier and Barrett Watten, has been identified as 'as much of an originary moment as language writing can be said to have', by Bob Perelman in *The Marginalization of Poetry: Language Writing and Literary History* (Princeton: Princeton University Press, 1996), p. 38.
7. Ron Silliman, *The New Sentence* (New York: Roof Books, 1989), hereafter *NS*.
8. Quoting Stein, p.135.
9. In this instance an extract from Bob Perelman's *a.k.a.* (Berkeley: The Figures, 1984).
10. The question of the relationship between irony and melancholy is an interesting one, which I cannot pursue here, but began to discuss in my thesis on Forrest-Thomson, 'Reading Between the Lines: Language, Experience and Identity in the Work of Veronica Forrest-Thomson' (University of London, 1996).
11. The first term was coined by Gilbert Adair, and widely taken up; the second I discovered in Charles Bernstein, *Artifice of Absorption* (Philadelphia: Singing Horse Press/Paper Air, 1987), p. 13, hereafter *AA*; the third I have tended to favour since being introduced to it by the Canadian poet Karen McCormack. All are vigorously contested, like 'Language', but perhaps less generally rejected by the poets and theorists concerned than 'experimental', or even 'avant-garde'.

12. A distinction also made by Perelman in *The Marginalization of Poetry*, p. 39.

13. A. C. Bradley, *Oxford Lectures on Poetry* (London: Macmillan, 1909), p. 19.

14. Jonathan Culler, *Structuralist Poetics: Structuralism, Linguistics and the Study of Literature* (London: Routledge & Kegan Paul, 1975).

15. Roland Barthes, *S/Z*, trans. Richard Miller (New York: Hill and Wang, 1974) is the text in which Barthes's influential theoretical formulations of the *lisible* and *scriptible*, the readerly and writerly text, are found. The distinction being that while the readerly text offers the 'consumer' readily assimilable meaning, is apt for immediate naturalisation, the writerly text requires the work of the (no longer passive) reader to produce from among the plurality of possibilities an open play of meaning, with profound consequences for the construction of subjectivity:

> *I read the text.* This statement ... is not always true. The more plural the text, the less it is written before I read it.... I is not an innocent subject, anterior to the text, one which will subsequently deal with the text as it would an object to dismantle or a site to occupy. This 'I' which approaches the text is already itself a plurality of other texts, of codes which are infinite or, more precisely, lost (whose origin is lost) ... Subjectivity is a plenary image, with which I may be thought to encumber the text, but whose deceptive plenitude is merely the wake of all the codes which constitute me, so that my subjectivity has ultimately the generality of stereotypes. (*S/Z* 10; Barthes's emphasis)

The structuralist poetics, a poetics of the always already written, of intertextuality, which Barthes is here articulating, also raises the question of the displacement of subjectivity by intertextuality.

16. The New Poets Award-winning collection, Veronica Forrest-Thomson, *Language-Games* (Leeds: School of English Press, University of Leeds, 1971), pp. 33–4; the poems and Note also appear in Veronica Forrest-Thomson, *Collected Poems and Translations*, ed. Anthony Barnett (London: Allardyce, Barnett, 1990), where this quotation appears on p. 263. My thanks to Allardyce Barnett for their kind permission to quote from this edition.

17. I am indebted to an email conversation with Barrett Watten, who in a message to me of 26 July 1998 wrote 'there is a wide gulf between self and "subject", the former being expressive and the latter discursive'.

18. Jacqueline Rose, *States of Fantasy* (Oxford: Clarendon Press, 1996), p. 144.

19. Fredric Jameson, *The Political Unconscious: Narrative as a Socially Symbolic Act* (London: Methuen, 1981), p. 107.

20. Anthony Rudolph, *Poems for Shakespeare*, 4 (London: Globe Playhouse Publications, 1976), pp. 24–5, p. 7. The edition is dedicated 'To the memory of Veronica Forrest-Thomson', who died the day before she was due to give her reading at the event this edition commemorates.

21. Ibid., p. 42; Rudolph's ellipsis.

22. Bice Benvenuto and Roger Kennedy, *The Works of Jacques Lacan: An Introduction* (London: Free Association Books, 1986), p. 119.

23. A poet associated with Language writing; Susan Howe, *Singularities* (Hanover, NH: Wesleyan University Press, 1990); *The Europe of Trusts* (Los Angeles: Sun & Moon Press, 1990); *The Nonconformist's Memorial* (New

York: New Directions, 1993), and other works.

24. Veronica Forrest-Thomson, *Poetry as Knowledge: The Use of Science by Twentieth-Century Poets* (doctoral thesis, University of Cambridge, 1971), pp. 2–7.

25. Maggie O'Sullivan, *In the House of the Shaman* (London: Reality Street, 1993), and other works; Maggie O'Sullivan (ed.), *Out of Everywhere: Linguistically Innovative Poetry by Women in North America and the UK* (London: Reality Street, 1996).

26. Forrest-Thomson, *Collected Poems and Translations*, p. 113.

12
Poetic Licence

Helen Carr

'You are a poem though your poem's nought,' Ezra Pound would quote to H.D. while he was courting her in Philadelphia in 1906, when both of them were at the beginning of their poetic careers.[1] Feminist critics in recent years have often seen such a sentiment as typical of the traditional place assigned by the male poet to woman in poetry: she is the passive image rather than energising creator, the object to be written about, not the subject who writes, the artefact, not the artist. But do women – or men – always see poetry as such a male-dominated genre and preserve? In many ways it has been, and some of the most illuminating feminist criticism of poetry has looked at women poets' recasting and subversion of male conventions within the poetic tradition: for example, Margaret Homans' exploration of how nine-teenth-century women poets negotiated a poetic language in which they as women were subsumed into Mother Nature, and Angela Leighton's subtle account of Elizabeth Barratt Browning's construction of a fatherly Muse.[2]

Men may certainly predominate in prestigious anthologies or on library shelves, but I am less sure whether the gender associations that cling to the concept of poetry, making the writing of it seem a legit-imate and appropriate activity for one gender or the other, are so monolithically male. What about the idea of poetry as soft and unmanly? The notion of art as dangerously emotional, moving away from the real world of business and action, more appropriate to women's concerns? Has that vanished? Why was it ever there? Surely the modernist poetics argued by someone like Ezra Pound were at any rate partly concerned with making poetry safe for men, escaping from the effeminate gender-bending nineties, or what Pound saw as the effete poetry of the 'ladylike' Tennyson or 'mincing' Meredith. He wanted to reconstruct the manly poet who would write poetry which is 'harder, saner ... "nearer the bone".... It will be as much like granite as it can be ... austere, direct, free from emotional slither.'[3] The sense of poetry as volatile, ready to slip dangerously from control becomes for Pound, as for most critics, pinned firmly on 'bad' poetry, that is sentimental poetry, hence associated with the feminine. In fact the elision between the bad, the sentimental and the feminine is so strong that even feminist critics tend to concur in condemning such poetry as a product of a distasteful ladylike tradition, what Alicia Suskin Ostriker has called 'the genteel poetry and the genteel ideal of femininity, which stressed the heart and denied the head', without always asking more deeply about the fears suppressed in such a struggle to repudiate 'emotional slither'.[4]

I want here to raise some questions about women and poetry, about poetry and 'emotional slither', and about the place of poetry writing in our society. Poetry is regarded in our culture in strikingly contradictory ways, and those contradictions are intimately bound up with gender. Poetry is seen both as a prestigious, élite and esoteric form, and as a private, intimate, intensely subjective one. And whilst considered in the former way women may feel intimidated, in the latter, they (and less privileged men) can regard poetry as a place in which they are enfranchised. Women writing poetry will not necessarily see it in only one of these two ways; more often both at once, or both at different times. Adrienne Rich in her influential essay 'When We Dead Awaken' talked of her sense of the forbidding weight of male poetic tradition, which she could only evade by constructing a counter-line of exemplary women.[5] I do not want to discount that sense of exclusion from the high literary tradition, but it is only part of a complex of ideas and assumptions, some of which are immensely productive for women. During the last two hundred years, even more perhaps than earlier, masculinity has been the place of the active, the public, the practical, the rational; femininity that of the contemplative, the personal, the dreaming, the emotional. Ever since the Romantics, poetry has had much closer associations with the latter than the former.[6] Why are those associations there, and how do they enter into the practice of poetry? I would want to argue that although these associations are cultural and historical, they also have roots in the different way, or perhaps one should say, more charged way, in which language operates in poetry from prose.

In the mid-eighties I was a co-editor of a national women's arts magazine, *Women's Review*, which appeared monthly and always carried some poetry, though by no means a great deal: generally only one poem per issue.[7] Notwithstanding this limited coverage, poems poured in, poems in whose writing women had clearly found a sense of freedom, a place where they felt they were allowed to speak. Poetry was an opportunity for them as women, not a privilege to be wrested from men. These poems were not necessarily overtly autobiographical poems, or concerned with traumatic events: some were, some were not. The sense of empowerment came, I would suggest, from the fact that in our tradition of lyric poetry, (by which I mean post-Romantic Anglo-American lyric poetry) writing a poem is a statement that, within those lines at least, the poet is a speaking subject whose subjectivity is taken seriously. In this Anglo-American, Western European tradition, poetry has become associated with the private and the personal. The office of Poet Laureate – however distinguished its holder – is considered a joke: public poetry is derided.[8] In many ways this is our cultural and political loss, yet precisely because in our culture poetry is associated with the private and the personal, it is a form which women can feel they have a right to use, even though elsewhere the social conventions they observe and the discourses they use may discount the subjectivity validated in their poetry. Our social mores dictate that we are circumspect in revealing emotion. The valued discourses in our culture – science and theory – are those which present themselves as objective and transparent, purged of subjectivity, emotion or ambiguity. In the deviant language of poetry all those murky areas, so culturally aligned with the feminine, can be allowed.

But, it may be argued, surely one must accept that all language, and specifically traditional poetic language, privileges the masculine position, and that these women in their poetry are constrained by this whether they realise it or not. In many ways, I would agree. But perhaps feminists have looked in the past so intensely at the potential coerciveness of poetic language that we miss other ways in which poetic language can be thought about more positively. Jan Montefiore suggests persuasively that the scarcity of women poets in the past is as likely due to their social lack of opportunity as to their sense that the language of Milton or Wordsworth was inhospitable to them.[9] I would not want to underestimate the problems women still find themselves up against both in the literary world and in literary language, though it is striking that in the 1990s, feminist discussion of women's poetry has more often been concerned to celebrate women's achievements than to catalogue their constraints. Neglected and forgotten women poets have been rescued, and their right to be seen as a significant part of our literary heritage persuasively asserted.[10] Admirable though this work is, such an attempt is not my object here. Instead. I want to suggest some possible reasons why the writing of poetry has been such a valuable practice for many women, regardless of whether their poetry is acclaimed or unknown, success-fully published or privately hoarded.

Poetic practice and critical theory

Feminist literary criticism – and here it is no less conservative than any other advanced radical criticism – has not rethought poetic writing in such wide-reaching ways as it has other literary forms. While else-where the concept of literature has been abundantly deconstructed, the old distinction between 'poetry' and mere 'verse' largely remains implicit and uncontested. Even critics whose theoretical stance makes such an idea problematic have stuck cautiously to the canon. Sub-liter-ary fiction – that is the kind of fiction that used to be regarded as part of 'mass culture', rather than 'literature', such as popular forms of romance, science fiction, detective novels – has been accepted as an area of criticism, but not sub-literary poetry, which is still belittled, and often scarcely considered poetry at all. There is, for example, surprisingly little feminist analysis of the lyrics of pop songs as opposed to the singers themselves.[11] Whether the Spice Girls should or should not be feminist icons may be hotly debated, but what they say rarely is. One area where this high art approach to poetry has changed is in the work at present being done on the writing of poetry as a ther-apeutic aid in the health service, but that is very much in its early days, and has hardly touched the academic literary world.

One effect of this conservatism is that poetry criticism has found it hard to move beyond the discussion of poetry in terms of close textual criticism. In the last few decades academics from a succession of crit-ical schools have made sure that every literature student learns – or at any rate is taught – to attend to and perhaps find pleasure in highly wrought and densely textured writing. Other ways of understanding the forms of pleasure or desire inscribed in poetry have been neglected. When we talk about pleasure in connection with detective novels or romance we accept that such pleasure does not necessarily come from the linguistic subtleties of the text. It has, perhaps, more, or as much, to do with the process of arousal and appeasing of desire. And in these postmodernist times, we are increasingly aware that to analyse such generic pleasures adds to our appreciation of more complex texts. To understand what gives pleasure in poetry we must take into account its distinctive use of language, but to deal only with the evaluation of the completed artefact can pre-empt examination of where it might be that the power of poetry lies.

What I want to do here is look at the writing of lyric poetry today as a comparatively widespread, even demotic, non-elitist practice, of importance to many people's lives, including a considerable number of women. Many women write poetry, at least sometimes. They may not publish it, or if they attempt to, it may be rejected out of hand; they may cyclostyle it along with the rest of a poetry group, or they may publish in little magazines or slim volumes; they may read their poems at events: some may even win literary awards. For many of them pleasure comes out of the writing or sharing of poems with a small group, whether or not they publish more widely. The reasons for writing poetry are what I want to consider, irrespective of whether the results are amateur or professional poetry, 'bad' or 'good'. I certainly do not want to talk about a tradition of 'women's poetry': to conceive of a monolithic women's poetic tradition in our multiethnic, multi-cultural, many classed society is impossible.[12] I merely want to speculate tentatively about some ways in which one can think of lyric poetry as process rather than product, and to suggest how that process may operate for women writing poetry today.

Yet there are other reasons why academic feminist theory has not always been welcoming to such questions. In 1989 Cora Kaplan, in an overview of the development of second-wave feminism up to that date, pointed out that in the seventies there was a three way alliance of creative writing, theory and politics, all closely interconnected, which broke down in the eighties as feminist criticism entered the academy.[13] At the time she was writing, a considerable rift existed between the highly theoretical language of academic feminism and the much more pragmatic way in which some poets, perhaps recently touched by feminist ideas, talked about their work. For feminist theorists influenced by post-structuralism, as many were, poetry could not be understood as the 'expression' of the poet's experience, and they were embarrassed by the comments of practising poets, particularly if they used a vocabulary which included such words as 'voice' 'experience' or 'inspiration'. Embarrassment is a response often prompted by poetry, particularly 'bad' poetry, though perhaps embarrassment is a signal that something has significantly reached us. But even worse, for an anti-essentialist post-structuralist, was talk of 'a female self' to be discovered by the woman poet through her art, the kind of argument put forward by a poet like Ostriker. Certainly 'the female self' it is not a term I could use myself – it makes even less sense in our fractured, disparate modern world than a 'women's tradition' – but reading a book like Ostriker's *Stealing the Language: The Emergence of Women's Poetry in America*, it is easy to sympathise with her impatience with the inadequacy of either New Critical or deconstructionist terms to describe what she wants to say about women's poetry in America. The critical tradition which most academics inhabited, going back to the modernists, and paramount for the New Critics, structuralists and post-structuralists, insisted that the poem must be read as an autonomous linguistic artefact.[14] Yet many women poets, like Ostriker, felt that they needed to speak in terms that acknowledged that their writing was important to them in finding some kind of identity as women outside, as it were, that poetry. Ostriker's common sense feminist reading produced a book which details fascinatingly the way American women poets began to write about the female body, revise male myths, explore how their female identities could be conceived. Ultimately, however, her terms are closed, unlike her observations of change and flux. She writes as if there is one way of being a woman, common to all, which has been buried and unspoken but which can be gradually recovered and displayed, although her very account presents women trying out shifting and evolving possible selves. What was important in her work, however, is the recognition of an intensely strong relationship between these women's poetic writing and their need to re-examine what it meant for them to be a woman in their world.

While Ostriker's universalist answers may now appear even less plausible than they did when her book was published in 1986, the questions she wanted to answer, about how one writes within and against a dominant tradition, and what happens as a result, are very much present. In the nineties the critical climate has changed again. The burgeoning of new literatures in English, and an increasing awareness of living in a postcolonial world and a multicultural society, have made the struggle of writers from different groups to revise and recast the dominant literary forms an important issue in recent years. The growth of postcolonial criticism on the one hand and of queer theory on the other have broadened and deepened the kind of questions feminists have asked about remaking language and identities. Difference, whether of gender, sexuality or ethnicity is now a central critical topic: history, and therefore politics, have a fresh importance to literary studies. Cora Kaplan's argument that, in political terms, the creative arts had played a significant role in the transformation of the sense of identity for women is now widely acknowledged to be true for post-colonial and ethnic groups. So it is within this broad framework of differences and resistances that I want to come back to question of poetic language. Unlike Ostriker, I would not want to abandon the insights of post-structuralism and psychoanalysis into the mutability and provisionality of meaning and identity. From postcolonial theory has come too the concept of 'hybridity', that complexity and many-strandedness of identity in the modern world that the late nineteenth-century French poet Tristan Corbière already recognised as a 'mélange adultère de tout' – an adulterated/adulterous mixture of everything.[15] We are each constantly changing, unstable, contradictory; formed, deformed, reformed by our personal histories, our social and ethic histories, our class and gender positions, our bodies, our hormones, our conscious beliefs and our unconscious drives. We are born into a maze of language through whose contradictions and ambiguities we come to what sense we can of ourselves and our world. As women in the western world our possibilities and expectations have changed with an extraordinary rapidity: how we recognise who or what we are or might be can be deeply problematic. Yet we are also at a moment of new possibilities. We are far more able than ever before to act as agents in our own destinies.

So how can we talk about the importance of poetry for women? What is the relationship between lyric poetry and subjectivity, between poetic and personal identity? The chasm between the speaker and speech, the poet and poem, the body and language is another of those insights, or one might say anxieties, so present in poetic writing since the romantics and now central to post-structuralist thought. Language is like a prison uniform, issued to us each and fitting none of us. The complex of history and flesh that we each are can never be represented accurately in a shared discourse. When Mallarmé says that poetry is made not of feelings but of words, on the literal level, so to speak, one cannot disagree. But I still think some way of understanding the relationship between words and 'feelings', between language and affect, still remains. Ostriker in her book ended up by dismissing the problem – no gap exists for these women, she asserts, between the 'I' of their poems and 'I' who writes. That statement does not seem tenable, but the link between those 'I's still asks for an explanation.

I want to get nearer answering these questions by first stepping away, looking at how poetry is used in quite a different culture, to evade, as much as anything, some of the constraints of my own critical training. Oral poetry is the main exception to the general critical reluctance to examine verse that might not be necessarily 'good'. Oral poetry is by definition composed by people different from the literate scholar, and does not raise the same embarrassed confusions. Even so, work on oral poetry has been much more aligned with anthropology and linguistics than with literature. But for that reason it has tended to ask quite different questions about poetry, seeing it as a social and discursive practice rather than an art-form. I have spent some time reading and thinking about one culture's oral poetry, that of the Native Americans.[16] At first I was most struck by how different the place of poetry was in their cultures from ours – there was no concept of an autotelic art practised for its own sake and admired in terms of its skill, it is part of social rituals defined in other ways – but I have increasingly felt that the kind of questions prompted there could be immensely liberating for talking about poetry in our culture. What is the social function of this poetry? What is its relation to the central myths and rituals of the society? Who composes or performs it? In what sort of circumstances, and why? What is the relation of the language used in this poetry to other discourses? That art is autotelic is perhaps a western cultural myth, even though the reasons for writing poetry in this culture are not as immediately apparent as in Native American traditions.

Poetry and cultural context

Distinguishing between verse and prose is not necessarily easy. The difference is one of degree rather than kind, but all cultures appear to have had special forms of language, set aside from everyday speech, that particularly exploit the physicality of words, most commonly through rhythm and metre, but also through sound, repetition, parallelism and patterning. In a literate culture the physical arrangement of script or print is important too: indeed, for some twentieth-century poetry, supremely important, as its only overt distinguishing feature may be that it looks different on the page. Because of the artificiality of its language, poetry is always a highly cultural rather than a natural form. That may seem a redundantly obvious statement, but the Romantic myth of poetry's origin in the 'savage tribes' ... mere expression of passion in the sounds which passion itself necessitates' still sometimes lurks in the western view of non-western oral poetry.[17] In many cultures poetry, as this special form of language, is associated with the same kind of areas of danger, disturbance and power that Mary Douglas investigates in her book *Purity and Danger*, in which she analyses the way taboos against pollution and rules of purity shape the conceptual order of cultures.[18]

The practice and the place of poetry, of course, vary enormously between and within different cultures. Several disparate forms existed in the different traditions of Native American oral poetry. I will mention three, of which two, as it happens, are male. Most of this Native American oral poetry was recorded in the late nineteenth and early twentieth centuries by anthropologists who (even if they were women) overwhelmingly chose men as their informants. Much more men's poetry than women's was taken down, but this certainly gives a distorted view of the balance within these cultures, though how much so is impossible to say. But at this stage in my argument, gender is not the immediate issue, especially as gender, as opposed to biological sex, has different constraints in different societies. The vision songs of the Plains and Woodland Indians were 'found' when boys at puberty were sent out to fast for a vision, which they would then describe in a song, or perhaps one should rather say, would come to them as a song. This vision song would remain their personal possession. They would sing it as they went into battle, re-invoking the visionary state, rather as if they were taking a psychotropic drug. On the one hand these songs could be described as highly individualised – each man has his own unique song – but on the other, the means by which the vision was gained, and the musical and linguistic form used in the song, were entirely traditional. A few words – generally poeticised or sacred archaic forms – would be repeated numerous times with additional vocatives and particles. When the core words are translated into English they can look like imagist poems (as they were claimed to be when first discovered by American poets): for example:

> As my eyes
> search
> the prairie
> I feel the summer in the spring [19]

Quite different are the Navajo chants, used to cure physical and psychic pain. These are traditional, shaped by repetition and parallelism, and accompanied by the telling of a long narrative myth and the making and destruction of the famous Navajo sand-paintings, which illustrate the myth and the chant. They are recited by a chanter, who has acquired his esoteric knowledge through a long apprentice-ship. He speaks on behalf of the patient, the whole ceremony lasting between two and nine days. This may sound like a church liturgy, but in fact it is never performed twice the same way. The selection of possi-ble elements is always fitted to the circumstances and problems of that particular patient, so his or her individual plight is placed within a group narrative which always ends with the centring of the individual within harmony and calm. This is a dynamic, not a static harmony: the principal verb in Navajo is 'to go', not 'to be'; the word for one of these chants is a 'way', and life is conceptualised as a 'walk': 'With beauty before me, I walk. / With beauty behind me, I walk. / With beauty below me, I walk,. / With beauty above me I walk. / With beauty all around me, I walk. / It is finished in beauty'.[20]

A third form is the poetry of individual shamans, the poet/priest/healers found among many pre-literate groups, particularly in Siberia and the Americas. A chanter is a shaman of sorts, but the more traditional shaman has undergone a personal crisis, experienced as a death and rebirth, a spiritual journey out of the body and back again. This journey can be re-invoked in the singing of the songs brought back from that journey, found there as the young boys found their songs in their vision. The patient in this case is cured by being 'led' by the songs through a similar journey. For example, there was an elderly woman shaman in the Papago nation whose songs were recorded in the twenties. Known as Owl Woman, she had experienced a period of acute depression following several bereavements as a young woman, which she recounts in her songs as a death in which she visits the spirit land, is strengthened and returns to life. As I describe it here this may sound a very individual voyage, but again the imagery and the para-meters of the experience are traditional in form. Owl Woman's songs about the white mountain in the spirit land at the edge of the world echo those that appear within Papago myths of origin and those sung by other shamans. Each song is at the same moment conventional and unique.[21]

Drawing parallels from other cultures can be dangerous: but aware as one must be of differences, I think it could be illuminating to compare our poetic practice with what happens here. There are four main points I would like to draw out. Firstly, in each of these Native American forms there is a complex imbrication of individual desire with a very specific traditional discourse, so that a group narrative or myth or way of symbolising can be appropriated by or on behalf of a specific individual for a specific situation. Secondly, the context of this poetry is that of an individual in a state of being which is in some sense abnormal, for example, sick or unhappy, or liminal, that is, on the threshold between two accepted states, like the boy at puberty passing from childhood into adult life. Thirdly, all these forms are transformative: they are concerned to change one state of being into another. But although their context may be that of pain, grief, or disorientation that is not what they 'express': their words have much more to do with the pattern of being that they wish to achieve. Although in the sequence of the Papago shamanic songs and in the Navajo chant, the symbolic story embodies the process of change, the poetry produces meanings rather than mirroring them. And fourthly, there is the role of the shaman, the voyager and cartographer of the descent into the depths and re-emergence, whose map provides a cure.

Poetic narrative

To return to the first point: in a literate cosmopolitan society with a proliferation of media, the available myths and discourses are much more various and intermeshed than those of an oral group: but our poetry too is formed of a culturally controlled range of discourses which the individual writer of poetry appropriates or subverts or enters This process is perhaps at present more usually and usefully talked about either as intertextuality, or, more politically, as in postcolonial criticism, as 'writing back' to a dominant form. All poetry rewrites other texts; perhaps one of the most striking changes in modernist, postmodernist and postcolonial poetry is that these pre-texts are much more overtly used, and increasingly are outside the poetic tradition. The surge of women's poetry this century specifically rewriting myths and fairytales – H.D., Anne Sexton, Stevie Smith are only a few of the names one could mention – is one very obvious example. So is the work of Caribbean poets, both men and women, who have so actively 'calibanised' European forms by drawing on traditional Afro-Caribbean figures and motifs – Grace Nichols on the Ashanti spider woman, or Fred D'Aguiar on Mama Dot.[22] In the introduction to her book *The Land of Look Behind,* the Jamaican/US writer Michelle Cliff talks about her emergence from an education which made her intellectually proficient but which, she says, 'almost render(ed) me speechless about who I am'. She discovered that to write as a Caribbean woman, or man, 'demands of us retracing the African part of ourselves, reclaiming as our own, and as our subject, a history sunk under the sea.... It means finding the artforms of these our ancestors and speaking in the patois forbidden to us.... It means ... mixing in the forms taught us by the oppressor, undermining his language and co-opting his style, and turning it to our purpose.' [23] But 'writing back' is often a less obvious process: the reworking of the woman-as-flower image, for example, which Jan Montefiore analyses in poems by Sylvia Plath, Alison Fell and others, or Emily Dickinson's subversion of Isaac Watts's hymns.[24]

Lévi-Strauss says of myth that it is always the transformation of another myth. The same perhaps applies to poetry. Even public poetry, such as school-songs or hymns, where the poet and the reader give themselves gladly to total absorption in a cultural or group myth, negotiates the same problem, which is not that of inventing a new narrative, but of making existing narratives your own, whether or not you need or wish to subvert them in that appropriation. The school song is a fusion of mythic elements which come together as a new and formative, some might say, deformative, construction. Even the toiler that Borges describes rewriting *Don Quixote* word for word is, as Borges insists, writing a completely new text.[25] Language cannot be static: it is this perhaps that the Russian linguist Voloshinov means when he talks, in the context of class and power, of the sign being the site of struggle. When poets, women or otherwise, speak of finding a voice and expressing their own experience, they are talking perhaps about this transformation of a narrative, or fusion of narratives, which then work as their own; they make the sign produce new meanings for them.

Barthes argued as long ago as 1957 that 'contemporary myth' was discontinuous, and postmodernists say that we are witnessing – have witnessed – the breakdown of the grand narratives of the western world: Christianity, progress, humanism.[26] Perhaps their loss has made the kind of provisional and partial narratives that a poem can hold all the more important. Lyric poetry is not often thought of as narrative: but just as Barthes argues today even a phrase can be mythic, so the single image can imply a narrative, although it may be a narrative free of the demands of cause and effect, direction or closure. There is a sense in which all our narratives are decentred, unlike the Native American mythic structures, where the central myths of the society shape the apparently more individual structures. But we all use, and need to use, narratives, as Lévi-Strauss argues, to cope with 'the inchoate and arbitrary' flux of existence. In an article which is one of his most fascinating, and in which he makes a rare attempt to come to terms with subjectivity, he tells the story of a Cunan shaman treating a woman through a difficult breech birth. The shaman tells her a myth whose progress, a struggle between spirits and animals within her, mimes the journey of the child down the birth canal, including turning it round so its head is in the right direction. It works: the baby is safely born, though after lurid descriptions of mythic alligators, a sticky-tentacled octopus and a black tiger. Lévi-Strauss goes on to make an analogy with Freudian psychoanalysis. For the successful outcome of psychoanalytic therapy, the analysands must find a narrative, their own personalised version of the Freudian myth, to provide an organising story of their lives, one which lets them escape the destructive private myths behind their neurotic compulsions. The point for Lévi-Strauss is not whether the elements of the Freudian myth are any more true that of the Cunan. It is that we need a narrative that make sense of unspeakable physical or psychic disturbance, reconciling the unconscious and the conscious, if we are to move on. Lévi-Strauss is well aware of the differences between psychoanalysis and Cunan shamanism, but he is fascinated by the power exerted by a symbolic structuring of experience, in each case through a socially accepted and acceptable narrative appropriated by or for an individual. The narrative orders the subjective experience, but it must do so by mapping that subjectivity on to a wider myth.[27]

Post-structuralist theory has often presented the narratives or myths of our society as primarily oppressive and constrictive. But we need narratives: they are where we start. Lyotard, one of those, of course, to argue most strongly that the master narratives have gone, puts forward in his book *The Postmodern Condition* a view of language which perhaps illuminates how the fragmented, vestigial narratives of poetry work. He draws on Wittgenstein's idea of 'language-games': language is not the bearer of absolute meanings, but a collection of different discourses or language-games, each of which has its own rules, a kind of pragmatic contract understood, explicitly or implicitly, between the players. But unlike Wittgenstein, Lyotard argues that those games and their rules are always a site to be contested. He sees them as struggle, a competitive game, a series of moves and countermoves, where each move shifts the nature of the game slightly. Once we speak we are players in the game, agents in our lives. We shift ever so little the power relations embodied in language. As Lyotard says, we are all born into stories already awaiting us. But we can negotiate the outcome of the plot.[28] In the rapidly changing modern world, it is not surprising that so much of contemporary women's poetry is occupied with re-charting male narratives, as so much postcolonial poetry is in re-charting European narratives, playing new moves, struggling to change the rules of the game. In poetry, as in any speech-act, the speaker produces him/herself as an agent. That is perhaps a way of looking at the Lacanian model positively rather than negatively, not at the failure of language ever to encompass a 'true identity' but at how language empowers the speaker to create a pragmatic or strategic identity that can enter the social world. Just to speak is in some sense to take control.

Rites of passage

So to the second point I drew from the Native American tradition: their verse is associated with disturbed or liminal states. So is much of our lyric tradition, though in more heterogeneous ways. Oral poetry is paradoxically further from ordinary speech and from direct individual communication than much written poetry. In a literate society the development of detailed autobiographical or individualised content becomes possible in a way only found in the briefest snatches in an oral tradition, so the scene of poetry becomes much more various. Yet living as we do in a society where we are both flooded with possible narratives and yet without any certain structures of meaning, how we cope with desire, death, love, bereavement, outrage, anger, anguish, impotence, despair, anxiety, fear, must perhaps be, for many of us, through fictive forms: films, novels, TV soap opera, romance, pop songs as well as lyric poetry. But lyric poetry remains an important strategy for some in finding an order to the chaos of responses those life-events bring with them; not making private sense of them – that would be psychosis – but finding a fiction which can be shared. For many women in our culture their whole identity is a liminal state. We are not the creatures we grew up expecting to be; lyric poetry is one way of trying out possible selves. 'Piece by piece I seem / to re-enter the world', as Adrienne Rich says.[29]

It has become a cliché now to note that our society is painfully destitute of rites of passage, rituals that accept, order and so mitigate or control the psychic distress or excess we all experience at some time or other. It is an impoverishment, but perhaps in a multicultural secular society inevitable. There are no accepted or stable myths that could provide a basis for such rituals. This, perhaps, is why fictional forms become so valuable; simulacra in place of icons. Ritual places the single sorrow or fearful moment of transition into a shared cycle of being. Take for example, the poem by Eavan Boland, 'The Journey', which she wrote after her small daughter almost died of meningitis.[30] This is not mentioned directly in the poem, which instead speaks (whilst saying such speaking for others is impossible) for all those mothers in the past who have lost their children. Boland places her poem in the centre of the western poetic tradition, beginning with a quotation from Virgil's *Aeneid*. As Aeneas follows the Sibyl down to the underworld he passes at the entrance the crying souls of babies: 'never had they had their share of life's sweetness for the dark day had stolen them from their mothers' breasts and plunged them to a death before their time'. But what her poem says has hitherto been unspoken:

> And then the dark fell and 'there has never'
> I said 'been a poem to an antibiotic'
> never a word to compare with the odes on
> the flower of the rare sloe for fever ...

In the poem that follows she falls asleep, dreaming that she is led, not by a Sybil but by Sappho ('it was she, misshapen, musical'), into that same underworld, where she is conscious not so much of the dead babies as of their stricken mothers:

> Then to my horror I could see to each
> nipple some had clipped a limpet shape –
> suckling darknesses – while others had their arms
> weighed down making terrible pietàs

The poem's narrative re-enacts her own descent into the shadow of bereavement and return; she sees the silenced women of the past, whose pangs at losing their children have never been adequately chronicled – the only acknowledged pietà, the word reminds us, was Mary's grief for her adult son. The narrative shape of this poem was there for her to take and reform, standing already as a literary device that symbolises the descent into the abyss, that claims to discover important truths about the world though that journey. Her traumatic journey follows an old pattern: yet her trauma is one hitherto unperceived, unspoken. Aeneas only saw the dead infants, not their mothers. Thanks to the antibiotic, she can return. Her isolated anguish becomes part of a historical narrative: her 'horror' turns to compassion and 'love', for those past women and herself.[31]

Much of twentieth-century verse has dealt with such highly charged subject-matter self-consciously, as Eavan Boland does here, aware of the structures that form the poem and its subject, aware of the gap between representation and being. The criticism of some feminist poetry ('bad' feminist poetry) has been that it is naively unaware of the problems of language, defiant perhaps about conventional representations of femininity but slipping into other clichés. I think that may sometimes have been true, but for my purposes here it is irrelevant. Such poetry can still be a valuable cognitive move for its writers even if not for all of its readers. It is often, however, the sort of poetry criticised in those terms which tends to be most popular at poetry readings. Perhaps it is hard to take in the shifting of more than one narrative at once. There is a possible parallel with some of the indubitably sentimental poetry which has been produced by well-established male poets in Britain on the New Man as father, which politically, if in no other way, one cannot but applaud, and which I have heard warmly clapped, for whatever reason, at London's National Poetry Society.

Transformations

The third characteristic of the oral verse, its transformative aim, is both like and unlike our cultural forms. The differences are certainly considerable. We do not expect a poem to 'cure' illness or induce hallucinatory trance in quite this way. Eavan Boland may write a poem to an antibiotic, but she would not use a poem as a substitute for one: Freud may have unsettled our mind/body dichotomy, but it still operates powerfully. The chanter and the shaman clearly have a role that combines priest, psychoanalyst, doctor and poet, and though such a combination of power has great romantic attraction, our poetry is a more marginal and comparatively fragile structure. Yet I have already argued that the transformation of narratives is central to our poetry, and that changing a narrative changes how we experience ourselves. We see this in contemporary poetry in postmodernist terms – a plethora of images that we catch and recombine. Julia Kristeva sees similar transformations in modernist poetry (changing from one sign system to another is how she puts it) and Isobel Armstrong has suggested that the transformation through poetic language of the 'categories' of subject and object is at the heart of Romantic poetry.[32] To some extent lyric poetry takes on, in a more tentative way, the role of religion in 'making sense', not by giving an explanation or answer, but by finding a way by which contradictions and confusions can be set down and found a shape, by finding words which draw the inchoate into signification. Michelle Cliff's first piece of writing, she says, other than a dissertation, was entitled 'Notes on Speechlessness' and was indeed just that, notes, 'jagged, non-linear, almost short-hand', though even that had a pre-text, the story of the wild boy of Aveyron, whose inarticulate wildness she could there make speak for her, and provide a first stage in her exploration.[33]

The significance of the narratives of fictive forms is not that they provide causally argued explanations like the narratives of science or politics, or absolute and comprehensive claims to truth like religion. Their narratives are not necessarily logically, not even in the case of poetry syntactically coherent: the narrative of a poem may be closer to that of a dream (and of course it has often been suggested that the principles by which Freud said dreams are ordered, displacement and condensation, are versions of metonymy and metaphor). Poetic images, like those of dreams, can stand in for the otherwise un-speakable, for conflicts which may be repressed below the level of consciousness, psychic or social, or in the realm of the pre-linguistic, or pre-conceptual. In Emily Dickinson's poetry, Cora Kaplan has argued, Dickinson explores imagistically her divided psyche, 'Ourself, behind ourself concealed' prefiguring any systematic psychoanalytic theory of the multiform personality.[34] But it is not just a question of imagery. In a poem like, for instance, 'Because I could not wait for Death', its poetic form immediately signals that the poem need not work in the terms of everyday narrative: we accept that its story need have no more conse-quentiality than a dream, but we know, as in a dream, that it is of consequence.

Some psychoanalysts suggest that 'areas of creativity' provide a space between fantasy and reality where psychic dramas can be worked through.[35] Poems do not reach a rational stasis: they move, in both senses, through symbolic patterning. They do not necessarily resolve or unify, but they are productive processes. Julia Kristeva suggests something like that when she argues that, after analysis, the analysand will reach, not a static cure, but the possibility of being a 'work in progress', constantly producing him/herself through imaginative speaking or writing, without being trapped by inner conflict either as a fixed self or in a meaningless void.[36] Kristeva, whose work is so alert to the inseparablity of the psychic, the social, the somatic and the linguistic, moves away from the ultimately commodificatory notion of texts as 'objects', autonomous or otherwise. She sees them as processes, whether written or as read, just as each one of us has to be understood as a subject-in-process. In her earlier writing what she stressed was the subversive force of 'poetic language', by which she meant avant-garde modernist writing, whether poetry or prose, to call in question the certainties of the dominant discourse. 'Poetic language' with its disruptions of usual patterns of signification and syntax, through its discontinuities, gaps and ruptures, through its exploitation of the materiality of language, destabilises meanings and speaks what before had no place in the symbolic structure which is our shared discourse. Poetic language alters, or any rate fractures, ideology because its physicality is in touch with the preconscious and the unconscious.

To put this another way, lyric poetry perhaps could be seen as a form of play, both in the deconstructionist sense of experimenting with the multiform possibilities of signification, and in the Kleinian sense of a symbolic acting out of psychic conflicts. To understand poetry, one would need to understand the interaction of those two forms of play. I am not sure we yet do, though Freud's suggestion that jokes, punning and wordplay throw up unconscious associations is often cited as a possible entry into the problem. Playing with the sounds and the patterns of words allows the unconscious to evade the censors of rational discourse. Language as a system may be shared and arbitrary, but as a practice it is for each of us libidinally charged: our desires are its energising force. Language registers our psychic drives (called in French so much more evocatively *'pulsions'* so they can be seen as waves pushing against the normative constraints of language, as Kristeva puts it, 'waves of attack against stases').[37] Poetry is perhaps, as Kristeva argues, where in language those *'pulsions'* can be registered most powerfully: but always, since it is through language, by fusing the psychic and the social.

The relationship between the psychic and the social is clearly very different in different historical matrices. In the Native American oral poetry there was no suggestion of reformulating social structures, only of evoking the mythic map which lies behind both the social and psychic order; the rhythms and sounds of oral verse work with its mythic images to achieve affective states in harmony with that imaginary cosmos. To make generalisations about contemporary poetry would be dangerous, but it clearly does not have the same agenda as either Native American traditional or European modernist poetry. For modernist writers it was imperative to use language explosively. They felt society and social practices as a carapace, or worse, a room like the one in Poe's story 'The Pit and the Pendulum', whose walls inexorably close in. They struggled, as it were, against an immensely powerful dominant language that systemised subjectivity like a railway time table. The situation for us is different. The explosion has happened, though most people would see modernist poetry as tracing the seismic shocks rather than causing them. What that explosion was we are not sure; it is variously explained as Freud, the First World War, Auschwitz, the loss of Empire, the crisis of reason, the growth of the multinational, the spawning of media – but we know it has taken place. Late capitalism has dispersed the familiar prison warders of nineteenth-century bourgeois culture. We have to make sense of our world before we know how to react. It is not that discourses of class, race, gender do not still oppress, but they do so differently, and at the moment we do not really know how. We are trying to pick up pieces of these shattered narratives and see what sense of them we can make, and what sense they make of us. I think at the moment most of us are deeply confused about where and how power operates in our society, in what way our social system continues the order of the past and how it has changed it, about what it means to be a person, let alone a woman. This is at any rate what I see behind the postmodern quest to remake compulsively our relation to the past. Perhaps that is the process celebrated in Amy Clampitt's poem about the car lot, 'Salvage', where

> the bag-laden
> hermit woman ...
> ... stoutly
> follows her routine,
> mining the mountainsides
> of our daily refuse
>
> for artefacts: subversive
> re-establishing
> with each arcane
> trash-basket dig
> the pleasures of the ruined.[38]

Finally, in looking at the transformative intention of the oral poetry, I want to draw attention again to the difference between the initiating context of distress or disorientation and the ordered poem. Because of the artifice inherent in all poetic language the divide between the impulses and conscious ideas and the eventual words is more striking than in a prose form. It is this divide that is perhaps describe by the Greeks when they speak of inspiration, or in the post-structuralist insistence that the subjectivity found in a poem is its creation not its creator. Even in the two examples I gave when the oral poet was composer as well as speaker of the verse, the important moment is not the creation of the song but its recital. Poets are most importantly their poems' first readers.

The shamanic text

I want to look finally at the role of the shaman, who is by definition a poet whose creativity speaks for more than him/herself, who is read, so to speak, by many. I suggested before that the shaman in an oral culture is priest, psychiatrist, poet and doctor all at once. (There are those who claim that the heart of Christianity is shamanic, with Christ's descent into hell and resurrection as its paradigmatic journey, which I find more attractive, but perhaps no less reductive, than the Frazer fertility myth.) Psychoanalysts have claimed that they fulfil better the role of shamans, making the journey to the recesses of their own unconscious and by their esoteric knowledge leading others through those Stygian paths. But I think in poetry too we look to a shamanic figuring, reading poetry that makes sense, at least within the poem, of where we are. Some poetry is pleasurable and empowering for the person who wrote it. That is a good thing; but some is also pleasurable and empowering for others. And perhaps this is where aesthetic value begins. I do not think we shall or ever should return to claims for the absolute value of works of art. Many of the terms in which art has been evaluated have been Eurocentric, bourgeois, patriarchal. Brecht suggests we should talk of 'weaker (simple) and stronger (complex) pleasures.... The last-named ... are more intricate, richer in communication, more contradictory and more productive of results.' The theatre must represent, he says, 'people's lives together in society' but the pleasure felt in watching that skilfully done 'must be converted into the higher pleasure felt when the rules emerging from this life in society are treated as imperfect and provisional'. Poetry that draws in the complexities of our psychic and social lives in all their intricate contradictoriness, providing a narrative while exposing its provisionality, is poetry that gives in Brecht's terms, the stronger pleasure.[39] I would like to think that this definition could be reconciled with our more usual formalistic criterion of pleasurable poetry as that which exploits most richly the resources of language.

Conclusion

Lyric poetry, I am arguing, is a process which enables writers to position themselves as agents, to claim a value for their subjectivity, to make sense, not logically but psychically of themselves in the world, to re-negotiate the relation between preconscious and consciousness, unconscious and conscious, psychic and social. Perhaps in the postmodern condition women poets, because they have to be so aware of he need to read the narratives and rewrite them, to find psychic maps, could claim to be the poets most typical of our age. Certainly I would want to argue they are at a moment of creative plenty. (I am tempted to say, with almost the whole of Western culture available for rewriting at the change of a pronoun, though of course it is not as simple as that.) Stephen Heath suggests that 'in the overall system of sexuality that is tightened to perfection in the nineteenth century and that still today determines so powerfully in so many ways the facts of our lives, male sexuality is repetition, female sexuality is query (darkness, riddle, enigma, problem, etc.)'.[40] As I suggested at the beginning, femininity is still conceptualised in many ways as the place of the private, the feeling, the dream. Our relation as women to those constructs of femininity and female sexuality is not a simple one, but, as Heath says, they still enter into our positioning of ourselves in the world. And that position, margin rather centre, mobile rather than fixed, questioning rather than certain, has been the place of poetry.

Poetry since the early nineteenth century has given a high value to a decentred and questioning subjectivity. Some critics on the left have condemned that tradition as one of the excesses of bourgeois individualism, whilst some feminist critics have seen it as high male egoism. But it is important not to forget the radical potential of that romantic legacy, which made possible the kind of oppositional strategies within bourgeois capitalism that Raymond Williams has argued have formed so much of the artistic tradition of the last two hundred years. The Romantic poetic position is sometimes read ahistorically; those poets were asserting the right of those without social power to speak; they claimed to be legislators, but that they knew they were unacknowledged.[41] Women in our Western cultures are still marginal to the central social formations, and often not even sure, as our position has changed so rapidly, about the place we have on those margins. So the tangential tolerance of poetry, its tradition as a site of resistance to the dominant social and economic forces, makes it a peculiarly helpful place for women to test out and explore their relation to the general culture.

The modernists were of course no less oppositional to the dominant than the romantics: but they wanted their share of the action; they wanted to move the position of artist back to the centre, to assert some kind of power. Hence the unease over the connotations of effeminacy that hung around the notion of poetry. When Pound condemns emotional slither, he is still aware that poetry has to be, in psychoanalytical parlance, language charged with affect. But he needs to see that affect or emotion as fixed and determinate. ('By hardness I mean a quality in poetry which is nearly always a virtue – I can think of no instance when it is not'). Bad writing is rotten, slushy, muzzy, bloated, loose; good writing is clean, 'sane and active ebullience', leading to 'clarity and vigour'; beauty is 'hygiene'.[42] The crusading bluster of his bludgeoning critical style and that emphasis on cleanliness is certainly impossible now to divorce from his anti-Semitism.[43] He fears his contamination by the taboo, the soiled, what Kristeva calls the abject and Mary Douglas ritual uncleanness, contagion or pollution. In oral cultures poetry is often integral to those periods or ceremonies which deal with the taboo, at once sacred and defiled, empowering and dangerous. I think something of the same hangs round our poetic practice. In our society we have strong taboos against the expression of overt passion (in the broadest sense) and lyric poetry is one place where those psychic energies are allowed to find a place. But our anxiety about the process is very great. As in the oral culture, it is a special discourse, limited to certain contexts. We demand order, control, the sanction of art, to protect us. Perhaps rightly so. The other side of what Rimbaud called poetry's power to change the world is madness.

One project of feminist criticism must be to examine that male anxiety aroused by poetry's place of 'query ... darkness ... enigma'. But it must also be to continue to explore the importance of poetry for women in all its complexity and contradictoriness and in all its forms. As Virginia Woolf wrote: 'The streets of London have their map; but our passions are uncharted.'[44] Maps are not identical with towns any more than poetry is with passion. But they each make further exploration possible.[45]

Notes

1. H.D., *End to Torment*, ed. Norman Holmes Pearson and Michael King, (Manchester: Carcanet, 1980), p. 12. 'From what? I did not ask him,' wrote H.D.

2. Margaret Homans, *Women Writers and Poetic Identity* (Princeton: Princeton University Press, 1980); Angela Leighton, *Elizabeth Barrett Browning* (Brighton: Harvester, 1986).

3. Ezra Pound, *Literary Essays* (London: Faber & Faber, 1954), pp. 276, 425, 12. The long quotation is from 'A Retrospect', published in 1918 but incorporating earlier work. Although so different in other ways, he reacts here as do the aggressively manly imperialists and public-school men, like Newbolt.

4. Alicia Suskin Ostriker, *Stealing the Language: The Emergence or Women's Writing in America* (London: Women's Press, 1987), p. 15.

5. Adrienne Rich, 'When We Dead Awaken', in *On Lies, Secrets and Silence* (London: Virago, 1980).

6. The relationship of women to poetry could be seen as a synecdoche of their relation to literary studies as a whole. Although men still dominate much of the teaching and administration of English studies in universities and polytechnics, though less so than even ten years ago, far more women study literature at 'A' level and in higher education than men. Our cultural norms make it a more appropriate place for them than it is for men: Lisa Jardine has suggested this is a problem even for radical male critics, whose 'tough', 'rigorous' language is always striving anxiously to reassert the masculinity of their profession. '"Girl Talk" (For Boys on the Left)', *Oxford Literary Review*, 8/1–2 (1986).

7. *Women's Review* was published in London between October 1985 and July 1987.

8. In recent years performance poetry and forms like rap that by their nature are shared rather than private have been increasingly popular, but they are certainly not public in any establishment way, rather the voice of an oppositional or minority group. The performance poet Benjamin Zephaniah was recently suggested – though not by anyone likely to influence the decision – as a possible Poet Laureate. Had he been appointed, it could have transformed the office into something meaningful.

9. Jan Montefiore, *Feminism and Poetry: Language, Experience, Identity in Women's Writing* (London: Pandora, 1987), p. 31.

10. See, for example, the two recent big anthologies of Victorian women's poetry anthologies: *Nineteenth-Century Women's Poetry*, ed. Isobel Armstrong and Joseph Bristow with Cath Sharrock (Oxford: Oxford University Press, 1996), and *Victorian Women Poets: an Anthology*, ed. Angela Leighton and Margaret Reynolds (Oxford: Blackwell, 1995), and collections of essays such as that edited by Angela Leighton, *Victorian Women Poets: a Critical Reader* (Oxford: Blackwell, 1996).

11. There are exceptions of course: for example, Suzanne Moore's perceptive analysis of Prince's 'Signs of the Time' in 'Getting a Bit of the Other: the Pimps of Postmodernism', in *Male Order: Unwrapping Masculinity* ed. Rowena Chapman and Jonathan Rutherford (London: Lawrence & Wishart, 1988), pp. 165–6, though perhaps it is significant that she

comments on the kind of play of ambiguity and paradox which traditional poetry criticism is best at handling. See also her 'Here's Looking at You, Kid?' in *The Female Gaze: Women as Viewers of Popular Culture*, ed. Lorraine Gammon and Margaret Marshment (London: Women's Press, 1988). The South Bank Centre Literature Department's 'More than Meets the Ear' season (1993) was an innovative exploration of the pop lyric.

12. I am not suggesting there are no traditions of women's poetry. There is a tradition of American feminist poetry; I have heard interesting arguments for self-conscious tradition of Victorian English women's poetry; there is a Maori tradition's of women's songs of loss. None is universal.

13. Cora Kaplan, 'Feminist Criticism Twenty Years On', in *From My Guy to Sci-Fi: Genre and Women's Writing in the Postmodern World*, ed. Helen Carr (London: Pandora, 1989).

14. For readers who have not been through this particular mill, I should explain that New Critics are not new, but a school of criticism, or perhaps approach to criticism, first identified by John Crow Ransom in 1941, which emphasised close reading and attention to the form of the literary object rather than its history.

15. Michael Hamburger, *The Truth of Poetry* (Harmondsworth: Penguin, 1972), p. 54.

16. Some Native American groups still have a living oral culture, and several present day Native American novelists and poets, such Leslie Marmon Silko, Louise Erdrich, and Gerald Vizenor, draw such oral traditions into their written works, again transforming the dominant cultural tradition as do the postcolonial groups I mentioned earlier. Here, however, I am talking about oral poetry taken down in the late nineteenth century and first half of this century. Some of these traditional forms are still in existence, but not all have survived the disruption of Native American cultures, the imposition of the reservation system and government efforts in the early years of the century to eliminate 'Indianness'.

17. Samuel Taylor Coleridge, 'On Poesy or Art', in *Miscellanies, Aesthetic and Literary* (London: George Bell, 1892), p. 42.

18. Mary Douglas, *Purity and Danger* (London: Routledge & Kegan Paul, 1966).

19. Frances Densmore, *Chippewa Music II, Bureau of American Ethnology Bulletin* 51 (1913), p. 254. I have discussed this further in my book, *Inventing the American Primitive: Politics, Gender and the Representation of Native American Literary Traditions, 1789–1936* (Cork University Press and New York University Press, 1996). The work I have done on Native American poetry has been largely on the way Euroamericans have misread it for their own purposes, so I am aware there is an irony in my attempt to use it. I do not want to claim here that I am giving a 'true' version. I am simplifying and selecting, but I hope I am treating this tradition with respect.

20. Washington Matthews, *The Night Chant, a Navaho Ceremony*, Museum of American Natural History, vol. VI (1902), p. 76. Navajo chants are still performed today.

21. Frances Densmore, *Papago Music, Bureau of American Ethnology Bulletin* 90 (1929).

22. Grace Nichols, *i is a long memoried woman* (London: Karnak House, 1983), p. 65, and Fred D'Aguiar, *Mama Dot* (London: Chatto & Windus, 1987).

23. Michelle Cliff, *The Land of Look Behind* (Ithaca, N.Y.: Firebrand Books, 1985), p.14.
24. Montefiore, *Feminism and Poetry*, pp. 16–20.
25. Jorge Luis Borges 'Pierre Menard, Author of the Quixote', in *Labyrinths* (Harmondsworth: Penguin, 1971), pp. 62–71.
26. Roland Barthes, trans. Stephen Heath, 'Change the Object Itself', in *Image–Music–Text* (London: Fontana, 1977), p. 166.
27. Claude Lévi-Strauss, trans. Claire Jacobson and Brooke Grundfest Schoepf, 'The Effectiveness of Symbols', in *Structural Anthropology* (Harmondsworth: Penguin, 1968), pp. 186–231.
28. Jean-François Lyotard, trans. Geoff Bennington and Brian Massumi, *The Postmodern Condition: A Report on Knowledge* (Manchester University Press, 1984), and with Jean-Loup Thébaud, trans Wlad Godzich *Just Gaming* (Manchester University Press, 1985).
29. Adrienne Rich, *The Fact of a Doorframe* (New York: Norton, 1984), p. 55.
30. Eavan Boland gave this information at a poetry reading that I attended.
31. Eavan Boland, 'The Journey', in *The Journey and Other Poems* (Manchester: Carcanet, 1986), pp. 39–42.
32. Julia Kristeva, trans. Margaret Waller, *Revolution in Poetic Language* (New York: Columbia University Press, 1984) and Isobel Armstrong, *Language as Living Form in Nineteenth-Century Poetry* (Brighton: Harvester, 1982).
33. Cliff, *Land of Look Behind*, p. 12.
34. *The Complete Poems of Emily Dickinson*, ed. Thomas H Johnson (London: Faber & Faber, 1970), p. 333, and Cora Kaplan, 'The Indefinite Disclosed', in *Writing Women, Women Writing*, ed. Mary Jacobus (London: Croom Helm, 1979), repr. in Cora Kaplan *Sea Changes* (London: Verso, 1987). She does not quote that particular line in that article, but did so when making the same point in a talk on 'Women and the Gothic' I heard her give some years before.
35. See Joyce McDougall, *Theatres of the Mind* (New York: Free Association Books, 1987), p. 10.
36. Toril Moi (ed.), *The Kristeva Reader* (Oxford: Blackwell, 1987), p. 14.
37. Kristeva, *Revolution in Poetic Language*, p. 28. She adds that these stases are 'themselves constituted by the repetition of these charges'.
38. Amy Clampitt, *The Kingfisher* (London: Faber & Faber 1986), pp. 93–4.
39. Bertolt Brecht, trans. John Willett, 'A Short Organum for the Theatre', in *Brecht on Theatre* (London: Methuen, 1964), pp. 181, and 205.
40. Stephen Heath, in Alice Jardine and Paul Smith (eds), *Men in Feminism* (London: Methuen, 1987), p. 13.
41. For an illuminating defence of the complexity of the Romantic view of the self and self-consciousness, see Armstrong, *Language as Living Form*.
42. Pound, *Literary Essays*, pp. 21, 47.
43. See Adorno et al.'s analysis of fascism in *The Authoritarian Personality* (New York: Harper & Row, 1950), and compare this language here with Pound's very similar descriptions of usury in the *Cantos*.
44. Virginia Woolf, *Jacob's Room* (Harmondsworth: Penguin, 1992), p. 82.
45. An earlier version of this article was published in Carr, *From My Guy to Sci-Fi*.

13
'Nothing to Do with Eternity'? Adrienne Rich, Feminism and Poetry
Janet Montefiore

A feminist heroine?

Adrienne Rich's readers have been variously admiring, grateful, hero-worshipping, occasionally sceptical or dismissive, but never neutral. She is the leading feminist poet, a 'heroine of the women's movement' (Nancy Milford), 'the Blake of American letters' (Nadine Gordimer), a feminist prophet who 'by recalling the ancient cthonic mysteries of blood and birth, by reconnecting daughters with their mothers, by drawing parallels between women today and their historical counterparts, and by envisioning the women of the future ... celebrates women's strength and possibilities' (Wendy Martin). Helen Vendler once wrote lyrically of her poetry's 'courage, generosity and self-forgetfulness', and for Charles Altieri she is 'one of the two strongest American poets' (the other being John Ashbery) who contests American ideology by her powerful ethical sense of community. More recently, Eavan Boland has celebrated her as one of the 'shape-makers of this century's poetry', and Michael Schmidt has praised her in similar terms.[1] Yet there has also been harsh criticism, most cogently from Helen Vendler criticising Rich's tendency to simplify her poetic world of innocent wronged victims *versus* wicked oppressors, but also crudely from reactionaries such as Professor Smithers who, after Rich was awarded $25,000 by the Mellon Committee, said publicly that she had only been honoured because the Mellon prize committee needed a lesbian poet for political reasons.[2]

My own feelings about Adrienne Rich are about as mixed as these paeans and snipings; I swing, irreconcilably, between admiration and gratitude for her best work and increasing irritation with the inflated claims made for her transcendent vision. I give here a detailed account of my mixed response not (I hope) out of egotism, but these because details of the reception of this poet represent a significant moment in recent intellectual history. I have bought, read and pondered all Rich's books and have written respectful criticisms of her work. As an (occasional) poet, I have learnt much from her (Eavan Boland is right, I think, to praise Rich for enabling other women to write about their own lives[3]); I have also taught her work to English Literature undergraduates and Women's Studies postgraduates. I first encountered her as a reader, through picking up her poetry collection *The Dream of a Common Language* in December 1978 while browsing the poetry section of Collett's bookshop (now defunct, then a left-wing haunt) in the Charing Cross Road. Enchanted, I bought the book (and wrote down the date on the flyleaf), even though I didn't understand all the poems nor recognise many of the women they celebrated. I was moved by the political exhilaration that fills the book, whose woman-centred feminism was obvious and congenial; I was deeply excited by the images and rhythms of the poems, by the energy and pleasure of their language, and by the autobiographical element, especially the open eroticism of the lesbian love poems (which in 1999 look rather restrained). I felt, much as Helen Vendler describes feeling about Rich's earlier poems,[4] that Rich's 'common language' was speaking both to and for me as a woman. I can still recapture some of that exhilaration when I read the book – though I now see how narrowly its 'common' language is defined by a lesbian-separatist rhetoric invoking a trans-historical fellowship of women and urging us 'to close the gap in the Great Nebula / to help the earth deliver.'[5] Good grief, I think now, reading that; but in 1978 those words looked exhilarating, not absurd.

Since that encounter I have written a good deal about Rich, who features in almost every chapter of my *Feminism and Poetry* (1987) as a feminist landmark, admired poet and acknowledged theoretician, but is treated less as a guiding star than as a target of (respectful) criticism. I applaud the radicalism and energy of her feminist commitment but criticise her account of women's poetry for its unmediated equation of poetry with experience; I praise the famous autobiographical fable of the young woman poet in 'When We Dead Awaken' but worry about the reduction of many different women poets into this single model; I admire her attempt to produce a 'whole new poetry' of the female Imaginary in 'Twenty-One Love poems' but criticise her essentialist notion of primordial lesbian identity.[6] All these reservations derive from my discomfort with the universality which Rich has habitually claimed for poetry, or for her own version of female identity, or both, although her definition of that universality has changed in the last twenty years in which she has publicly acknowledged her own homosexuality and her Jewishness, identifying herself with African Americans, Native Americans, the colonized Irish – in short, with the victimized. Although I still love much of *The Dream of a Common Language* – 'Power', 'A Woman Dead in Her Forties', the end of 'Cartographies of Silence' and 'Transcendental Etude', and still admire (with reservations) 'To a Poet' and 'Natural Resources' , I no longer feel that identification with the poet's interrogation of her own experience, because the terms in which she conducts that interrogation have come to seem rather questionable. The grandiose statements of 'Splittings' – 'I am choosing / not to suffer uselessly and not to use her / I choose to love this time for once / with all my intelligence'[7] arouse my scepticism. '*All* my intelligence?' What about the intelligence of the unconscious self, that writes itself in dreams and puns and slips and isn't amenable to the will? What meaning has this claim to be in total command of one's psyche, other than that very American ideological wish-fulfilment, the yearning to accomplish one's escape from history simply by saying one does so? (Besides, how can you claim 'not to use' another person when making poetry out of desiring her?) Above all, what does all that self-conscious poetic agonizing have to say to those millions, not so lucky as the poet, who don't have her options, can't choose their suffering, and do suffer uselessly?

These are tougher questions than I asked in *Feminism and Poetry*, but even that was regarded as insufficiently reverential, provoking a letter from an American fan of Rich denouncing me, more in anger than in sorrow, as a brainwashed tool of academic patriarchy who couldn't appreciate great feminist art. Without taking that too seriously, I did come to wonder whether, given Rich's importance for feminism, I might have been over-hard on her. So my chapter on post-colonial poetry in the book's second edition contains unalloyed praise both for Rich's questioning of American ideology and her memoir of her own Jewishness, which I read as a forerunner and intertext for Eavan Boland's celebrated 'Outside History'.[8] I also wrote a rave review of her prose book *What Is Found There* (1993), preferring its ethical challenge to American culture and ideology over Robert Hughes' acclaimed *The Culture of Complaint* (1993) whose 'Orwellian' denunciations of PC-speak invited the reader to join the author as a superior, balanced person: '*We're* not like those self-pitying, self-righteous, muddle-headed, philistine idiots.'[9] Yet afterwards I had doubts; the more I

looked at Rich's arguments for poetry as *the* form of political interven-
tion, the more I felt she was making claims for 'the power of language'
that simply weren't valid in the world of real power and action. I was
moved to write her a long meditative letter about poetry and the Gulf
War, which she didn't answer. Not that I blame her for that; it's
entirely reasonable for famous poets not to reply to unsolicited criticism (and mental dialogue with her ended up positively by inspiring a
dissenting poem of my own). Also, I began to think that Rich's poetic
identification with the insulted and the injured bore a worrying resemblance to that self-righteousness which tainted Hughes's critique of
'political correctness' in the arts: '*We're* not like those insensitive patriarchal racist heterosexist ruling-class brutes.'[10] My dissatisfaction
produced a more critical review of her *Dark Fields of the Republic*,
praising the poet's brilliant visual imagery but attacking her self-
righteousness and too-easy identification with victims, notably in
'Deportations' in which the secret police are imagined arresting the
poet and her lover:

> four men walk through the unlatched door
> One in light summer wool and silken tie
> One in work clothes browned with blood
> One with open shirt, a thin
> thong necklace hasped with silver round his neck
> One in shorts naked up from the navel
>
> And they have come for us, two of us and four of them
> and I think, perhaps they are still human
> and I ask them *When do you think all this began?*

The following poem 'And Now' claims that this horrible scenario of
rape and torture merely witnesses 'who was in charge of definitions /
when the name of compassion / was changed to the name of guilt'.[11]
Yet the poet is never in truth likely to risk danger from the state, and
to claim identity with victims implies a disavowal of the real differences of class and privilege between herself and the people whose fate
she fantasises sharing.[12] Equally dubious is that line ' perhaps they are
still human'. Sadism and silk ties are not part of animal behaviour,
and we cannot suppose that these thugs are sci-fi aliens. Surely the
'Blake of American letters' ought to know that cruelty has a human
heart and terror the human form divine? It is comforting for a feminist to believe that cruelty has a misogynist heart and terror an

imperialist face; but that half-truth is too limited for good politics, let alone good poetry.

Students, however, don't see Rich at all this way – or so I've found when teaching her poems over nearly twenty years, with mixed success. Many can't cope with her deliberate fragmentariness or her erudition (her poems often inspire them to better written commentaries than verbal discussions) and are simply baffled by 'Snapshots of a Daughter-in-Law', which I used to teach alongside an improvised anthology of the masculine Great Tradition sources (Shakespeare, Horace, Dr. Johnson, Baudelaire etc.) which the poem quotes from and twists, with a wit that is inevitably blunted by explanation. Resenting being made to go a long way round to prove what they reckoned they knew anyway – that patriarchal poetic tradition oppresses women – students tended to conclude, dishearteningly for me, that canonical male poets were simply a waste of time when they could be reading Judy Grahn or Grace Nichols. They also found difficult the allusions to political issues which the lapse of time had made obscure: 'The Burning of Paper Instead of Children' needed nearly as much explanation as 'Snapshots'. Those who did like Rich, usually a minority of gifted or sophisticated students (mostly postgraduates), never shared my worries about her essentialist or universalist shortcomings – cavils which they thought picky and unfair. (Feminist students make no bones, quite rightly, about disagreeing with their teachers). It was, precisely, Rich's bold claims and her 'experiential' vision that appealed to those young women, and a very few men, for whom she released intellectual possibilities. I remember particularly one intelligent and sensitive student dying of cystic fibrosis, who in her final year was inspired by Rich's essay 'When We Dead Awaken' to find her own voice as a poet. These enthusiasts felt, as I had done in 1978, that she spoke both to and for them, her vision opening up theirs.

A visionary poet?

Vision is what Adrienne Rich's major poetry most characteristically offers her readers. That sounds obvious – doesn't most post-Romantic poetry, not to mention most creative writing do the same? (One thinks of Conrad defining his task as 'before all, to make you *see*'[13].) Yet for few major poets writing today is the idea (and metaphor) of sight so crucial as it is for Rich. She has always excelled at invoking visual images, from early poems like 'Aunt Jennifer's Tigers' with its 'bright topaz denizens of a world of green' – the phrasing a little arty but very vivid, as are the old lady's fingers that 'fluttering through her wool / Find even the ivory needle hard to pull.'[14] There is nothing naive about these poetic invocations of visual images; they live, very consciously, in the mind's eye and the imagination, bodily as well as mental – what Wordsworth calls 'sensations sweet / Felt in the blood and felt along the heart.'[15] (Bitter ones, too). It was this sophisticated awareness of the gap between word and referent that prompted my remark that 'Adrienne Rich is more subtle in her poems than in her essays'.[16] For at her best, the poet avoids claiming 'I am a camera', though she may take the camera as her metaphor, sometimes with a finely ironic effect, as in the recent 'Take' which describes a film scenario taken over successfully by the poet's desire to turn images to words and to follow their meanings into history beyond the reach of any film director.[17] Similar meditations empowered her brilliant 'The Photograph of the Unmade Bed' (1969), which ponders

> how poems are unlike photographs
> (the one saying   *This could be*
>
> the other   *This was*)
> The image ... is intentionless
>
> A long strand of hair
> in the washbasin
>
> is innocent and yet
> such things have done harm[18]

Here the visual image represents both the transformation of literal into figurative *and* the transforming powers of the imagination – which Rich now considers 'the only hope for a humane civil society',[19] although her younger self was more cautious – 'such things have done harm.' The verbal image is not literal truth (*'This was'*); rather (*'This could be'*) it represents (1) the figurative possibility of metaphor, or (2, just conceivably) the utopian possibilities of political transformation, or (3, much more likely here) the obsessive fantasies of a betrayed lover.

Similar meditations, though political rather than personal, structure the long contemporary prose poem 'Shooting Script'. This contemplates a dream landscape of American desolation, to be abandoned 'when I give up being paraphrased, when I let go, when the beautiful solutions in their crystal flasks have dried up in the sun, when the lightbulb bursts on lighting, when the dead bulb rattles like a seed-pod.' The poem achieves resolution by refusing the authority of the projector (= the means by which film is shown, but also 'political authority', the witty pun on 'beautiful solutions' being as near as Rich gets to humour), and choosing 'to see instead the web of cracks filtering over the plaster. / To read there the map of the future ... To read the etched rays of the bullet hole left years ago in the glass; to know in every distortion of light what fracture is.'[20] 'To *see*, to *read*, to *know*' – film and dream are rejected, but only in order to achieve a truer vision in poetry. Visual images are equally powerful in 'Planetarium', whose title is a brilliant pun. A planetarium gives an adjustable image of the night sky, just as the poem does for its readers as it contemplates both the efforts of human scientists to understand a universe whose vastness makes the imagination shrink, 'ribs chilled / in those spaces of the mind', and the special effort for 'a woman in the shape of a monster' to map her universe. The astronomer Caroline Herschel did this in one way by 'riding the polished lenses' while the poet does it by translating 'pulsations / into images for the relief of body / and the reconstruction of the mind'.[21] That last phrase 'the reconstruction of the mind' is significant: Rich's feminist radicalism implies re-inventing herself, as in the better-known 'Diving into the Wreck' where she discovers a lost self ('I am she: I am he').[22] But the subtlety of thought in Rich's best visionary work demands close reading rather than survey. To this end I shall examine two long quotations from Rich at her strongest: first, an extract from the beautiful but little-remarked meditation 'Woman and Bird' which opens *What Is Found There* with an understated epiphany. The poet sees a large bird alighting on her house; she greets it, tentatively identifying it as a Great Blue Heron, and then, wishing 'to be sure I could name what I had seen,' looks it up in her guide to Pacific Coast ecology:

> Then, as I sat there, my eye began to travel the margins of the book, along the names and habitats of creatures and plants along the 4,000-mile Pacific coastline of North America. It was an idle enough activity at first, the kind that sometimes plays upon other, subterranean activities of the mind, draws thinking and unfiltered feelings into sudden dialogue. Of late, I had been consciously thinking about the decade just beginning, the last of the twentieth century, and the great movements and shudderings of the time; about the country where I am a citizen, and what has been happening in our

social fabric, our emotional and sensual life, during that century. Somewhere beneath these conscious speculations lay a vaguer desire: to feel the pull of the future, to possess the inner gift, the unsentimentality, the fortitude, to see into it – if only a little way. But I found myself pulled by names: Dire Whelk, Dusky Tegula, Fingered Limpet, Hooded Puncturella, Veiled Chiton, Bat Star, By-the-Wind-Sailer, Crumb-of-Bread-Sponge, Eye Fringed Worm, Sugar Wrack, Frilled Anemone, Bull Kelp, Ghost Shrimp, Sanderling, Walleye Surfperch, Volcano Barnacle, Stiff-footed Sea Cucumber, Leather Star, Innkeeper Worm, Lug Worm. And I felt the names drawing me into a state of piercing awareness, a state I associate with reading and writing poems. These names – by whom given and agreed on? – work as poetry works, enlivening a sensuous reality through recognition or the play of sounds (the short *i*'s of Fingered Limpet, the open vowels of Bull Kelp, Hooded Puncturella, Bat Star); the poising of heterogeneous images (*volcano* and *barnacle*, *leather* and *star*, *sugar* and *wrack*) to evoke other worlds of meaning. Sugar Wrack: a foundered ship in the Triangle Trade? Volcano Barnacle: tiny unnoticed growth with explosive potential? Who saw the bird named Sanderling and gave it that caressive, diminutive name? Or was Sanderling the name of the one who saw it? These names work as poetry works in another sense: they make something unforgettable. You will remember the pictorial names as you won't the Latin, which, however, is more specific as to genus and species. Human eyes gazed at each of all these forms of life and saw resemblance in difference – the core of metaphor, that which lies close to the core of poetry itself, the only hope for a humane civil life. The eye for likeness in the midst of contrast, the appeal to recognition, the association of thing to thing, spiritual fact with embodied form, begins here ... I began to think of about the names, beginning with the sound and image delivered in the name 'Great Blue Heron', as tokens of a time when naming was poetry, when connections between things and living beings, or living things and human beings, were instinctively apprehended. By 'a time' I don't mean any one historical or linguistic moment or period. I mean *all* the times when people have summoned language into the activity of plotting connections between, and marking distinctions among, the elements presented to our senses.[23]

Rich goes on to deplore the fact that poetry, science and politics which ought to flow in and out of each other, have become disconnected, and ends by offering the creative imagination as a potential solution rather like Leavis on the Two Cultures. Speaking impersonally yet intimately of her own poetic imagination works, and helped in the original by an elegant Bembo typeface and generous spacing, Rich here makes an important statement of her own poetics. Certainly her love and knowledge of her art appear in her informed attention to vowel sounds and her unpicking of the metaphors in the names, but more telling is that 'state of piercing awareness' into which she is 'pulled', and even more the human and ethical significance she attaches to 'the act of naming'. She is clearly writing in that tradition of American utopian and religious thought which goes back to the Pilgrim Fathers. As Wendy Martin has observed, 'The Puritans believed that God's elect were destined to reform the Satanic wilderness ... Rich calls for a similar dedication to the feminist vision that will bring about "the transformation of our society and of all our life"'.[24] Rich is also drawing, how consciously I do not know, on Transcendentalist thinking. The significance which she sees in names is very close to Emerson's remark in 'The Poet' that 'the poets made all the words, and therefore language is the archives of history ... Language is fossil poetry' – not to mention the verbal echo of his famous 'Natural facts are symbols of ... spiritual facts' in her celebration of the matching of 'spiritual fact with embodied form'.[25] Rich's feminist preoccupation with naming and reality goes further back, to her early manifesto urging women to see 'how the very act of naming has been till now a male prerogative, and how we can begin to see and name – and therefore live – afresh'.[26] This notion of 'the act of naming' as a form of new vision which takes possession of the thing seen and named, and of the poet who names as an exemplary because universal figure, re-enacts, in terms of female rhetoric, the myth of Adamic language ('I nam'd them, as they passd, and understood / Thir Nature, with such knowledge God endu'd / My sudden apprehension'[27]). The later invocation of 'a time when naming was poetry' invokes a (potential) American Paradise, defined not as a 'real' place but as as an ideal moment that occurs when language is used creatively to understand the world by invoking likeness in difference. Though Rich doesn't share Shelley's Platonism, her belief that poetry is 'the best hope for a humane civil life' is also very close in thought to his 'Defence of Poetry' which argues that the 'imagination, that great instrument of moral good', works through poetry to unite material with spiritual realities, thus potentially redressing the evils of mechanical industrialism.[28] Also, of course, her belief in the visionary imagination recalls Whitman. Possessed by the beauty and hugeness of

America, wanting to imaginatively grasp not only 'our century, our country' but more specifically (and so in a way more ambitiously) its '4000-mile long Pacific coastline', she resembles a female version of Whitman's ideal poet as described in the lyrical 'Preface' to *Leaves of Grass* (1855): 'His spirit responds to his country's spirit ... he incarnates its geography and natural life and rivers and lakes ... when the long Atlantic coast stretches longer and the Pacific coast stretches longer he easily stretches with them north or south.' And compare her long enchanting list of seashore plants and animals with the famous catalogues in 'Song of Myself', or (an even closer parallel) with his list of American seas and lakes in the same essay.[29] And here, greatly though I admire Rich's prose, is a source of unease for me. Totalizing vision is a Platonic metaphor, whose phallic universalism has become rightly suspect ever since Luce Irigaray's deconstruction of the sexual politics of visionary metaphors in *Speculum*.[30] Yet Rich seems to believe, as a post-Irigarayan could not, in the innocence of the visionary mind; which I think explains those lapses into self-righteous identification with victims which I have criticised above.

That said, I do not want to deny Rich's feminism or her break from her American masters. It is important to note that 'Woman and Bird' leads *not* to that prophetic vision of the USA's future for which the poet was consciously seeking at the outset, but to the pleasures of language, towards which she was pulled sideways by looking for the bird's name in a reference book. *This*, the anecdote says, was where she should have been looking, not towards a grandiose abstract future but towards metaphors and names. And though she may agree with Emerson that metaphor is the base of poetry, her ideal of poetic metaphor as a model of 'a humane civil life' , an enactment of 'likeness in difference' comprising both a political model of the USA as Rich would like it to be (*e pluribus unum*), and her poet's love of language, does not derive from him. These ideals, feminist and multi-cultural, as well as American, interestingly parallel Nicole Ward Jouve's more recent meditations on metaphor and the maternal body in. Like Rich, though in psychoanalytic rather than political terms, Ward Jouve envisages poetic metaphor as a source of humane possibilities, defining it in Winnicottian terms as a 'transitional space' between the maternal body and the external world, within which likeness and difference can freely and creatively play.[31]

Visionary feminism

Feminism is, of course, an explicit preoccupation of Rich's 'Trans-cendental Etude' whose meditations enact the poet's pilgrimage towards self-discovery and a female language which preoccupy *The Dream of a Common Language*. The poem begins, in the post-Romantic tradition of 'occasional' poems like 'Tintern Abbey' (or more recently, Seamus Heaney's *Station Island*) with the poet driving 'one August evening' through Vermont backroads. She passes a 'great soft sloping field / of musing heifers' and through woods of 'dark maple' and a startled doe with her fawns, which in three months will be 'fair game' for male hunters,

> But this evening deep in summer
> the deer are still alive and free,
> nibbling apples from the laden boughs
> so weighted, so englobed
> with already yellowing fruit
> they seem eternal, Hesperidean
> in the clear-tuned cricket-throbbing air.

Rich's vision of rural America as an all-female Eden momentarily regained corresponds to that phase of 'women's time' defined by Kristeva as the moment of 'separatist and utopian' women's writing which constitutes a '"female society" as a sort of alter ego of the offi-cial society ... imagined as harmonious, without prohibitions, free and fulfilling'.[32] In the poem's utopian space, the 'real' summer evening becomes an all-female Paradise, a 'happy rural seat of various view'

> Groves whose rich Trees wept odorous Gumms and Baum,
> Others whose fruit burnisht with golden Rinde
> Hung amiable, *Hesperian* fables true
> If true here only, and of delicious taste.
> Betwixt them Lawns and level Downs, and Flocks
> Grazing the tender Herb, were interposed ...'[33]

Of course Rich, far from directly imitating *Paradise Lost*, has rejected patriarchal epic and its 'striving for greatness'. Yet her paradisal land-scape mirrors Milton, point for feminized point: the diversely wooded and pastoral landscape of 'various view', the maples which run with sugar sap in spring and the Hesperidean apple-trees, interspersed with open meadows grazed by does and heifers 'alive and free'. These subtextual echoes are perhaps less surprising than they at first look. The inheritance of the Puritan fathers and the myth of America as paradise regained pull powerfully in Rich's poetry, especially in *Dream of a Common Language*, her most utopian collection. 'A Woman Dead in her Forties' in the same book begins with a comparably Edenic moment: 'the women I grew up with' are sitting half-naked on the rocks in sunshine – 'we look at each other and/ are not ashamed'. For a fleeting moment they are innocent and happy, Eves before the Fall, until the mastectomized woman pulls on her blouse, a 'stern statement' of shame, pain and mortality.[34]

Nevertheless, the meditations on the relation between art and a woman's life occupying most of the six-page 'Transcendental Etude' constitute a determined rejection of the male world and all its works, especially the Great Tradition of patriarchal texts like 'Genesis' and *Paradise Lost*. We cannot, says Rich, train ourselves towards mastery of language as a pianist masters her instrument because life doesn't fit the prescribed rules of craftsmanship. Instead, our life is 'trying to sightread / what our fingers can't keep up with, learn by heart / what we can't even read', faithful only to 'a half-blind, stubborn / cleaving to ... what we are'. And a woman's self-realization demands a painful cutting loose from her old life, a free fall into 'utter loneliness ... her being a cry / To which no echo comes or can ever come'. Yet 'we were always like this, knowing it makes the difference'. Our psychic histories universally repeat a Fall from sensual unity with our mother into the alienating condition of compulsory heterosexuality. That primordial lost mother and lost self can, be rediscovered through love between women, the realization that *'this / is how I can love myself / as only a woman can love me'.*

> Vision begins to happen in such a life
> as if a woman quietly walked away
> from the argument and jargon in a room#
>
> and sitting down in her kitchen, began turning in her lap
> bits of yarn, calico and velvet scraps,
> laying them out absently on the scrubbed boards
> in the lamplight, with small rainbow-colored shells
> sent in cotton wool from somewhere far away,
> and skeins of milkweed from the nearest meadow -
> original domestic silk, the finest findings

and the darkblue petal of the petunia
and the dry darkbrown lace of seaweed;
not forgotten either, the shed silver
whisker of the cat,
the spiral of paper-wasp-nest curling
beside the finch's yellow feather.
Such a composition has nothing to do with eternity,
the striving for greatness, brilliance –
only with the musing of a mind
one with her body, experienced fingers quietly pushing
dark against bright, silk against roughness
with no mere will to mastery,
only care for the many-lived, unending
forms in which she finds herself,
becoming now the sherd of broken glass
slicing light in a corner, dangerous
to flesh, now the plentiful, soft leaf
that wrapped round the throbbing finger, soothes the wound
and now the stone foundation, further forming
rockshelf underneath everything that grows.[35]

This passage has received much admiration and commentary, never to
my mind quite adequate because all its critics to date have equated the
poem, over-literally, with its stated manifesto. For Wendy Martin it
amounts to 'an acceptance of life for its own sake. Rejecting ontologi-
cal hierarchy, Rich's poem does not attempt to rise above ordinary
experience.' Charles Altieri likewise finds that the poem 'makes available for public thought the many-sidedness of the woman's potential,
while allowing the poet to recognise the naturalness that moves her to
realise her powers'.[36] Even those 'equality' feminists who rejected the
poem's embrace of women's 'difference' agree with this account of the
poetry, while doubting its arguments. So Kate McLuskie, aptly comparing the passage with 'the art of collage, of the family quilt, of the
postal event, of the fence round Greenham Common' and praising
Rich for her commitment to 'collectivity and resistance to élite art',
less convincingly criticises her feminist rhetoric for ignoring 'the gap
between experience and language'.[37] Similarly, Margaret Homans
argued that in celebrating the 'absent musings' of a woman in the
kitchen table as the bedrock of the world, Rich is re-inscribing the
woman's old enemy the 'cthonic feminine object ... Rich knows that
her language is lovely enough to persuade us that she embraces

inarticulateness, and that we should too; [the] woman in the lamp-light, turning her back on "argument and jargon" is as much of a threat to the life of the female mind as Dickinson's "Mother Nature" who "Wills Silence – Everywhere".'[38] (Though surely not, if she can stimulate such lively disagreement?)

All such literal readings of 'Transcendental Etude' overlook the fact that this poem belongs, far more than its argument suggests, to a tradition of mastery, beginning with its title. This is the name of a famous piece for the piano by Frédéric Chopin (incidentally a male composer). One cannot play Chopin well without first undertaking exactly the kind of fierce, disciplined study that Rich (officially) rejects with the disclaimer that 'we're not performers like Liszt', or like 'the 79-year old pianist [who] said, when I asked her / *What makes a virtuoso? – Competitiveness*'.[39] Moreover, Adrienne Rich's own mother was a pianist (was she that 79-year-old player?) who taught her daughter to play Mozart on the piano at four years old (a discipline the girl later defied, preferring to pick out 'Smoke Gets In Your Eyes' on the keyboard devoted to Mozart[40]). These unspoken facts, combined with the poem's invocation of the joy and terror of the primordial mother, the 'heavy or slender / thighs on which we lay, flesh against flesh, / eyes steady on the face of love'[41] all imply a complex rejection and affirmation of the poet's mother and the traditions she represents.

The other point missed by the critics who accept the poem at its own anti-formalist valuation is that the lovely language describing its fragments of the natural world is a classic instance of the art that conceals art. Those two long sentences that follow the mind's movement across thirty lines are full of subtle verbal links and transformations as the poet's gaze moves unobtrusively from general plural nouns – 'bits' of yarn, velvet 'scraps', to the more sharply seen 'small rainbow-coloured shells … from somewhere far away', and then to the close-up focus on the 'darkblue petal of the petunia'. Note the aural repetition and transformation of 'petal' into 'petunia', and the way the self-coined adjective 'darkblue' is likewise repeated and transformed into 'darkbrown' in the next line, almost like a rhyme. The word 'lace', suggesting the seaweed's intricate branching complexity, relates to other metaphors of precious things: the 'silk' of the milkweed (a near-rhyme here) and the 'silver' of the cat's whisker emphasised by enjambment. These half-buried metaphors of decoration subtly turn rubbish into beauty, as does the imagined matching of the dark colours contrasting with the straight silver line beside the spiral shape and dull white of the wasp's nest, seen against the yellow feather. (The repeated 'f' has a lovely resolving effect here, the skilfully interposed colour-adjective preventing the alliterative 'feather' from coming too soon after 'finch'.) And the focus on the woman's hands at their work pushing 'dark against bright, silk against roughness' is beautifully tactile as well as visual, its oppositions suggesting both pain and pleasure. So do the connotations of cutting and comforting in the penultimate images of the glass splinter and the bandage, disliked by Homans for being 'both a dangerous object and the cure for it, the traditional types for the woman as whore and as saint'.[42] Yet the glass 'slicing light' acts as a prism, splitting light into rainbows, echoing the small coloured shells envisaged twenty lines before. Such a composition has nothing to do with stumbling amateurism; it implies a long apprenticeship to the art of words, like the disciplined skill of the pianist making itself so unnoticeable that her listeners become aware only of the lovely sounds.

Yet the relation of 'Transcendental Etude' to the patriarchal tradition which it rejects goes deeper than this brilliant, disavowed technical skill. It is not only that the woman in her kitchen leads outwards, to the whole world, nor even that the 'forms in which she finds herself' reinscribe a Whitmanesque identification between self and world. Such intensely visual poetry, the poet's gaze creating what her mind's eye imagines, has a long, distinguished and largely masculine ancestry, looking back most obviously to Whitman's catalogues, but also to the poet's acknowledged first 'master' Wallace Stevens,[43] and beyond him to the Keats of the great Odes where the poet's mind moves from perception of a 'here and now' to the imagined visions which come before us through his words: the lover on the urn, the visions conjured up by the nightingale's song. Of course, Rich is rejecting that tradition most emphatically, since her own imagined composition 'has nothing to do with eternity / the striving for greatness, brilliance'. To repudiate the 'will to mastery' is nevertheless to define oneself in relation to that ideal. As Cora Kaplan said of another woman's poem, 'the ghosts of the meanings she wishes to resist shadow her words';[44] but this means strength, not her weakness. To resist a tradition can be as creatively enabling as to inherit it – if not more so.

Precisely because the poem's oppositional feminist aesthetic of process, as opposed to artifact, *needs* the existence of patriarchal ambition and traditions of greatness to make its own informality significant, it has a great deal to do, dialectically, with the ideal of the 'artifice of eternity'.[45] The poem's movement from coloured detail to detail resembles and anticipates Baby Suggs contemplating the patches on her quilt in Toni Morrison's *Beloved*.[46] A similar point was suggested by Kate McLuskie, shrewdly comparing that imaginary collage to the collective, anti-establishment art of the 'family quilt' and the fence at Greenham Common. (This was the famous all-female anti-nuclear camp set up there in 1981 to protest against the (now defunct) US airbase for cruise missiles. The 'Greenham women' used to weave leaves, bracken, ribbons, family photographs and other fragments of their lives into the wire perimeter fence in a collective gesture of feminist defiance.) Yet without the elite art of masters like Yeats or Milton to oppose, the new tradition of 'alternative', dissenting feminist art would become unpolitical and merely decorative, an aesthetic blind alley.

Nothing to do with eternity?

W.H. Auden once wrote that good criticism is rare because it depends on acknowledging that 'Mr A's work is more important than anything I can say about it', which few critics can bring themselves to say.[47] Of course Auden's language here is sexist, assuming that critic and poet alike are bourgeois males courteously referring to each other as 'Mr' – just what you might expect from the man whose 'Foreword' to Rich's first poetry collection notoriously patronised her as a good little girl.[48] And it will certainly be viewed with suspicion by those for whom criticism means deconstructing the sexist assumptions underpinning the great masculine tradition(s), a task which makes the critic, the knowing subject more powerful and so more important than the poet whose sexist unconscious her commentary contains and analyses.

Yet criticism which sees writing merely as the site of ideologies or product of discursive formations (whether patriarchal, heterosexist, imperialist, racist, or politically correct feminist) will never do justice to the pleasures and possibilities of language. I have here written many admiring and some harsh things of Adrienne Rich; but her best poems remain more important, and will outlast, anything I can say about them.

Notes

1. Nancy Milford 'This Woman's Movement', 1975, repr. in Barbara and Albert Gelpi (eds), *Adrienne Rich's Poetry* (New York: Norton, 1975),

pp. 189–202 (hereafter *ARP*); Nadine Gordimer, on blurb of Adrienne Rich, *Dark Fields of the Republic* (New York: Norton, 1996) (hereafter *DFR*); Wendy Martin, *An American Triptych: Anne Bradstreet, Emily Dickinson, Adrienne Rich* (Chapel Hill, NC: University of North Carolina Press, 1984), p. 227; Helen Vendler, 'Ghostlier Demarcations, Keener Sounds', *ARP*, (1973) pp. 170–1; Charles Altieri, *Self and Sensibility in Contemporary American Poetry* (Cambridge University Press, 1984), pp. 165ff.; Eavan Boland, 'Reading Adrienne Rich', *PN Review* 114, (March–April, 1997), pp. 17–18; Michael Schmidt, *Lives of the Poets* (London: Weidenfeld and Nicolson, 1998), pp. 817–21.

2. Helen Vendler, *Soul Says: On Recent Poetry* (Cambridge, Mass.: Belknap Press, 1995), pp. 215–17; A.L. Smithers, *MLA Newsletter* 48 (Spring 1990), p. 8.

3. Boland, 'Reading Adrienne Rich', p. 17.

4. Helen Vendler, *ARP*, p. 160.

5. Adrienne Rich, 'Natural Resources', *The Dream of a Common Language* (New York: Norton) (hereafter *DCL*), p. 67.

6. Jan Montefiore, *Feminism and Poetry: Language, Experience, Identity in Women's Writing* (London: Pandora, 1987), pp. 11–14, 58–60, 89–91, 144–5, 160–7.

7. Rich, 'Splittings', *DCL*, p. 10.

8. Jan Montefiore, *Feminism and Poetry*, 2nd edn (London: Pandora, 1994), pp. 205–7, 210–15.

9. Jan Montefiore, 'Troubling the Waters', *The Nation* 4 Feb. 1994, p. 169.

10. It is fair to add that Rich's 'Notes Towards a Politics of Location', 1984, in *Blood, Bread and Poetry (London:* Virago, 1987), pp. 210–32, did struggle with these questions; I wish that she had kept up this self-questioning inquiry.

11. Rich, *DFR*, pp. 30, 31.

12. Jan Montefiore 'Fine Words but False', *TLS*, 2 Jan. 1997, p. 27. Helen Vendler has similarly observed that Rich 'presents herself less as a champion or leader than a co-sufferer, pitying herself (indirectly) in others': *Soul Says*, p. 217.

13. Conrad, 'Preface' to *The Nigger of the 'Narcissus'* (London: Heinemann, 1897), p. i.

14. Rich, 'Aunt Jennifer's Tigers', *ARP*, p. 2.

15. Wordsworth, *Tintern Abbey*, ll. 28–9: 1798, repr. in *Romanticism: An Anthology*, ed. Duncan Wu (Oxford: Blackwell, 1994), p. 241.

16. Montefiore, *Feminism and Poetry*, p. 4.

17. Rich, 'Take', *DFR*, pp. 41–2; cf. my commentary in *TLS*, 2 Jan. 1997, p. 27.

18. Rich 'The Photograph of the Unmade Bed', in *The Will to Change* (London: Chatto and Windus, 1972) (hereafter *WTC*), p. 45.

19. Adrienne Rich, *What Is Found There: Notebooks on Poetry and Politics* (New York: Norton, 1993) (hereafter *WFT*), p. 6.

20. Rich, 'Shooting Script', *WTC*, pp. 65, 67; *ARP*, pp. 56, 57.

21. Rich, 'Planetarium', *WTC*, pp. 13, 14; *ARP*, pp. 45–6.

22. Rich 'Diving in the Wreck', *ARP*, p. 67.

23. Rich, 'Woman and Bird', *WFT*, pp. 6–7.

24. Martin, *An American Triptych*, p. 170.

25. Emerson, 'The Poet', from *Essays, Second Series*, 1844, repr. as *Emerson's Essays* (London: Everyman, 1906), p. 215; 'Nature', 1836, repr. as *Nature* by Dent, 1908, p. 11 ('Particular natural facts are symbols of particular spiritual facts').
26. Adrienne Rich 'When We Dead Awaken: Writing as Re-Vision', 1971; *ARP*, p. 90.
27. 'Paradise Lost', Book VIII, ll. 352–4, in *John Milton: The Complete Poems*, ed. B.A. Wright (London: Dent, 1908), p. 299.
28. P.B. Shelley:'The great instrument of moral good is the imagination, and poetry administers to the effect by acting on the cause', from 'A Defence of Poetry', 1821, repr. in Wu, *Romanticism*, p. 759.
29. Whitman, 'Preface' to *Leaves of Grass* 1855: repr. in *The Viking Portable Whitman*, ed. Mark van Doren (New York: Viking, 1945), pp. 31–2.
30. Luce Irigaray, 'La Tache aveugle d'un vieux rêve de symétrie', in *Spéculum de l'autre femme* (Paris, Editions de Minuit, 1977).
31. Nicole Ward Jouve,'Metaphor and Narrative', in *Female Genesis: Creativity, Self and Gender* (Cambridge: Polity Press, 1998), pp. 196–200.
32. Julia Kristeva, 'Women's Time' in *A Kristeva Reader* ed. Toril Moi (Oxford: Blackwell, 1990), p. 202.
33. Milton, *Paradise Lost*, Book IV, ll. 246–53, in *Complete Poems*, p. 221.
34. 'A Woman Dead in Her Forties', *DCL*, p. 53.
35. Rich, 'Transcendental Etude', *DCL*, pp. 72–7: quotation taken from pp. 76–7.
36. Martin, *American Triptych* p. 215; Altieri, *Self and Sensibility in Contemporary American Poetry*, p. 172.
37. Kate McLuskie 'Women's Language and Literature: A Problem in Women's Studies', *Feminist Review* 14 (Summer 1983), p. 59.
38. Margaret Homans, *Women Writers and Poetic Identity: Dorothy Wordsworth, Emily Brontë and Emily Dickinson* (Princeton, NJ, 1980), p. 229.
39. Rich. 'T.E.', *DCL*, p. 74.
40. Rich, 'A Poet's Education', *WFT*, pp. 184, 187.
41. 'T.E.', *DCL*, p. 75.
42. Homans, *Women Writers*, pp. 228–9.
43. Rich, 'Rotted Names', *WFT*, 197–205.
44. Cora Kaplan, 'Language and Gender', 1977, *Sea Changes* (London: Verso, 1985).
45. W.B. Yeats, 'Sailing to Byzantium', *Collected Poems* (London: Macmillan, 1950), p. 218.
46. Toni Morrison, *Beloved* (London: Chatto, 1988), p. 1. I am grateful to Alison Mark for suggesting this point.
47. W.H. Auden, 'Reading', in *The Dyer's Hand* (New York, Vintage, 1968), p. 9.
48. W.H. Auden, 'Foreword' to Rich *A Change of World* (New Haven, CT: Yale UP, 1951), repr. in *ARP*, pp. 124–5. See also Schmidt, *Lives of the Poets*, p. 818.

14
Marking Time: Fanny Howe's Poetics of Transcendence

Clair Wills

> ... consciousness has nothing to do with me either
> I'm just moving inside it, catch as catch can.
>
> Fanny Howe, *Introduction to the World*

In recent years critical discussions of contemporary poetry have suggested the implausibility of any straightforward distinction between the traditional lyric – dominated by the notion of the authentic personal voice – and avant-garde work which strives to disrupt or even eliminate the role of the 'I'. It has become clear that even the most confessional of poets – Lowell and Plath, for example – create a poetic self that isn't simply autobiographical. Furthermore, despite the apparent centrality of individual experience, modern confessional poetry is far from asserting a sovereign subject – its presuppositions are emphatically post-Freudian. The self which is laid bare is fractured and opaque, traversed by all kinds of unconscious forces, and reverberating with cultural and historical echoes and memories which are beyond its control.

Among the writers who have questioned this notional opposition between the lyrical and the anti-subjectivist or experimental, women poets have played a prominent role. The reasons for this are not hard to discern. Arguably, the representation of an inner life in lyric poetry, through personal address or solitary meditation and reflection, has always also been a mirror of social and cultural forces. But, given the nature of the poetic tradition and the history of poetic practice, this mirroring has also been gendered. This has led some contemporary women poets to seek to 'reclaim' the lyric, by making explicit within the lyric itself its relation to the broader external forces which pervade it, and which have traditionally defined the poetic persona – among other things – as maculine. Writers such as Adrienne Rich and Eavan Boland, for example, have explored within their poetry women's experience of finding themselves in an occluding, even silencing, cultural location experienced by women, and have sought to bring to light the unspoken – often painful – histories which have shaped the individual self.

Whether we speak in terms of a personal and cultural unconscious, or in terms of 'hidden histories' which shape the self, we are concerned with a relation to an outside which is also an inside, an overlapping of interior and exterior which unsettles conventional notions of the essential privacy and sovereignty of the subject. But traditionally, of course, one domain in which the experience of these reversals of inside and outside has been central is the domain of religious experience. Theology is another way of transgressing the boundaries of inwardness, of addressing the subject's relation to an encompassing reality which is nevertheless not simply external, another means of thinking about what 'unbounds' or 'de-limits' the self. And in the work of the contemporary American poet Fanny Howe, an often spare, denuded mode of writing, which has affinites with the radical anti-subjectivism of the Language poets, is employed to create an opening onto a transcendent dimension, a meaning which does not entirely eliminate, but immerses the self. Howe has said of her own work: 'I was at no time the only one writing these poems, for the taking of the language from the outside heralded a further loss of myself.'[1] She doesn't entirely disown the notion of agency here. She merely denies her uniqueness and solitariness (typical of the posture of the traditional lyric self), and suggests a more complex relation between selfhood, poetic writing, and self-loss, than the standard categories of subjectivism and anti-subjectivism are able to capture.

Loss of self is, of course, a long-established category of theology and religious meditation. But in Howe's work it enters into a new conjuncture with a specifically feminine sense of the rhythms of traditional practice and everyday life. While she is careful not to romanticise the oppressive and demeaning aspects of inherited female roles, she also offers a positive exploration of the temporality of mundane domestic ritual. Women's everyday activities are plotted against the cycles and thresholds of femininity, the stages of growth from girlhood to womanhood and maternity. Howe seems to be hinting that the very anonymity and immemoriality of such activities – cooking, providing, mending, sewing – can be seen as a kind of spiritual discipline. Furthermore, for Howe this submission to the unassuming constraints of routine, typical of women's experience, has a deep affinity with the disciplines of poetry. In poetry, too, we are subject to the contraints of an immemorial practice – that of language itself – and the way in which we experience these constraints is in terms of the determinism of a temporal sequence. Each word limits the possibilities of its succes-sor so that, in Howe's phrase, the poetic sentence becomes 'an image of the pressure of temporality'. Only by surrendering fully to this pres-sure, she suggests, can we glimpse that liberating dimension beyond the self from which it flows.

Time and transcendence

> I figure we are intended to experience time exactly as we do, even if it is *wrong*, because it is the only way we can measure the value and meaning of our actions here. This is where I link letters and sentences with time; they are analogous to minutes and hours and aspire to a justice which is also analogous to our quest for the promised land.[2]

The cover of Fanny Howe's most recent volume of poetry, *O'Clock*,[3] shows two young girls (perhaps sisters) mid-hop in a traditional Irish dance. This country dance competition appears to be actually taking place in the Irish countryside, in a marquee erected over temporary boards. The photographer has snapped an instant in time when the two girls hover simultaneously above the earth, and they are thus caught forever above ground. Both the notion of the temporary or makeshift, and that of immediacy and the fleeting moment are central preoccupations in this book, as well as in the sequence 'Q',[4] and in this essay I want to explore the implications of these concerns.

Howe's preoccupation with the concrete pressure of time can be interpreted in several ways. In recent art and poetics the measurement of the temporal is associated not only with contingency, with fugitive moments and the play of surfaces but also with a concomitant sense of the material world's resistance to interpretation or 'poetic' signifi-cance. While in the work of a poet such as Frank O'Hara this exploration of the momentary is still associated with a self (dialoguing with another), in more recent American poetry – particularly in the work of the Language poets – this impulse has been clearly tied to a conviction about the absence of interiority in contemporary life, and the disappearance of the arena of privacy. Rather than a secure grounding for the subject in the material world, all we have to go on are surface images and the experience of the moment. Fanny Howe's work has been referred to in the context of experimental linguistic work, and Howe herself has expressed admiration for a poetics which attempts to empty out 'content' from the verbal field.[5] Yet Howe has also commented that unlike the group of poets associated with Language she is 'unable to free myself from the charged vocabulary of a romantic'.[6] The lyric, expressive impulse evident in her work is undoubtedly at odds with Language's focus on the primacy of the linguistic medium, and the deconstruction of the possibility of a coherent or consistent lyric voice. However, despite this expressive impulse it would be untrue to say that Howe's work is representational in any simple sense. Her interest is not in articulating the contours of a private or individual subjectivity, but in giving voice to forms of spiritual experience which lie beyond the self. This gives us another way of understanding the preoccupation in her work with time, duration and the sequence. As a convert to Catholicism Howe is interested in what might be called the aesthetics of incarnation – she is searching for ways to move from the temporal and material to the eternal. Poetry and art can offer a moment of fusion of the material and the transcendent – a moment when, as in the cover photo, there is a leap from one element into another. This search for correspondence between the natural and human world (including the realm of language) and the spiritual world seems totally opposed to the concerns of other linguistically innovative contemporary writers. Although the poetic structure of her work could not be termed 'symbolic' in any simple sense Howe uses rhyme, pattern and metaphor as part of her poetic quest for a linguistic 'fit', or adequacy in relation to the spiritual realm. Such adequacy is, however, dependent on the encounter with a God who is immanent in experience, experience which may be expressed in language. As Howe has said, 'I feel that we are already occupying divine territory, on earth, and that we can't escape it once we are consciously in it. The Buddhists are the most enlightened purveyors of the experience of being *in heaven* – of *God* as experience rather than object – but I feel no contradiction between their expression of enlightenment and the traditional Western doctrine of incarnation.'[7]

Yet if Howe's work differs from that normally associated with Language, by virtue of its lyric, expressive impulse, it also differs from 'traditional' lyric poetry. Howe's interest in incarnation does not lead her to make symbolic or mythological connections between earthly and spiritual realms. Instead there is a counter-impulse in Howe's work which, though equally based in spirituality, does accord with more avant-garde anti-representational concerns. In her essay, 'The Contemporary Logos' Howe discusses two twentieth century writers whose work pushes language to the limits of its ability to 'express' eternity or the alienness of God: Simone Weil and Samuel Beckett. What she finds valuable in their work is the drive to fuse human speech with the voice of eternity, the anonymous or prophetic voice which speaks out of the void and is therefore as articulate in silence as in symbolic language – and a similar drive to fuse the eternal and the temporal, the human and the heavenly, lies behind her own work. Yet for Howe it is not so much the voice as the written word which must bridge the gap – and this is precisely because writing is a temporal phenomenon. Through submission to the laws of time poetry can articulate the silences which are those of eternity. Howe quotes Simone Weil: 'Total obedience to time obliges God to bestow eternity.'[8] It is eternity which places temporality in an allegorical relation to itself, which makes bounded time the window onto another liberatory reality. For Howe poetic writing is privileged in its 'obedience to time' through form and letter, and it is thus able to enact a form of resolution between the eternal voice and the voice of human thought: 'Poetry writes twice, and produces another sound from the ordinary.'[9] In other words, poetry, by representing both the language of ordinary human interaction, and its temporal and spatial limitations, can reach outwards towards the eternal. Both the rhythm and the shape of the lyrics on the page are of fundamental importance to Howe's work, as these formal elements embody for the reader the boundedness of poetic language. It is only by experiencing the disciplines of temporality that the leap into timelessness (like the leap of the dancers) may be made. This emphasis on the formal dynamic of measure, sequence and duration differs markedly from traditional lyric's use of image and metaphor to bridge gaps and make connections. In what follows I want to explore the tensions and frictions between these uses of language and look at the ways in which Howe both theologises and genders Language poetry's preoccupations, as she moves between attempts to 'rewrite the word "God" by filling up pages with other names'.[10]

The moment

Poetry may be the written equivalent of the dancing which is represented on the cover of *O'Clock* – creativity within the confines of strict obedience to time. The poems which make up the sequence are each 'titled' by a time: hours and minutes, days of the week, months or occasionally seasons. Those poems (the majority) titled by temporal markers such as '7:30', '5:26' or '21:09' are perhaps the most intriguing since the suggestion is that the poem takes place within, or records, this specific moment. Time is collapsed into the instantaneous moment, even as it is clear that the poems themselves cannot be produced within this moment. At one level Howe seems to be playing with ideas of inspiration, suggesting that the poem arrives in its completed form in an instant of transcendence or what Howe elsewhere calls, after Coleridge, 'the contemporaneous moment'.[11] Many of the lyrics in the volume explore the way in which encounters with the natural world (in particular the Irish landscape) can open onto a spiritual dimension, and it is tempting to interpret Howe's preoccupation with transcendence through nature (space and time) as a form of pantheistic neo-romanticism. But it may also be possible to understand Howe's recent work within the terms of a revolutionary Marxist perspective, which is referred to more than once in the volume. In particular Howe seems indebted to Walter Benjamin's concept of the 'Now' time – a moment of revelation or illumination – which he sets against the idea of a developmental or teleological mechanism of history. Both romantic aesthetics and revolutionary Marxism offer images of an alternative to the idea of *progress* through time.

It is clear, however, that though Howe feels drawn to the rhetoric of transcendence she is equally aware of its limitations, and a tension between imaging the transcendent and the material runs through her work. One of the consequences of attributing the poems to contingent times through their titles is, paradoxically, that the possibility of illumination, transcendence or universality is denied. The sequence as a whole explores the nature of time as development and teleology, as ideas and images progress from moment to moment, line to line. The poems' formal and rhetorical strategies are meant to raise questions and to propose the terms of the debate for they are temporal phenomena (both written and read according to the laws of sequential time). In her essay 'The Contemporary Logos', Howe stresses the importance of poetry's submission to temporality:

> any poetic line is composed under the compulsion and constraint – the sentence – of syntax.
> Just as, in one sentence *you* cannot turn into *she, run* cannot turn into *ran*, you can't, in your desire to be free of a certain moment, be somewhere else immediately. This is the judgement of time, history

and gender as it is reflected in any written line.

And just as the sentence contains only as much language as it can bear, so can it be viewed as an image of the pressure of temporality. The facing of what is in front of you, by sorting out what is behind, goes into the careful syntactical processing of a sentence. Law and grammar must coexist in that cell. This coexistence requires the exaction of judgement.

Poetic language goes to the extreme with this exaction, and the more extreme, the more otherly it becomes. It transforms the state of being lost into that of being free, by making judgement on judgement itself.

There is thus a tension within each individual section of the poem sequence between the linear sequential character of language, and the desire to offer an escape from the laws of temporality. But as Howe suggests, it may be precisely by conforming to the laws of the temporal, sequential world that transcendence, or 'freedom', may be acheived. She doesn't simply counterpose time and eternity as though they were discreet entities – but instead shows how they intertwine, how eternity may be glimpsed through the evanescent, unstable and momentary.

Exaction

The first poems in the sequence *O'Clock* focus on the differences and distances between 'human' and 'sacred' time – in this case the fairy world deemed in myth and legend to be accessed through the Irish countryside. The natural world, and traditional ritual is a point of connection, or a route from one to the other, and indeed the efficacy of the fairy world is measured by success in the human one – the fairies should ideally help sort out the human problem of loneliness for example:

> Set golden butter out in a dish
> Beside a mill, a stream and a tree.
> Say: oh my love, loved by me,
> Give me your heart, your soul, your body.
> Then see.

Drawing on pantheistic Irish fairy lore, Howe explores a form of correspondence which allows the sacred to be accessed through the natural world: a parallel with the aesthetics of incarnation, in which the temporal moment 'contains' the eternal. As long as there is both friction and association between spiritual and material realms there may be revelation. However, rather than an immediate fusing of the human and the sacred (as in myth), the emphasis here is on activity, process and duration (Do this, and then *wait*). In fact the submission to the dictates of traditional ritual is similar to confinement within the contours of dance or poetry – it requires obedience to time. Striking in this lyric, and throughout the volume, is the attention paid to poetic measure and the achievement of balance through rhyme (both signs of Howe's indebtedness to William Carlos Williams). It is as though the sing-song element is an embodiment of the beat of time, a form and structure which has to be gone through in order to reach a moment of revelation. A later poem, '6:30', clarifies this desire to achieve a balance, or a fusion between the material and the spritual world through the rituals of time;

> A full Irish breakfast
> consists of sausage, black pudding, brown bread,
> butter, jam and some kind of egg.
>
> The tea bag is dropped
> into a stainless steel pot
> and you pour steamed water on it.
>
> Now the light behind the clouds is rinsing them blue.
> And gales on coasts and hills
> will fly from such a sky.
>
> The earth will suffer, drop,
> then enter eternal doubt
> and those soft clouds
>
> will be its literature.
> Space in time goes against nature.
> This condition is called 'the future'.

The title of this poem, unusually for this collection, does seem to refer to its literal contents – breakfast at dawn in Ireland. The description of the Irish breakfast is meticulous in its unromanticised materiality (tea bag rather than tea, for example). This is an unchanging domestic ritual, repeated at the same time each day, but it also offers a vision of change, as the boiling water poured onto the tea-bag in the pot issues in clouds of steam. This witty image of transsubstantiation is mirrored by the transformation of the sky as dawn breaks and the weather turns. The final six lines draw an analogy between the dropped tea bag and the earth, an anlogy made manifest by the mobile 'fleeing' clouds which balance the image of the clouds of steam in the second stanza. Howe seems to be suggesting that the 'dropping' of the earth into temporality, the cycles of day and night, is at once the cause of suffering through distance from the divine ('eternal doubt') and at the same time the condition for change and transformation. This ambivalence may be the explanation for the paradoxical last lines in which we are told both that the material world ('space in time' – what another poem calls 'As the World Turns') is both 'unnatural' and that it is the condition for the future, for time as possibility. One intriguing aspect of the poem, however, is that the temporal and material state of the earth is itself placed in the future ('the earth *will* suffer, drop'). It is as though the earth's fall into 'eternal doubt' has not yet taken place. Or perhaps this is this the eternal present, in which human life is bound ever to repeat the fall from grace, like the endlessly repeated morning ritual of making tea. If this endless falling suggests lack of progress, the poem makes clear that it is also the precondition for 'literature'. Like the steam and clouds, the creative transformation of language is dependent on this fall. Without temporality there would only be stasis, without change.

Though the temporality of the material world necessitates exile from God and eternity, it also makes possible poetry and the creative arts, which in turn may embody the possibility of transcendence. (As Howe says elsewhere in the sequence, 'My vagabondage/is unlonelied by poems'.) For it is the embodiment of time and the temporalization of space in poetry which causes the 'exaction' which can lead to freedom. Grammatical markers can overcome their syntactical boundaries when bounded by space and time, and this paradox is made explicit in an untitled poem (hence one of the few poems in the sequence with no temporal marker).

> Where is when
> every time.
>
> When is where
> I and she combine.

> No she without a where, no I without a when.
>
> Body, place, time.
>
> Likewise the same for it and them.
> Condensation and diffusion.

A rather different, though related, exploration of 'the contemporaneous moment' occurs in 'Thursday One'. Here too place becomes synonymous with time – or at least time-travel and jouneying through space become equivalent:

> Next time I'll travel by dream.
> Quick forward into first person.
> I'll try to avoid the world
> where bombs obviate everything.
>
> The twelfth century was when?
>
> If I close my eyes my brain
> rises with the train.
> I'm in a town called Pontefract
> where the men who bombed it
>
> are only remembered for their technique.
>
> Still I wonder if the birds
> perched along the bridge
> are singing – or were-
> *Oh let them burn!*

The poem ostensibly explores the desire to avoid the 'world', characterised by the 'bombs' of human violence and mortality. The way to do this is to travel 'by dream' rather than conventional travel, as the poem sets up a contrast between dream or imaginative journeys and journey by train. While the dream may protect the individual 'first person', conventional forms of transport confront the person with otherness. Attempting to evade contemporary violence (perhaps the bombing of Iraq?), the train journey she regrets brings her to Pontefract, where she is reminded of the 'bombs' of history, and the unjust society of twelfth century feudalism. (Pontefract was an important town in the feudal battles of the later middle ages, and is mentioned in the Domesday Book.) Finally, as in many of the other poems in the book, Howe offers a contrast between the natural world (the birds) and the destructiveness of human society.

Yet like '6:30' this poem is confusing in its use of tense. As Howe puts it in another poem in the sequence, 'Past, Present, Future. No such things.' For the initial projection of an alternative form of travel into the future ('next time'), turns out to be redundant since the dream journey is happening in the present. The journey to Pontefract is not a real but an imaginary one, or it is transformed in dream. For it is, in fact, not generally possible to travel to Pontefract by train (the town is not served by a rail network unless passengers are travelling only from the town of Hull). The train seems to be a fantasy – a train of thought. Indeed the whole of this journey seems to be governed not by fact but by linguistics: etymology and word association. While Pontefract means literally 'broken bridge', there is no river and no bridge in the town. Nontheless through the name Howe uncovers or imagines a history of violence and bombing which is analogous to the contemporary world of bombs she wishes to avoid. So perhaps the lesson of this journey is simply that there is no progress, that the twelfth and the twentieth centuries mirror one another. In this case the answer to the question 'The twelfth century was when?' is not only, as it first appears, the place 'Pontefract', but also the time, 'now'.

Through the dream principles of condensation and diffusion which she refers to in the poem 'Where is when', Howe creates another world outside the limits of space and time. Through linguistic exaction she creates another (future) history, and other meanings for Pontefract, at the same time offering an alternative perspective on contemporary bombs. This imaginary time-travel is also the subject of the poem 'Again Sunday':

> You travel a path on paper
> and discover you're in a city
> you only thought about before ...
>
> How can you be where you never were?
> and how did you find your way – with your mind
> your only measure?

At one level Howe is referring here to the mind's creativity, and the imagination's ability to transform everyday surroundings into something else. But the emphasis here is also on 'measure', reminding us that the marking of time in the poetry is in itself an attempt to heal the broken bridge between the temporal and the eternal, heaven and earth. The duration of the sequence and the rhythms of language, like the rhythms and rituals of everyday life are not simply the vehicles for the journey, they are the journey itself; they are not simply the material from which the bridge is made, but the passage over the bridge as well.

One of the final poems of the sequence, 'Sundayed', also collapses notions of time, splitting it in two directions. In the process of preserving or constructing history and the future, the present disappears – or is it all there is?

> On azure seats
> chopped lights and limbs, big white sheets.
>
> My day might be the museum of itself
> Like I am an ancient mummy.
>
> The avant garde worships history, the others
> choose mystery. So far, God, this may be my last
> book of unreconstructed poetry.

The title is the past tense of the putative verb 'to Sunday', but also perhaps suggests death in 'Sundied'. The pastness of her present experience, and her distance from it, is suggested by 'My day might be the museum of itself'. The poet seems to be looking at herself from a distance. The 'chopped lights and limbs' are images of disconnection and dislocation yet at the same time there are intimations of future resurrection, not only in the Christian symbolism of Sunday, but also in the Egyptian mummy and the resurrection of the sun god. Here though the after life is lived in the present (perhaps all mothers, not just 'ancient mummies', exist in a sort of after-life, immersed in domestic ritual and distanced from their own present). On the one hand the poem suggests that you can only know the past at its moment in the present, when it is 'present' to you (indeed this is the implication of the precisely timed poems). At the same time the present is lived as though it were the past, as though it were an act of preservation . Yet this problematises the idea of future possibilities, even puts the whole notion of the future into question. This is made clear in the last three lines where Howe seems to be setting up a choice

– between the worshipping of history, the radical transformation of the past, (the idea of historical progress as a route to liberation) and the worshipping of mystery and religious ritual. Howe doesn't seem to be clear about her own choice here. She is caught within temporality ('so far, this may be my last'), within a present precariously balanced between an unreal or distanced personal history, and an uncertain future.

Home and homelessness

Howe's ambivalence or uncertainty about the value of the temporal may be related to her interest in revolutionary or Liberation Theology and the drive towards the realisation of heaven on earth in terms of justice and social inequality. As she says in 'Saturday Night', she can't ignore the human temporal world in favour of the eternal:

> I still can't kill
> my hopes before the strangeness of change
>
> and so I've come to stay
> where Camillo Torres says:
>
> 'Every Catholic who is not a revolutionary
> is living in a state of mortal sin.'

Howe's sympathy with Liberation Theology's emphasis on issues of poverty and social justice suggests that, so far from purely abstract and theological, her preoccupation with spiritual alienation and exile can also be understood as a reflection on material homelessness. For many in Central and South America 'exile' and 'alienation' conjure very human and material experiences such as border-crossing, illegal domicile in the U.S., and the loneliness of separation from family. Perhaps paradoxically, throughout *O'Clock* Howe evinces a desire or a need to be lost, to suffer dislocation from home, in order to experience liberation. She quotes Simone Weil: 'We must take the feeling of being at home into exile. We must be rooted in the absence of a place.' One of the ways this is explored is in relation to familial roles, both her own as a mother, and her relation to god as parent. In '6:07' she addresses heaven:

> Parent above, look down and see
> how far from you I've travelled.
> From the swell in your firmament
> you'll see the way that the light
> has diffused the location of home …

But home and human relations – both of family and community – keep crowding back in, so that in '10:18' Howe writes of the difficulty of becoming lost:

> Into the forest I went walking – to get lost.
>
> I saw faces in the knots
> of trees, it was insane, and hands
> in branches, and everywhere names.
>
> Throughout the elms
> small birds shivered and sang
> in rhyme.
>
> I wanted to be air, or wind – to be at ease
> in outer space. but in the world
> this was the case:
>
> *Human* was God's secret name.

Here the lesson is similar to that of Liberation Theology – that the infinite exists in time and in human society – shares the materiality of the natural world.

The tension between the desire to be lost and 'in solitary confinement', and to embrace the human and material world, is perhaps clearer in Howe's sequence 'Q'. The epigraph to the sequence is a line from Tagore: 'Where roads are made I lose my way'. Howe's poetic interpretation of this statement is complex. The sequence does not so much oppose loss and displacement on the one hand with man made routes or routines on the other, as suggest that loss occurs through such rituals. While this might seem a decidedly negative view of human endeavour, we should perhaps bear in mind Howe's ambivalent attitude to the state of loss and absence, and her sense of the necessary balance between the ecstasy of the experience of God's absence, and the need for human community and communication.

The work on language which poetry necessitates can bring these two poles together, not as symbolic representation but as linguistic action. It may be helpful to think of this project as one of 'demythologising' incarnation. In this view it is not that the balance and order of poetic language represents mimetically the eternal world in the material, but that the soul's desire for and distance from God is both enacted and revealed in language through its submission to temporality. As such Howe's own poetic roads are a means to the 'diffusion of home'.

'Q' has the structure of a quest – indeed perhaps 'Q' stands not only for 'Queue' but for 'Question' (as in 'Q and A'). Such restlessness is the preserve of humans, but it is also their curse, as Howe's frequent comparisons between the human and the natural world attest:

> Lambs are lower to the ground
> but closer to heaven than humans are.
>
> They don't try being itinerant
> or to be where there are no minutes or questions
> like, "Why be obedient to a world that will end?"
>
> Wool walks in the agriculture
> ignorant of its colouring.
>
> Patented in blue, yes, as food and clothing
> for persons and their furniture.

The lambs' lack of concern about time, endings and death is to be envied, yet it is also the reason why their lives can be treated in such a utilitarian manner. The poem leaves us with a question too, for are the lambs 'patented' by man (in the blue brands burned onto the fleece), or by God in the colour of heaven? The sequence repeatedly plays with images of nature's artificiality, as the natural world is 'read' and ordered through urbane signs. Indeed it seems as though nature is dictated by humans: 'apple-red as a school'; 'neon green / early spring leafing on Hampstead Heath / and midwinter flowers in the same season'; 'Temperate gales blew from the jets / at Heathrow'. As in *O'Clock*, it is not possible to escape temporality by immersing yourself in nature as our experience of nature is filtered through our human-ness.

Unlike the lambs, the voice in these poems is both questioning and itinerant, asking not only which is the road and what the vehicle for the journey, but where does it end. The sequence enacts a pilgrimage from exile to 'home' which is imaged as the migration of birds. The 'family' with which the sequence begins keeps moving in and out of makeshift homes – digs, caravans, and the many forms of temporary home used by travellers and tourists, even the shoe belonging to the old woman who had so many children she didn't know what to do. The home within a shoe is particularly apt as a makeshift residence, of course, since the shoe is both shelter and a means to travel the road (as well as, when dancing, the way to tap out a beat or measure). These temporary, movable dwellings bring together the two poles of home and homelessness, in a kind of allegory of the dislocation or loss of self which Howe seeks in God: 'You will find the way to get lost/if you're lucky, blessed.'

One literal basis for this preoccupation with travel may be Howe's experience of living in England and Ireland in 1993–95, while acting as academic adviser for American students in Britain. Certainly there are many references to London (Hampstead Heath, Westminster Cathedral), as well as British culture. However the sequence is also concerned with the state of being 'at home' in a more general way, in terms of taking on both the roles of girl-child and mother. In both 'Q' and *O'Clock* the exploration of time – in terms both of temporal exaction and of temporariness – is tied to gender. The temporary home-making in 'Q', for example, is presided over by the old woman who lived in a shoe, by lone mothers, by a woman stealing half-price shoes for her daughters. The rhythms of femininity are also those of more mundane domestic ritual however – making tea, shopping, preparing meals and providing, as in 'Tuesday One' from *O'Clock*:

> Today she bought new nightgowns
> for the girls
> and a pair of suspenders
> for the child whose pants fall down.
>
> Then she went to the market
> in the rain
> for gooseberries to bake a pie
> which she did, after she was finished
>
> sewing dollclothes from the old nightgowns
> and watching *As The World Turns*.

These rituals which mark the passing of time (children outgrowing their clothes) are themselves plotted alongside the moments of a woman's life: young girl, mother, old woman, ancient mummy – all balanced by the rhythms and rhymes of the mundane, the everyday and the traditional.

It might be helpful at this point to compare Howe with another woman poet for whom constraint – and the relation between spiritual and poetic constraint in particular – is fundamental: the Belfast poet Medbh McGuckian. McGuckian, who comes from a Northern Irish Catholic background, shares with Howe a deeply religious sensibility, though for her poetry represents an alternative to religious forms of succour, since she has rejected the organised Catholicism of her childhood. She has compared the practice of writing poetry to the habit of the confessional:

> I love the feeling of control over my life that [poetry] gives me. Instead of events just passing you, for me its in amber. Poetry is about desire, maybe it's sublimating desire, but I think desire is at the heart of it. If I didn't express those desires and exorcise them, I think it would be very unhealthy for me – to keep it bottled up. I guess I feel pretty guilty about all those inner yearnings and so I had to write them – like a confession. I think that my Catholicism is very deeply embedded in me and that the poems are confessions of ... sins of thought.[12]

At first glance McGuckian's poetry seems to be securely autobiographical; it offers lineations of the female self, of the experiences of pregnancy, motherhood and domestic life. Yet in spite of its personal tone, the poetry is typically split between multiple voices, the 'I' is oblique and elusive. McGuckian's analogy of the confessional should not be taken to suggest an emotional outpouring; instead the implication is that the alleviation of distress comes not through open, uninhibited expression, but through articulation within a particular codified structure. Release comes through containment, through acceptance of the constraints of poetic form.

A poem entitled 'Waxwing Winter' in her most recent volume, *Captain Lavender*, explores this process through the image of an imprisoned bird:

> It bathes in smoke and windswept flight.
> If it is found towards the end of the day

> you must put its wing out of action
> until it is healed or free
> of flesh in a fume-cupboard.
>
> Its heat is what for us would be fever:
> of you use the fingers of one hand
> to form a 'cage', can you hear
> through the leaf litter and imagined open space
> the light-proof birdsong
> as the bird itself might hear it?

One of a series of poems in elegy for her father, whom McGuckian describes as having lived his life as a 'second-class citizen' as a Catholic in Northern Ireland, the poem equates death with liberation. To be healed is to be free of flesh (ie. a skeleton), but – as the line break insists – it is also to be simply free. The last stanza suggests that it is no more possible to tell sickness from health than to distinguish inside from outside, the state of being caged from that of being free. Like the poem itself, the cage is created by hand; it is a small enclosure, yet inside it is open space and song. This image conjures up the many different sorts of metaphysical freedom which are somehow realised, rather than being limited, by physical constraints – the soul in the body, the prisoner in the jail, lyric transcendence in the strict lineation of words on the page.

McGuckian's work is thus clearly committed to an idea of metaphysical release through poetry, of healing through poetic form. Yet it would be a mistake to associate this with the expressive release of the conventional lyric voice, and with ideas of balance and integration. Instead healing seems to depend on dislocation. As the lines from 'Waxwing Winter' suggest ('you must put its wing out of action'), there is a need first to break in order to heal. Despite her preoccupation with stages of woman's life, with motherhood and domesticity, McGuckian poetry is marked by a sense of alienness, homelessness and internal exile. In part this reflects her conviction that we come to know ourselves not through *finding* ourselves in familiar surroundings, but through encounters with foreignness, through conflict and dialogue with strangers. But there is undoubtedly also an Irish dimension here, a sense that the home is always divided and unstable, and the question of belonging uncertain.

So despite the very diverse backgrounds which have formed Howe and McGuckian, not to mention their differing attitudes towards religion and their different poetic styles, the comparison between them has an unmistakable cultural logic. As the girls dancing on the cover of *O'Clock* remind us, the journey home being traced here is a female one, but it is also Irish. If the issues of exile, homelessness and diaspora are central material concerns within Liberation Theology, they also hold a distinct place within the history of Ireland. Howe herself is Irish American through her mother, Mary Manning, a playwright who left Ireland as a young woman. At a certain level then the 'return' to Ireland in *O'Clock* can be read as part of a personal exploration of a female Irish past – a 'homeland' which never will be her own. Yet while the female figures are temporal signposts to alternative pasts, and maybe futures, the images struggle with the weight of metaphorical meaning ascribed to them. In the poem 'Monday the First', the girl becomes symbolic of the distressed Irish nation, but the poem works to show what underlies that metaphorical connection – a mismatch between temporal and cultural registers:

> After this girl was grown
> the tedium of the nursery began.
>
> Either overdressed or a mess
> she was a metaphor
> for the suffering of the Irish.
>
> Seven boys and seven girls, a harnessed pony
> and a clay pipe, delinquency laws and bad thin boys.
>
> Out like a scout, she tackled the fields
> in her hem or heels.
> When she was dragged and staked
> she called the story of her life
> *Where My Body Went.*

The girl is schooled in the disciplines of femininity after she has grown – and she carries the signs of control marked out on her clothes and body – these are the measure of gender. Her refusal or inability to submit to the dominant cultural requirements of temporal development ('growing up') lead her to be condemned as a witch. Yet Howe's work as a whole seeks a balance between discipline (obedience to time) and freedom. This poem foregrounds another aspect of both 'Q' and *O'Clock*, which is the recurrent image of women as witnesses to and recorders of history. The 'story' that is charted through the girl's body is not only the sexual and reproductive story of femininity, but a 'history' (signified by the clay-pipe and delinquency laws) which is accessed through the marking of time within the family.

There is a danger, for both McGuckian and Howe, that the exploration of the possibilities of liberation hidden within constraint may appear to be romanticising traditional female roles, even underwriting a form of female masochism. Yet in McGuckian's case this suspicion is allayed by the strange, dislocated sensuousness and luxuriousness of her lyricism, while the very restraint and sparseness of Howe's poetry gives it a light , transformative quality which is both astonishing and illuminating. Indeed there is something joyous in the way Howe's poetry explores new ways of writing the experience of God, as she both theologises and genders the language of poetry. She is a vagabond on earth, lost to God, but by taking the road of poetry she is able to lose her way rather than trace a familiar route – and it is this loss which 'unlonelies' her. The 'wobbly caravan' in 'Q', like the dream time and space travel in *O'Clock*, are the vehicles for her journey, but so too is the beat and rhythm of the poetry itself, which is remarkable for its clear and fairy-tale-like quality. Indeed one of the aspects of Howe's poetry which has been clouded over in this essay is this lyric simplicity, for the poems themselves seem at ease with the weight of epistemological and theological inquiry which I have suggested lies behind them. The steady measure and childish rhymes are an integral part of Howe's exploration of the rhythms of a woman's everyday life, but they are also redolent of that discipline or obedience to time which is the pathway to God. In the same way, if these common roads are the routes which Howe's poetry follows, part of the routine, the discipline, of the work is that of the poetic sequence itself- an exploration of the regularities of time as much as of narrative.

> If I follow a sequence of dares
> each one will be part of
>
> the final product.

It is important therefore to think of Howe's use of the precise moment, and linguistic exaction, as tropes rather than themes within the poetry. Even while 'hammered down into a sequence', following the dictates of traditional ritual (whether fairy lore or Catholic doctrine) and the predetermined pattern of rythym, the poetry effects change and transformation. The 'unlonelying' of poetry, its reaching beyond the bounds of the self, is a process which the work enacts, rather than a state which may be described.

Notes

1. Fanny Howe, *Introduction to the World* (Gt Barrington, MA: The Figures, 1986), p. 22.
2. Manuel Brito, *A Suite of Poetic Voices: Interviews with Contemporary American Poets* (Santa Brigida: Kadle Books, 1992), 99.
3. Fanny Howe, *O'Clock* (London: Reality Street Editions, 1995).
4. Fanny Howe, *Spectacular Diseases* (forthcoming, 2000).
5. See Wendy Mulford, '"Curved, Odd ... Irregular": A Vision of Contemporary Poetry by Women', *Women: A Cultural Review* 1.3 (1990), p. 273.
6. See Brito, *A Suite of Poetic Voices*, p. 102.
7. Ibid., p. 101.
8. Fanny Howe, 'The Contemporary Logos', in Michael Palmer (ed.), *Code of Signals: Recent Writings in Poetics* (Berkeley, CA.: North Atlantic Books, 1983), p. 55.
9. Ibid., p. 54.
10. Fanny Howe, 'Well Over Void', *Five Fingers Review* 10 (1991).
11. Howe, 'The Contemporary Logos', p. 54.
12. See Kimberley S. Bohman, 'Surfacing: An Interview with Medbh McGuckian, Belfast, 5th September, 1994', *Irish Review* 16 (Autumn/Winter 1994), p. 96.

15
Body and Soul:
The Power of Sharon Olds
Vicki Feaver

The power to 'tell'

> I say
> Do what you are going to do, and I will tell about it.
> 'I Go Back To May 1937[1]

Olds' declaration of a poet's power to speak out, to bear witness, comes at the end of a poem which she described in an interview as 'a little manifesto (womanifesto)' and the poem, up to that date, by which she would most want to be known.[2] Initially, I was puzzled as to why she considered it so significant. It was only as I read her poems over and over that I realised how central to her work is the power of that threat – 'I will tell about it.' It is why totalitarian states lock up dissident writers and ban publication of their works. It is why Tereus tore out the tongue of Philomena – so she couldn't tell her sister that he had raped her. It is why the abusers of children – parents mostly – terrify them, or blackmail them, or shame them into silence.

In poem after poem Olds 'tells' about the abuse of power. Like Anna Akhmatova,[3] or other poets of post-war Eastern and Central Europe collected in *The Poetry of Survival*,[4] an anthology to which Olds contributed some translations, she is a poet of witness: to state terror, to the terror inflicted on his victims by the rapist,[5] but above all to family terror. At the core of her work are poems that testify to the experience of being 'the one survivor' of an abusive family. That this is Olds' experience seems to be confirmed by the fact that the narrator of the poems is variously addressed as 'Sharon', or '*Shar*', or '*Sharry*'. The father of the poems is an alcoholic, both wounded – 'a stuck / buffalo, baffled, stunned, dragging/arrows in his hide'[6] – and wounding: in a

140

repeated image he is the god Saturn who 'unconscious on the couch every night'[7] was 'eating his children'.[8] The mother is revealed as emotionally and sexually abused. However, Olds is not the poet as victim, exhibiting her wounds 'to the peanut crunching crowd', but the poet as survivor. She is more interested in describing extreme sensations of the body – in childbirth, in the ecstasy of sex – than in morbid states of mind. The poems about abuse in her childhood family are juxtaposed with poems in which she celebrates her capacity in her own family to love and nurture. She speaks out about what was done to her not to show how damaged she is but to demonstrate her power to confront the past.

Writing about the survivors of political terror in his introduction to *The Poetry of Survival*, Daniel Weissbort argues that 'to say nothing may, in effect, be to collude with the forces of destruction. To speak out, on the other hand is not only proof in itself, evidence of a kind of survival, but also a vindication of it.'[9] Olds makes a similar connection between silence and compliance in an article she wrote on the 'silenced voices' of Turkish dissidents, revealing that 'as a child I had seen wrong things and wanted to stop them, and I hadn't'.[10] Again and again in her poems, as if the power of her voice as a poet depended on it, or as if *telling* was evidence of her survival, she refers to the 'silenced voice' of her childhood. Even in her latest book, *The Wellspring* (1996), there is a poem[11] about her silence and passivity in the house where 'there was required silence, / twenty-four hours of silence for a child / or silence at the table for a mother and three children', where she stood in the corner in silence and lay across her mother's legs in silence ('as I grew bigger and bigger over the years / I began to hang over the ends of her lap / in massive shame'). She would only be *asked* to speak to provide entertainment at Sunday Lunch ('the membrane of the pig / crackling in the skillet, the knots of fat / undoing' in an echo of that other famous poem that connects Sunday lunch and torture, Plath's 'Mary's Song'), to repeat the phrase chosen for her by her father to demonstrate her lisp, 'Sharon sswallowss ssaussagess'.

The significance of 'I Go Back to 1937' is that it is the poem in which Olds gives herself retrospective permission to end her silence, to transform herself from dumb and passive victim into the powerful narrator of her own story. The 'you' she threatens with exposure – 'Do what you are going to do, and I will tell about it' – are her parents, just before they were married, before she was even conceived. Viewed separately outside the gates of their colleges, as if in graduation photographs, her father 'strolling out', her mother standing with 'a few light books at her hip', they are presented as innocents, Adam and Eve figures in the garden before the Fall, carefree, careless, unaware of the unhappiness that will follow. The poet-daughter in the role of seer, she transfers her prescience of what the future holds for them to their portent-loaded backgrounds – 'the red tiles glinting like bent plates of blood' behind her father's head, the 'wrought iron gate still open' behind her mother, 'its sword-tips black in the May air'. Seeing what her parents are unable to see – the damage they will do and, at that point, the possibility of avoiding it, the gate 'still open' – she wants to go up to them and stop them, to tell them

> you are going to do bad things to children,
> you are going to suffer in ways you have not heard of,
> you are going to want to die.

Momentarily the poem fills with a child's illusory omnipotence, as if the poet really is powerful enough to prevent the coming together of this couple whose tragedy she can see written in the disparity between their flawed human faces and 'beautiful', innocent bodies ('her hungry pretty blank face turning to me, / her pitiful beautiful untouched body, / his arrogant handsome blind face turning to me, / his pitiful beautiful untouched body'). Then the adult's reasoning takes over, not in the obvious form of her acceptance of her powerlessness to change what happened before she was born but in a witty recognition of the logical implications of doing so. She doesn't do it because, as she says, 'I want to live'. Instead, in a pantomimic, Punch and Judy-style image that reverses the usual situation of parents battering their children she describes how, in a kind of kangaroo court in her head,

> I
> take them up like the male and female
> paper dolls and bang them together
> at the hips like chips of flint as if to
> strike sparks from them, I say
> Do what you are going to do, and I will tell about it.

As a poet, Olds has the imaginative power to reduce the towering, all-powerful parents of childhood to the size and substance of harmless cut out paper dolls. But, characteristically, almost as soon as this image is formed, it is metamorphosed to get closer to the truth. As she bangs the paper figures together – how could parents ever permanently be reduced to something so flimsy? – they become 'like flints', indestructible. But this truer perception, instead of rendering her powerless, becomes a source of renewed power. As the chiming, one-syllable, harshly consonant-stopped words, 'hips', 'chips', 'flint', strike off each other, they articulate, in the allusion to the creation of fire, the sense that in the mimetic enactment of her anger she creates the spark that will fire her creation. Her actual power, as the last line of the poem bears out, consists not in the ability to destroy her parents but to save herself, through her testimony, through the power of her writing.

It is interesting to compare 'I Go Back to 1937' with the title and opening poem of Olds' first collection, *Satan Says* (1980), which is also concerned with confronting her parents but which ends with her back in the position of abused child, silent and powerless. Shut in a little cedarwood jewellery box with a ruby-eyed ballerina pin and 'the pain of the locked past', she is tempted by Satan with the promise that if she repeats a series of shocking and forbidden phrases – '*My father is a shit*', '*My mother is a pimp*', '*fuck the father*', '*torture*', '*the father's cock, the mother's cunt*' – he will get her out. At first, she complies and the lid begins to open. But suddenly, struck with the realisation that 'the exit is through Satan's mouth', her courage fails. 'Oh no, I loved / them, too,' she pleads. At this point, Satan loses patience with her. '*It's your coffin now*,' he says, and the poem ends with her still locked in the box, describing, unconvincingly, how she is left 'warming my cold / hands at the dancer's ruby eye – / the fire, the suddenly discovered knowledge of love'.

Although the jewellery box makes an apt analogy both for the 'prison' of the abused child's house as well as for the imprisonment of the adult with 'the pain of the locked past', Olds has not included 'Satan Says' in subsequent selections of her work. Its allegorical drama evoked the isolation and powerlessness of a child of abusing parents. It unstoppered some of her suppressed anger. But it is too staged, too cosily closed, and as her strategy 'to write my way out of the closed box', or to escape 'the pain of the locked past', it didn't work. The poem's central premise that any threat to parental authority on the part of a child must be instigated by the devil was a denial of her valid anger. As the psychoanalyst Alice Miller points out in *Thou Shalt Not Be Aware: Society's Betrayal of The Child*, the taboos against survivors of child abuse 'telling' on parents are reinforced by the fact that for the child, especially the abused child, idealisation of the parent is 'essential to survival'.[12] This would explain why the mechanism by which the box begins to open – the voicing of a stream of parentally directed obscenities – is counteracted by the stronger, because more familiar, mechanism of replacing the critical, 'cold', angry feelings by the 'warmer', more comfortable and silencing feelings of love. The cause of the poet's anger that nearly slipped out in the almost buried word 'torture' remains untold. The only resistance remaining is in her body that betrays the truth her mind suppresses.[13] The words 'I loved them, too' are immediately followed by a description of physical tension: 'I brace my body tight in the cedar house.' Earlier in the poem, she described how, as her anger is released, 'her spine uncurls'. In her subsequent work, Olds' method is almost always to rely on the power of the body to tell the story.

The power of the body

> The body on earth is all we have got
> 'I wanted To Be There When My Father Died'[14]

The body as text

The focus of almost every Olds' poem is a body or bodies: her own body – abused in childhood, or with her lover's body (a series of poems that in their erotic variety constitute a rival female Kama Sutra), her daughter's ripening body, her son's sick or injured body, her father's body as his cancer progresses, or bodies connected to her only in the evidence they provide of the abuse of power – for example, the rope-swaddled bodies of young dissidents about to be executed in Iran.[15] Her characteristic poetic method consists of 'reading' a body, or bodies, in a language that is both sensual and exploratory, that discovers meaning by making connections with other bodies and other discourses and texts. For instance, the human body is often read in relation to the body of nature (to plants and animals, or the body of the earth) or vice versa, as in 'The Connoisseuse of Slugs':[16]

> When I was a connoisseuse of slugs
> I would part the ivy leaves, and look for the
> naked jelly of those gold bodies,
> translucent strangers glistening along
> the stones, slowly, their gelatinous bodies
> at my mercy. Made mostly of water, they would shrivel

to nothing if they were sprinkled with salt,
but I was not interested in that. What I liked
was to draw aside the ivy, breathe the
odour of the wall, and stand there in silence
until the slug forgot I was there
and sent its antennae up out of its
head, the glimmering umber horns
rising like telescopes, until finally the
sensitive knobs would pop out the ends,
delicate and intimate. Years later,
when I first saw a naked man,
I gasped with pleasure to see that quiet
mystery re-enacted, the slow
elegant being coming out of hiding and
gleaming in the dark air, eager and so
trusting you could weep.

The poem's wit, signalled in the title by the deliberate misappro-
priation of the word 'connoisseuse' (signalling works of art) to slugs
(initially signalling disgust), is to read the slugs in a way that doesn't
spoil our astonishment at the surprising shift from slug to penis and
yet has all the time prepared us for it, leading to the words 'delicate
and intimate' that are applicable to both. It is also contained in the
playful juxtaposition of readings of slugs and penises that emphasise
the striking likeness of their physical characteristics and physiologi-
cal mechanisms. But the readings uncover more than just superficial
similarities. In both experiences – discovering slugs and sex – there is
a revelation: something hidden is revealed. In both, there is a sense
of wonder: both explicit ('I stand there in silence' and 'I gasped with
pleasure') but also implicit in a discourse that mixes factual scientific
language ('gelatinous', 'telescope') with the language of aesthetics
('gold bodies', 'umber horns') and religion (the 'quiet mystery re-
enacted'). In both, there is a reversal of the received female response:
disgust at slimy slugs and a reaction ranging from disgust to a reti-
cence at revealing any kind of response, and certainly one that
betrays the woman's pleasure, except in crude, women-can-be-as-
filthy-as-men-style jokes, to the exposed male organ. In both, the
poet is aware of having discovered something totally 'other' than
herself ('translucent strangers', 'the slow elegant being coming out of
hiding') and – an example of the way nearly all Olds' poems are at
some level political – of her power to reverence or destroy it. The risky

cliché at the end, 'so trusting you could weep', succeeds because it clinches the poem's discovery that the penis is as much at her mercy as the slugs.

Slug and penis are also, of course 'at the mercy' of Olds' readings of them. Her power as a poet could be to 'shrivel' them; or, as she does, to inscribe them with value, literally to let them grow. Reading the body is a means of both discovering meaning and manipulating meaning. Even an abstraction as problematic as the love between her and her father ('Love Between Us')[17]comes under her control when it is *embodied* (literally 'the Word made flesh') in a being she has created. Described first as 'a stillborn hung by the feet', it evolves to become a creature, loaded with ambivalent associations of horror and nurture, that 'Like a bat opens its leather cloak / and wraps it again around itself, / ... that feeds itself, swerves around things, / and nurses its young'. The abstract word 'torture' that slipped out, emotively but meaninglessly, in 'Satan Says', is, in subsequent poems, both personal and political, given substance through the reading of specific bodies. In 'Ideographs',[18] for instance, the body of a man 'twisted' on a scaffold as he awaits execution, is read as a combination of crucified Christ and angel: 'the spikes through his ankles / holding them up off the ground, / his knees cocked, the fold of his robe flowing / sideways as if he were suspended in the air / in flight, his naked legs bared'.

In 'Burn Centre'[19] the tortured body is the poet's as a child. In the first four lines the poem shifts from literal anecdote to a shocking, because sudden and totally unexpected, metaphorical image that draws its terrible analogy directly from the anecdote:

> When my mother talks about the Burn Centre
> she's given to the local hospital
> my hair lifts and wavers like smoke
> in the air around my head.

The literal abuse of the mother's physical assault on the child in bed, interpreted so powerfully in a later poem, 'What if God',[20] as an eruption of the earth's body ('her long adult body rolled on me like a tongue of lava from the top of the mountain'), is here converted into a metaphor of being burned that both establishes what was done to her as 'torture' and, by locating the pain in her body, shockingly identifies the source of pain as the person a child normally turns to for comfort in pain:

> I would stick to doorways I
> tried to walk through, stick to chairs as I
> tried to rise, pieces of my flesh
> tearing off easily as
> well-done pork, and no one had
> a strip of gauze, or a pat of butter to
> melt on my crackling side, but when I would
> cry out she would hold me to her
> hot griddle, when my scorched head stank she would
> draw me deeper into the burning room of her life.

The horrific literal details – 'well-done pork' and 'my scorched head stank' – are so seamlessly interwoven with metaphors that derive from the same discourse of cooking and burning – 'her hot griddle' and 'the burning room of her life' – that the story of the body becomes *the* story, a narrative that by its controlling wit puts the poet in control of her own pain.

Overall, the story told by the poet's body in the poems is one of liberation. The restrained, or abused, and always powerless body of the child ('tied to a chair', or 'force fed', or sexually assaulted by her mother) is replaced by an adult body that celebrates its freedom and sexual energy and powers of creation. It is a type of fairy tale, though one in which the happy ending is infinitely prolonged, in which a powerless and silenced girl, defeating the power of evil through the power of good (sexual love, as in fairy tales), is transformed into a powerful and powerfully-voiced woman. It is also, of course, if you define evil as phallocentrism, the story of the woman poet in history; and the laughing story of Cixous's Medusa – 'undoing the work of death' through a writing that, proceeding from the female body and its sexuality, celebrates life.

In one of Olds' earliest published poems, 'The Sisters Of Sexual Treasure',[21] the sexual act becomes the agent not only of the poet's liberation but also a model for a reversal of the received myth about sexual power relations between male and female:

> As soon as my sister and I got out of our
> mother's house, all we wanted to   .
> do was fuck, obliterate
> her tiny sparrow body and narrow
> grasshopper legs. The men's bodies
> were like our father's body! The massive

hocks, flanks, thighs, elegant
knees, long tapered calves –
we could have him there, the steep forbidden
buttocks, backs of the knees the cock
in our mouth, ah the cock in our mouth.
                    Like explorers who
discover a lost city, we went
nuts with joy, undressed the men
slowly and carefully, as if
uncovering buried artefacts that
proved our theory of the lost culture:
that if Mother said it wasn't there,
it was there.

By reducing the abusing mother to a frail bird, and reading the men
– whose bodies 'were like our father's body' – as massive cattle, and
herself and her sister as the controllers of these huge beasts (it is they
who perform the active sexual function, who take 'the cock in our
mouth', not the men who penetrate them, they who undress the men
almost like dolls), the poet assumes all the power. The analogy of the
women as explorers of men's bodies that follows is an exuberantly
witty, twentieth century feminist appropriation and reversal of
Donne's tongue in cheek but still shamelessly colonising seventeenth
century male's reading of his mistress as 'O my America, my new found
land'. Donne's poem[22] could be the archetype for a male writing about
sexuality that, as summarised by Cixous, stems from 'the power relation between a fantasized obligatory virility meant to invade, to
colonize, and the consequential phantasm of woman as a "dark continent" to penetrate and to "pacify"'.[23] But Olds' poem, although
deriving much of its imaginative energy and wit from subverting
Donne's argument, is as much about discovering a sexuality that has
been lost to women, denied them by their mothers, as it is about
reversing a male myth. As in 'Connoisseuse of Slugs', along with the
humour there is a serious reverence for men's bodies. The female act 'to
fuck' is represented not as an act of penetration and plunder but one of
oral pleasure (taking the 'cock in our mouth') and, after the initial
excitement (going 'nuts with joy'), of slow and admiring discovery.

In later poems Olds' project of reading the body becomes a serious
quest to discover existential meaning. In 'I cannot Forget the Woman
In the Mirror',[24] for instance, the poet studies the reflection of her
naked body as she approaches her lover: 'the flanks and ass narrow and

pale as a deer's' and 'her tongue long and black as an anteater's going towards his body'. What she sees initially is 'a human animal'. Then, as she raids the body of her knowledge and language (in this case the history of the American Indian) to get closer to the truth of what she perceives, she discovers, in 'an Iroquois scout creeping naked and noiseless', an even better image for a human body crawling on hands and feet and possessed of the acute senses of an animal. It reminds me both of Coleridge's demand, in a definition that privileges 'Tact' over 'logical coherence', that the great poet should possess 'the *eye* of a North American Indian tracing the footsteps of an enemy upon the Leaves that strew the Forest',[25] and of Irigaray's account of women's language as 'a process of weaving itself, at the same time ceaselessly embracing words and yet casting them off to avoid becoming fixed, immobilised', of 'touching (upon)'.[26] There is a sense of the poet *feeling* her way, of using what touchstones she has, of approaching closer and closer, until, in a moment of illumination and self-affirmation that could only have been arrived at through the patient readings of the text of her body, she observes:

> when I looked at her
> she looked at me so directly, her eyes so
> dark, her stare said to me I
> belong here, this is mine, I am living out my
> true life on this earth.

Body and soul

Although Olds frequently employs the language and imagery of the Bible in her work, it is made clear that she doesn't believe either in the Christian God or in the Christian concept of an eternal soul. Describing the moment after her father's death in 'The Feelings',[27] for instance, the poet states: 'Everyone else in the room believed in the Christian God, / they called my father *the shell on the bed*, I was the / only one there who knew / he was entirely gone, the only one / there to say goodbye to his body / that was all he was ... '. There are no 'out of body' experiences in Olds' poems. The 'central meanings' of 'Prayer'[28] are found in childbirth and sex. The 'still waters',[29] the calm pond / silent as if eternal',[30] and the other world of 'Ecstasy'[31] ('we did not know where we were, we could not speak the language', 'we were far beyond what we knew', in 'a place from which no one has ever come back'), are arrived at through sexual acts of the body. 'If I had a God,' she declares to her lover in 'Greed and Aggression',[32] a poem in which she 'reads' her body, in an apparently deliberate allusion to Blake, as being like a tiger eating an eland, 'it would renew itself the / way you live and live while I take you as if / consuming you while you take me as if / consuming me, it would be a God of / love as complete satiety, / greed and fullness, aggression and fullness'. In other words, it would be a paradoxically devouring and renewing God of sexual love, created in the image of their lovemaking – almost the complete opposite of the Christian God of Agape (spiritual love) who creates man in His image.

This Blakeian concept of the divinity of the body and sex is developed further in 'Love In Blood Time'.[33] During an act of simultaneous cunnilingus and fellatio ('the large hard bud of your glans in my mouth, the dark petals of my sex in your mouth'), the poet experiences first a sense of immortality ('I could feel death going farther and farther away, forgetting me, losing my address his / palm forgetting the curve of my cheek in his hand'). Then, as she 'reads' her lover's body in the 'small glow of the lamp', his 'lower lip / glazed with light like liquid fire', (the spread of alliteration and assonance creating a verbal equivalent of the circles of light in a Rembrandt or de la Tour), she moves towards a radical vision of God which draws on Christian concepts of goodness but, in a reversal of conventional Christian theology, locates this goodness in the human body and its sexual acts:

> I looked at you and I knew you were God
> and I was God and we lay in our bed
> on the dark cloud, and somewhere down there
> was the earth, and somehow all we did, the
> blood, the pink stippling of the head, the
> pearl fluid out of the slit, the
> goodness of all we did would somehow get
> down there, it would find its flowering in the world.

No poet I can think of has written so powerfully about sex: finding a language that precisely conveys physical details and at the same time invests them with an allusion and symbolism that makes use of existing systems of meaning in pursuit of discovering new meaning. For example, the verbal stream of 'pearl fluid out of the slit', beginning slowly with the repeated liquid 'l's and drawn out double-vowels of 'pearl' and 'fluid' and then rushing towards the explosive consonants of 'slit', provides an almost onomatopoeic impression of ejaculation. But it is also a reading that imbues the male sexual act with the values inherent in the language employed to describe it. 'Pearl' conveys exactly the colour and size and shape of the drop of semen that first emerges from 'the head'. But it also carries associations of something found in nature that is precious, as well as Biblical associations of purity.[34] The wit and wonder of the poem's final revelation that 'the goodness of all we did ... would find its flowering in the world' – bringing together the earlier botanical descriptions of the body's sexual parts as well as the spiritual connotation of pearl – are arrived at by a genuine process of exploration that involves a *touching* of the physical body and of the body of language.

Through the body and its sexual acts, Olds seems to be saying, we can reach not only a transcendence that is equivalent to the transcendence claimed for religious experience but also the 'goodness' that is more usually attributed to religious than sexual practices. 'The body on earth is all we have got', she states categorically in 'I Wanted To Be There When My Father Died'.[35] So what is the soul – normally regarded as the antithesis of the material body – doing in her poems? In the bitterly ironic 'What If God', for instance, she envisages the kind of god that might exist in her mother's abusive world, a world in which 'she said that all we did was done in His sight so / what was He doing as He saw her weep in my / hair and slip my soul from between my ribs / like a tiny hotel soap'. This witty but reductive image of the soul seems to parody the Christian idea of the divine 'body's guest'. 'Did He / wash His hands of me as I washed my hands of Him?' she goes on to ask. But earlier in the poem, in the startling personification of God as 'a squirrel with His / arm in the yolk of my soul up to the elbow, / stirring, stirring the gold', the image of the egg yolk evokes an idea of the soul as the creative essence of the body. Like the world 'pearl' in 'Love in Blood Time', gold describes both the colour and value of what has been violated. It is an image that connects closely with Olds' account of her creative process: her feeling that the poem forms behind her breastbone and that writing it is the 'effort to get it out of me and onto the page without distorting it – like a very very over easy egg out of the pan onto the plate without breaking the yolk'.[36]

Olds' other analogy for the relationship between her body and the poem is of a dance: her body's dance as she writes the poem ('When I am writing a poem, it's true that I am often hearing it, my lips move, but I am also, in a way, dancing with it') and 'the dance that goes on between the language and the line and idea or narrative' in the body of the poem. She illustrated this with a diagram which superimposes the shape of a dancing body whose multiple arms represent its movements on the shape of one of her ragged-edged poems. As she explained:

> I see the body likeness (as if in a mirror): the left-hand margin is the still left arm; the caesura is the midline of the body (the spine); the right-hand margin shows the right-hand's freedom.[37]

This image of a vertically dancing body appears in a more surprising but related context in 'Am and Am Not', the penultimate poem in Olds' last published collection, *The Wellspring* (1997). An addition to her topos of 'morning after' poem – a celebratory alternative to the also post-coital, but usually male-voiced and regretful, Aubade – it begins with the poet brushing her teeth and proceeds, with the concentric female logic identified by Irigaray,[38] to an enquiry of the performance of her vagina in the sexual act of the previous night and thence to an investigation of the soul:

> When I am tilted forward, brushing my teeth,
> I glance down. We do not know
> ourselves. My cunt, like a hand, stroked him,
> such subtle, intricate movement. Central
> inside me this one I am and am not,
> not only like a palm, more like a snake's
> reticulated body, rings of muscle –
> like the penis outside-in, its twin.
> Who is it? I lean against the sink, mouth open
> and burning with Colgate, nixie palate
> scoured with pond-mint; is it my soul
> in there, elastic as an early creature
> gone out on its own again, is it
> my soul's throat? Its rings ripple
> in waves, as if it swallows, but what it
> swallows stays, and grows, and grows,
> we become one being, whom we hardly know,
> whom we know better than we know anyone
> else. And in the morning I look down. Who? What has –
> what?! Seeing just the skin of the belly –
> she is asleep in there, the soul, vertical,
> undulant one, she is dancing upright in her dream.

Questioning and exploratory, the poem approaches the unknown (the central question of identity 'Who Am I?') and unseen (the vagina) through a reading of the body that begins with what is known and seen: the movements of a hand, a snake, and the penis. It employs language as a kind of a raft in the process of discovery: the pond-mint flavour of Colgate toothpaste (a product of the linguistic elasticity of contemporary advertising) leading by a process of natural association and post-modern wit to an image of the soul, 'elastic as an early creature', in the unformed, unfixed, watery world at the beginning of creation. It sets a precise and wittily paradoxical description of the empirical evidence ('Its rings ripple / in waves, as if it swallows, but what it / swallows stays, and grows and grows') against a language that breaks down in inarticulate speculation ('Who? What has – what?'). In defining the vagina as 'central inside me this one I am and am not', it playfully acknowledges phallocentric assertions of identity – the unquestioning 'I AM THAT I AM' of the God of Exodus, or the tortured self-examining of John Clare's 'I Am' – and at the same time discovers the female 'hole' (brilliantly epitomised as 'the penis outside-in, its twin') as symbolising not 'lack' but a source of mystery and paradox: an identity, a self, a 'soul', that together with the phallus becomes 'one being' but that exists separately, joyously, inside and as an integral part of the female body. It also embodies ideas about the body as the source of female creativity. The unfinished or delayed meanings of the line endings that propel the poem forwards give it the impression of being a writing of a body that, in Olds' admiring words about Ruth Stone, 'swivels its hips and moves'.[39] The suggestion that the vagina soul has a throat implies that it also has a voice. The lyrically ecstatic final lines with their hypnotic, rhythmically repeated 'I's' create an image of the dancing soul that not only demonstrates Olds' power to put 'body and soul' into her work but is a literal embodiment of her concept of the poet's/poem's dancing body.

A radical feminine interpretation of the dance of creation, the poem makes a brilliantly anarchic addition to the poetry of the soul, rivalling Marvell's 'A Dialogue Between the Soul and Body' in its wit and the Emperor Hadrian's 'Animula, vagula, blandula'[40] in its power to create an image of the soul that is vivid and comprehensible. Hadrian and Marvel both drew on Christian neo-Platonic thought to personify the soul. Olds' image of the soul as the vagina asleep after sex, 'dancing upright in her dream', is her own original construction.

*

The power of Sharon Olds consists in her fearless investigation and recording of her experience, even when it exposes the most intimate details of her life and relationships, or challenges, or completely reverses previously accepted codes or narratives. It arises from the sensuousness and physical texture of a poetic discourse that in focusing on the body draws attention to the animal, vegetable and mineral constituents of 'matter'. It resides in her ability to call on all her knowledge and all the resources of the existing body of language as she knows it to investigate and illumine the nature of her experience. It is in the structure of her poems: their aliveness and suppleness; the way they plunge in and change direction and don't stop moving until they have both embodied an experience and arrived at an interpretation. It is in the power of a voice that 'calls out to, whispers to, sings to'[41] the reader; that like Lorca's *Duende* 'gives a sensation of freshness wholly unknown', that 'burns the blood like powdered glass'.[42] Finally, it is in her power to give her work a resonance beyond her personal story. Her nakedness in her poems is not, in the usual sense of the term, the confessional nakedness of an exhibitionist: and yet it is exhibitionist. 'Our species needs (poetry), perhaps, to survive', Olds argues. She offers the poetry of her survival – her courage to speak out, to 'tell about it', her refusal to accept powerlessness, her quest to identify good and evil, her celebration of sexuality and love – for the survival of humanity.

Notes

1. *The Gold Cell* (New York: Knopf, 1987) (hereafter *GC*), *The Sign of Saturn* (London: Secker & Warburg, 1991) (hereafter *SoS*), p. 61.
2. Interview by Sue Stewart in 1991, *Talking Verse: Interviews with Poets*, ed. R. Crawford, H. Hart, D. Kinloch, R. Price (St Andrews and Williamsburg, VA: Verse, 1995).
3. In a foreword to her poem 'Requiem' Anna Akhmatova describes being asked by a woman standing beside her in a prison queue in the years of the Yezhov terror 'Can you describe this?' Her reply was: 'Yes, I can.'
4. Ed. D. Weissbort (London: Anvil Press Poetry, 1991).
5. 'The Girl', *GC*, *SoS*, p. 56.
6. 'The Pact', *The Dead and the Living* (New York: Knopf, 1984) (hereafter *DL*), *SoS*, p. 32.
7. 'The Sign of Saturn', *DL*, *SoS*, p. 45.
8. 'Saturn', *GC*, *SoS*, p. 62.

9. Ibid., p. 17.
10. 'Silenced Voices: Turkey – Ismail Besikci', *American Poetry Review* (July–Aug. 1986), pp. 29–30.
11. 'The Lisp', *The Wellspring* (London: Cape, 1996), p. 12.
12. (New York: Farrar, Straus & Giroux, 1984), pp. 62–3.
13. Ibid., p. 318. 'The truth about our childhood is stored up in our body, and although we can repress it, we can never alter it.'
14. *The Father* (London: Cape, 1993), p. 67.
15. 'Aesthetics of the Shah', *DL, SoS*, p. 19.
16. Ibid., p. 33.
17. *Satan Says* (Pittsburgh: University of Pittsburgh Press) (hereafter *SS*), *SoS*, p. 2.
18. Subtitled 'a photograph of China, 1905', *DL, SoS*, p. 15.
19. *DL, SoS*, p. 26.
20. *GC, SoS*, p. 63.
21. *SS, SoS*, p. 3.
22. 'Elegy: To his Mistris going to Bed'. The whole section reads: 'Licence my roving hands, and let them goe / Behind, before, above, between, below. / Oh my America, my new found lande, / My kingdome, safeliest when with one man man'd, / My myne of precious stones, my Empiree, / How blest am I in this discovering thee.'
23. Note to 'The Laugh of the Medusa', transl. Keith Cohen and Paula Cohen, in Isabelle de Courtivron and Elaine Marks (eds), *New French Feminisms* (Minneapolis: University of Massachusetts Press; Brighton: Harvester, 1981).
24. *GC, SoS*, p. 81.
25. '... the great Poet must be, implicite if not explicite, a profound Metaphysician. He may not have it in logical coherence, in his Brain & Tongue; but he must have it by *Tact*: for all sounds, & forms of human nature he must have the *ear* of a wild Arab listening in the silent Desert – the *eye* of a North American Indian tracing the footsteps of an enemy upon the Leaves that strew the Forest; the *Touch* of a Blind Man feeling the face of a darling Child.' Letter to William Sotheby, in *Collected Letters of Samuel Taylor Coleridge*, ed. E. L. Griggs (Oxford: OUP, 1956–71), vol. ii, p. 810.
26. de Courtivron and Marks, *New French Feminisms*, p. 103; from 'Ce sexe qui n'en est pas un – This sex which is not one', 1977.
27. *The Father*, p. 39.
28. *SS, SoS*, p. 14.
29. 'Sex Without Love', *DL, SoS*, p. 37.
30. 'Sunday Night in the City' *SS, SoS*, p. 4.
31. *DL, SoS*, p. 38.
32. *GC, SoS*, p. 77.
33. Ibid., p. 82.
34. E.g. Matthew 13: 45, 'The kingdom of heaven is like unto a merchant man, seeking goodly pearls: Who, when he had found one pearl of great price, went and sold all that he had and bought it.'
35. *The Father*, p. 67.
36. Sue Stewart interview, p. 188.
37. Ibid.

38. Ibid., p. 149.
39. 'Ruth Stone and Her Poems', in *The House Is Made of Poetry: The Art of Ruth Stone*, ed. Wendy Barker and Sandra Gilbert (Carbondale: Southern Illinois UP, 1996).
40. 'Little soul so sleek and smiling / Flesh's friend and guest also / Where departing will you wander / growing paler now and languid / And not joking as you used to?' (Stevie Smith's translation).
41. Sue Stewart interview, p. 191.
42. 'Theory and Function of the *Duende*', in *Lorca: Selected Poems*, trans. J. L. Gill (Harmondsworth: Penguin, 1960).

16
Beyond Interpellation? Affect, Embodiment and the Poetics of Denise Riley

Carol Watts

In her critical work *Am I That Name?* Denise Riley suggests that women are only women sometimes. If the range of possibilities of what it means to 'be' a woman is vast and indeterminate, and the 'historical crystallisations' of identity always denser and more extravagant than the appellation 'woman' can identify, then there will be times when it is right to refuse it:

> she can always say, in good faith, 'here I am not a woman',
> meaning, 'in this contracting description I cannot recognize
> myself; there is more to this life than the designation lets on,
> and to interpret every facet of existence as really gendered
> produces a claustrophobia in me; I am not drawn by the
> charm of a sexually distinct universe'.[1]

This refutation of a necessarily gendered prism on 'every facet of existence', and Riley's interest in the discursive constitution of identity and corresponding suspicion of the cohesive subject 'women', has been much discussed, not least in debates about the politics of her poetry. For the demand of that ventriloquated and dissenting voice in *Am I That Name?* – for self-recognition in the designations of language despite a resistence to its claustrophobic containment and seductions – also shapes the lyric drive of her poetry, and it is there that the rich materialism of her account of identity and language is made visible. The difficulty of her poetry resides in a passage of thought and allusion of which the critical work is also, differently, an index. What is offered in the latter as a meditation on the limitations of identity politics emerges more extensively in her poems as a scrupulously reflective and yet abandoned encounter of the self with, and by means

157

of, the constitutive force of language; in which its calling out – interpellation – is seemingly all there is and yet in its inevitable failure never enough. To read her poetics in terms of gender is thus to acknowledge the working through of something catachrestical, named and inappropriate, invoked and refused: women's experience. It is also to discover in the lyric mode the site of that working through.

Recent discussions of Riley's work have focussed on her use of the lyric for a number of reasons. As Linda A. Kinnahan has usefully explored, it is a form that has been much contested in contemporary poetry: the romantic legacy of an expressive private and authentic voice now exposed as discursive strategy, an ideological instanciation of authority. Critics and practitioners, most notably those associated with Language poetry, have explored the ramifications of the poststructuralist dethroning of the subjective self; feminists in particular have been alive to both the dangers of the rhetorical inscription of gendered power relations in the lyric form and yet its possibilities as testimonial: 'a necessary formulation for asserting a suppressed or erased identity'. For Kinnahan, Denise Riley's work is signal to a shared concern amongst experimental women poets (she analyses in detail the work of Geraldine Monk and Wendy Mulford alongside Riley) to 'refuse culture's dominant expression of the feminine while insisting on gender's inseparable link to the the project of language experimentation and the necessary reconsiderations of the lyric "I"'.[2] In an incisive article that informs Kinnahan's own, Clair Wills has questioned the seeming divide between the artifice of experimentalism and the expressive voice, arguing that the work of such poets 'reveals not the absence of a sphere of privacy but the ways in which that private or intimate realm of experience is constructed "through" the public, and [that] therefore elements of "expressivity", though radically divorced from notions of authenticity, are present'. The point, then, is not to suggest that the lyric voice is a means of representing a coherent self secreted 'beneath the discourses of the texts', just awaiting its moment of expression, but rather, as Wills explores in Riley's 'When It's Time to Go', the figuring of an 'interiority … without representation' in which 'the cultural construction of the subject meshes with interiority'; a cultural field, which in Wills's view, is shaped by 'the clashing and fragmentary forms of familial life and contemporary commodity culture'.[3] In what follows I want to explore the situating of the lyric in that field opened up by Denise Riley's poetry, and to consider the questions it raises about what might be seen as the 'cost' of identity, marked in the affective dynamics of its identifications. In particular, I am interested in what senses gender can be said to be 'inseparably' linked to the experimentalism of her work, in its catachrestical formulation of a relationship between a developing poetics and 'women's experience'. A relationship that I will suggest depends not upon representation, but on a characteristic affective syntax.

'She' is 'I'

The movement from 'She' to 'I' is repeatedly traversed in Riley's poetry. It is nevertheless possible to trace shifts in emphases, and a changing sense of what it means to articulate such a movement. In the poems from the 1970s, collected in *Marxism for Infants* and, with Wendy Mulford, *No Fee: A Line or Two for Free*, and later in her selection *Dry Air*, it is easier (to paraphrase a phrase of Raymond Williams) to see what is being broken from than broken towards.[4] If speech is 'as a sexed thing' – 'the tongue as a swan's neck / full and heavy in the mouth' – the very voicing of self depends upon its distinctions.[5] Alison Mark discovers here the 'erotics of absorption and repellence' theorised by Charles Bernstein, and in its fleshy provocation a central question: 'whether language is itself gendered, or whether that inflection is delivered in its use'.[6] The choice for the speaker is silence or collusion, registered in another poem as the double bind of identification:

> she's imagining her wife & how she will live her? when
> the wife goes off to endless meetings in the rain
> she'll say aah I admire her spirit bravo la petite
> & when her belly swells into an improbable curve
> the she-husband will think Yes, it was me who caused that,
> and more generously, Biology, you are wonderful
>
> (*DA*, 9)

Here, avowedly, is an acting out of parts, the compacted lines playing out the claustrophobic theatre of the family romance. It suggests the complicity of a feminine identity that anticipates the gestural etiquette of the determination of sex; her autonomy (and thus that of the lyric voice) split dialogically into coupledom. Identity is 'lived' here in the transitive sense of the word, externalised in the gendered social imaginary. What has too quickly been labelled a disabling narcissism in Riley's work precisely involves the drama of such a condition, begging the question of both the comedy and violence of misrecognition: what it takes to be social, to become a 'woman'. In another poem the 'she-wife' is incorporated and the 'I' emerges, having re-occupied her bodily space as if by political protest:

> she has ingested her wife
> she has re-inhabited her own wrists
> she is squatting in her own temples, the
> fall of light on hair or any decoration
> is repossessed. 'She' is I.

> (*DA*, 11)

The passage from 'She' to 'I' is here revealed less as a movement (or liberation) than an acknowledgement of the trial of identity. Despite the autonomy suggested by this literal incorporation of the self into the body as building, that 'I' remains within the protection and yet constraint of enclosed spaces (and thus the prison-house of language). The lyric form is unravelled as topography. The reader is invited in another sequence to 'assume a country / held by small walls' (echoes of Whitman here?), and later, 'the house in the landscape / which roads irradiate / the hand that rocks the cradle / erect at every crossroads' (*DA*, 20). If the house is synonymous with the self, as in the poetry of Emily Dickinson, it cannot escape its gendered coding: domesticity, hearth, shelter, prison, tomb. At times Riley's work suggests the gothic intensity of Dickinson: 'I am in several cupboards / deep, and wish well out, / wish out from this / dark air of china' ('What I do' *DA*, 50), or 'The house had its teeth in her leg. Her sorrow had made a cloud rose / and the cloud rose encompassed them' ('The Cloud Rose', *DA*, 57). Like Dickinson, whose dissociated 'I' fears being trapped in a house where she cannot recognise herself, there are fantasies of escape in Riley's work, the rope let down into the roofless small room: 'It looked impossible but I was not / disheartened' (*DA*, 14). Yet its ambivalence is specifically directed here at the figure of the mother, which the 'I' inhabits and resists: both a sign of comforting enclosure and 'erect at every crossroads', a phallicised symbol of control (the hand that rocks the cradle rules the world). Thus the house connotes maternal security that is a refuge, or, as in 'Affections must not', a fiction of domesticity and sign of entrapment:

> the houses are murmuring with many small pockets of emotion
> on which spongy ground adults' lives are being erected & paid
> for daily

while their feet and their children's feet are tangled around
                                             like those of fen larks
in the fine steely wires which run to & fro between love &
                       economics

affections must not support the rent

I. neglect. the. house.

                                                              (*DA*, 27)

Enacted in these movements of identification and refusal, protection and restraint, is a drama of interpellation: the way in which
language hails identity and brings it into social being, forming subjects
'between love & / economics'. It is an affective drama that depends not
simply on recognition of the law, but on desire and collusion, and thus
love for the designation that subjects you: '"women" can also suffer
from too much identification', as Riley puts it in her 'Short History'.[7]
Exposed as a fiction it can be contested, endstopped. In 'Affections
must not' the construction of one model of the feminine – the myth
of the mother, 'what stands up in kitchens' – is disclosed, with the realisation that 'inside a designation there are people permanently startled
to / bear it, the not-me against sociology'. There is a resistance here not
only to the ideological formulations of language, but also to the
abstractions that reduce those inhabiting them to ciphers; in Riley's
view, feminism, as a form of knowledge akin to sociology, takes just
such a risk in its use of the designation 'women'. The 'fine, steely
wires' that bind the feet of adults and children alike run from the intimate heart of familial relations to the very workings of the state:
exposing the constitutively public nature of the private sphere.
Acknowledgement of the 'not-me' (ironically itself just such an
abstracting concept) thus becomes in every sense a mark of political
consciousness.

'I am from the start outside myself and open to the world'

If the lyric voice is to be defined against the binding of language in
terms of negativity – the 'not-me' – the question arises nonetheless as
to what its 'self' recognition might involve, or indeed, whether such a
question and the concept of identity that underpins it remain at all
credible. Recognition is at issue, but predicated on otherness, not
selfhood. In one poem from *Marxism for Infants* the voice declares

wildly that it '"will write / & write what there is beyond anything"'. This lyric anticipates the 'beyond' as a state of being, that it will not – cannot – articulate: 'saying It's true, I won't place or / describe it It *is* & refuses the law.' In what sense is it possible to inhabit – or even imagine – such a beyond, a truth that has refused the law and also escaped its counter-identification? Here it is figured as a knowledge of the 'spirit' that 'burns in & / through "sex"', leaving the 'old, known' body behind (*DA*, 19). Yet the topography of the earlier poems does, seemingly, 'place' the scene for such a possibility; unlike the domestic enclosure of the house, it points to a space of transformation: outside, 'irradiated' by roads, 'constant and receptive as a capital city' (*DA*, 18). Metropolitan, fragmentary, crammed full of light and change. Identity here increasingly comes to embrace its necessary contingency, both exhilarated and yet materially battered in the encounter with what lies 'beyond' the refuge of self and the 'law' of language: noise, buzz, words 'flocking not through the brain but through the ear', as Riley puts it in a recent essay.[8] It is as if the representative drive of the poetry – the attempt to validate the 'I' (so central to a particular phase of feminism) – begins to be put under pressure by the charged bombardment of 'radio voices', the 'impersonal hazard' that will become 'Disintegrate Me'.[9]

In the lyrics of the later *Mop Mop Georgette* the earlier landscape is formally overrun, and a potential nomadism of the 'I' developed which is only hinted at before. At times this suggests a form of spectatorship which promises a welcome form of detachment, as here, in 'A Shortened Set':

> When I'm unloaded and stood in dread
> at home encircled by my life, whose
> edges do show – then I so want it to run
> and run again, the solitary travelling perception.
> Road movie: Protectedness, or, Gets through time.
>
> (*MM*, 22)

Yet the distanced control of such cinematic perception – 'that held sense of looking out' – is not to be had. The poems of *Mop Mop Georgette* repeatedly interrogate the security of poetic vision – the visual primacy of the I / eye – as if life has pressed in too close. Eyes 'film over' in 'Metallica', or blur and smear: 'a / corner of the eye's unsteady streak' ('A Drift', *MM*, 48). In 'Red Shout' the eye is assaulted by waves and tides of colour. In 'Pastoral' a damaged eye is taped shut, and underneath the lid the show of lightless colour and movement –

'like sunspot photographs' – is 'a poor video I can't turn off' (*MM*, 45). 'Wherever You Are, Be Somewhere Else' recalls the child's belief that covering your eyes means that you disappear, even as a Nintendo Game Boy slogan is made to evoke a more deathly 'gothic riff'. Here the looks and glances of others cut their 'tracery':

> ... all faces split to angled facets: whichever
> piece is glimpsed, that bit is what I am, held
>
> in a look until dropped like an egg on the floor
> let slop, crashed to slide and run, yolk yellow
> for the live, the dead who worked through me.
>
> (*MM*, 27)

The disruption of the sovereignty of vision – whether in terms of the imperfection of sight or its surrender to the powerful gaze of others – entails the fragmentation of the self. In the above it takes an almost Buñuelian form (reminiscent, too, of that Lacanian 'hommelette'); while the fear emerges in 'Pastoral' of a similar dissolution, 'what if the / pupil's black should slop and run across its / sheeny brown and green' (*MM*, 45). Yet these scenarios provide what might be seen as the verso of a desire central to Riley's lyrical form; one that aims precisely for such dissolution. What if that lyric voice could be 'only transmission', imagined in 'Wherever You Are ...' as a cabling between the wordprocessor and the head? A vision of technological shamanism otherwise only available in dreams: 'in sleep alone I get to articulate to mouth the part of / anyone and reel off others' characters' (*MM*, 28). Aware, and at times 'guilty' of the persistence and theatricality of that 'I', Riley's lyric seems to work towards its own coextensiveness with 'the sliding skin of the world' ('Glamour', *MM*, 57). In 'Lyric' this desire emerges as a plea:

> Take up a pleat in this awful
> process and then fold me flat
> inside it so that I don't see
> where I was already knotted in.
>
> (*MM*, 36)

And in 'A Misremembered Lyric' such concealment comes as a recommendation, like an afterthought: 'Oh and never / notice yourself ever. As in life you don't' (*MM*, 31). The dilemma for the lyric – of the desire for the loss of self and yet the prospect of extinction of consciousness that accompanies it – suggests a romantic paradox, but one that is transformed here. What is at stake concerns not the perils of transcendence but the externality of that lyric self in the world, the acknowledgement of its embodiedness. The line from Maurice Merleau-Ponty that surfaces on a number of occasions in Riley's critical writing – 'I am from the start outside myself and open to the world' – is testimony to a movement in her poetics in which such seeming decentring figures the situatedness of identity.[10]

Riley's poems hold out, occasionally, a reassuringly concrete sense of the material world, finding 'Things packed with what they are'. Perhaps it is only in a brute sense – 'heart's meat' – that the embodied self can take on such solidity: as flesh, the extinction of self ('So Is It?', *MM*, 52). Yet there is a movement at work that circumvents such an intimation of mortality, or rather, makes it part of another dialectic. The disturbance of the visual suggests a realignment of the hierarchy of the senses, in which the lyric 'I' becomes an assemblage of bodily sensations, a place of synaesthesic interchange. Mouth, ear, eye, touch. The effect of this is to site consciousness in bodily terms, to see the passions as a means of speculation: 'It is called feeling but is its real name thought?' ('A Shortened Set', *MM*, 20). This is not, however, to realign the embodied self with a traditional lyric expressivity.[11] Significantly, even as her poetry mines its intense introspection, it acknowledges a radical externality within identity itself, which works through the affective material that appears to take the most personal of forms. At times this acknowledgement is suggested in the uncertainty of the encounter with the world – 'the shakiness, is it inside the day or me?' ('Rayon', *MM*, 41) – which is manifested too in reflection about the place of language and memory in that encounter: 'suppose you stopped describing / something, would stopping free you from it, almost as it hadn't happened? / so is that shiver down the back water, or is it memory calling water' ('Oleanna', *MM*, 58). More radically, that 'I' is extended into the world almost prosthetically (often through technological means), picking up past and present frequencies of sound and imprints of sense – the lyrics of songs, the 'stammering' of the motors of language, the shapes of clichés, lines from film scripts, and slips of the tongue – through which it comes into being. Such dissociation might be seen as an index of the alienation of commodity culture in which emotional life and meaning is reified. But it is also the apprehension of something more, a phenomenological drama central to the lyric condition, here reworked.

In Riley's later poems affect becomes, at times, autonomous, disrupting the conventional ties between the lived body and the perceived world and the laws of language that secure them. It would be interesting to explore to what extent this has always been the risk of the lyric form. In this context it is what leads to the rich materialism of Riley's work. Affect is that mass of material sensations, impressions and impulses that has not been assimilated into consciousness, which, as Brian Massumi puts it, 'is not exactly outside experience ... it is immanent to it – always in it but not of it'.[12] In this poetry affect does not emanate from 'outside' in any simple sense, but it demands the recognition of the otherness of the self which makes it, by definition, social. I suggested earlier that while it was clear what Riley's early poems were breaking from, it was much more difficult to ascertain what they were breaking towards. If it is possible to trace a development in her work, it is perhaps that the demand for identity, and its refusal of the designations of language – the shift from 'She' to 'I' – gives way to the exploration of a much more fluid subjective space, the continual assessment of what it means for interpellation to fail, and the repeated encounter with the other's independence: in short, the subjective drama of sociality. What I want to call the nomadism of *Mop Mop Georgette* is in some sense a measure of this: an affective movement or figurative process that charts the desire for recognition by the other. This process is 'what forces the lyric person to put itself on trial' ('Dark Looks', *MM*, 54). At its most fluent it resembles a situation, in the words of Gilles Deleuze and Félix Guattari, of 'sensory becoming': 'the action by which something or someone is ceaselessly becoming-other (while continuing to be what they are)'.[13] Yet the passage of such becoming is not as smooth as this might imply; and to suggest how and why this might be the case, I want to examine aspects of one lyric sequence from *Mop Mop Georgette*.

The verdict of sociality: 'A Shortened Set'

The lyric sequence of 'A Shortened Set' puts into play a number of concerns central to Denise Riley's poetics: the nature of memory and the embodied self; the act of writing; the movement of that self through social space, characteristically here the landscape of the city. While these concerns are voiced in a series of lyric blocks, there is something vertiginous about the sequence as a whole, which works both as a kind of passage – the working through of affective material – and as a simultaneity, in which each theme is read in terms of the other. The body of the writer opens the space for these crossings, which force the reader at times unexpectedly to jump cut between frames of interpretation. The effect resembles montage: while the disjunction of frames can produce new connections, it also prevents a kind of expressive homology, in which the body of the lyric 'I', the text, and the wider world become one. This is a sequence that deals with a process of 'becoming-other', in which the reader is also brought to participate. But while enacting such a sensory process, like an affective physics, the poem is also about that process; the effort and the cost of it.

What is clear from the outset is that this a sequence about return: the need to remember again, to rework. In this sense 'A Shortened Set' is involved not with the experience of simultaneity – though in the sense of existing in the moment it is a state sought out – but with the demand for and melancholic cost of retrospection:

> All the connectives of right recall
> have grown askew. I know
> a child could have lived, that
> my body was cut. This cut
> my memory half-sealed but glued
> the edges together awry.
> The skin is distorted, the scar-tissue
> does damage, the accounts are wrong.
> And this is called 'the healing process'.
> Now nothing's aligned properly.
> It's a barbarous zone.
> The bad sutures
> thicken with loss and hope –
> brilliant, deliberate
> shaking patients in an anteroom
> refusing the years, ferocious to be called
> so I'll snip through the puckered skin
> to where they tug for re-aligning. Now
> steady me against inaccuracy, a lyric urge
> to showing off. The easy knife
> is in my hand again. Protect me.

> (*MM*, 16)

The poem's opening wager works like a metaphysical conceit, in which metaphors of surgery and incision emphasise the physicality of memory and the lyric text. Memory is like a wound, its skin misaligned, the scar-tissue thickening. Its medium is at once corporeal and linguistic, suggested in the 'connectives' of the first line; while the 'bad sutures' that 'thicken with loss and hope' pick up not simply on the surgical and linguistic themes – in which the connectives of language are what hold the wound together – but also on the notion of the suturing of subjectivity, which holds the subject in place. These sutures and the memories they bind are 'ferocious to be called', their demand for recognition 'refusing the years', still fresh. The poet-surgeon, then, recognises the insistence of the 'inside-other' in Jean Laplanche's terms – the unconscious – and begins to cut.[14]

The call for recognition also comes from outside. If the journey inaugurated by the opening section suggests an inward movement, into the dark and 'purplish' terrain of a 'small history', it takes place nonetheless 'in life', out in the colour and heat of the city, where the 'I' waits 'to get back something'. That 'something' may be a response – the voice attempting to provoke dialogue ('Am I alright you don't ask me') – but also the security of a shared identification with the world: 'My heart takes grateful note / to be in life, the late heat shaped in bricks of air / stuck out, hot ghosts to catch my hand on. / The slap of recognition that you know' (*MM*, 17). However even as the poem plays out the conventional forms of a belonging that is also a 'perfectly democratic loneliness', it finds the terms for the other journey, in which the textuality of the colours of the city registers the 'puckered skin' of that earlier wound:

> How can black paint be warm? It is. As ochre
> stains slip into flooding milk, to the soft black
> that glows and clots in sooty swathes.
> Its edges rust, it bleeds lamp-black
> slow pools, as planes of dragged cream
> shoot over it to whiteness, layered.
> Or the cream paint, leaden, wrinkles: birch bark
> in slabs, streaked over a peeling blue. A twist
> of thought is pinned there. A sexual black. And I
> can't find my way home. Yet wandering there I may.
> By these snow graphics. Ice glazed
> to a grey sheen, hard across dark grass spikes.
>
> (*MM*, 18)

This irruption of sensuous detail is an instance of the density of affect that appears to achieve a kind of autonomy in Riley's poetics, though not one that can be sustained. It suggests a sensory overload, part of the 'crammed-fullness of the place / too dense for story threads to pierce' (*MM*, 22). What begins as a question – about the synaesthesic properties of colour – leads to a tactile unravelling of the visual: black connoting heat, light, movement, age, clots and pools of blood, sex. The nomadism of the 'I' is apparent here. Amongst its densities come fragments of songs, like truncated telegrams, and 'snow graphics': scripts waiting decipherment. The poem deals in part with the inevitability of the reminder of the repressed, which unsettles like 'the underside / of a brushed wing' whenever it appears firmly under wraps (*MM*, 18). But the question of how this is to be lived (and its damage limited) is immediately pleated into the act of writing itself, which for Riley crucially involves a process of return, and continuously copes with the demand for recognition: 'It's to you. Stop' (*MM*, 19).

In the essay 'Is There Linguistic Guilt?' Denise Riley has discussed her own sense of the process of writing, and in particular its retrospective quality:

> There's a feeling of being seized against your will by too much language, of being inscribed by language, when the sounds and shapes of what you've written, not their meaning, determine what comes next – an untidy, semi-conscious, vacillating affair after which you have to dust yourself down, maybe to realise 'what's really going on here' only in retrospect. If you do – perhaps the writer is the last person to know.... What does it mean, to come to know what you 'meant to say' only after it's written down?[15]

'A Shortened Set' makes this process evident. The image of a stream of water, hard and white like heavy snow, switches to the process of cutting in which 'Deletions are sifting down/ onto the study floor' (*MM*, 20). Elsewhere the text is weighed with literary clichés (allusively Shakespearean), and lines from songs that twist in meaning or seem heavy with import, while the 'ex-poet' busies herself with choices, lines sloughing off into inverted commas or arbitrarily changing mid flow. It is not just that the act of writing resembles the attempt to edit the 'active materiality' of a language that brings the 'I' into being. It is also that these poems – with their stress on need to listen, to wait 'until word may finally arrive', and their constant anticipation of a call that comes from outside – register the *interpellative* force of that language without always understanding (or needing to understand) what it signifies. And, seemingly, also expose such interpellation where it might be thought to be absent. Lacan famously described the signifier as resembling a sign in the desert, which still manages to signify *to* someone, even though what it is a signifer *of* is unknown. As Laplanche puts it, 'we know that *there is 'a signifying'* somewhere, but there is not necessarily any explicit signified'.[16] The fragments of song can sound like imperatives – 'Mother of children, don't go into the house in the dark' – but the address is ambiguous, its 'signifying' both a naming and, potentially, a reverse warning about such positioning (*MM*, 20). What happens to identification here? Might this enigma not be a way of thinking the historicity of the interpellative process, its situatedness in time? If the earlier poetry registers its resistance to that interpellative power to name 'women', the later work appears to explore the grammar of that power; the labour that goes into (mis)identification with it; and the potential, in time, for designification.

Riley points out in her essay the similarity between her sense of the scene of writing and a psychoanalytical account of self-knowledge. What comes to mind here for me is Jean Laplanche's theorisation of the unconscious in terms of the alienated 'fragments of communication' that endlessly demand translation: 'the untranslatable but endlessly retranslated … upon which the auto-theorisation of the human being seizes but which it cannot reduce except in an unstable and asymptotic fashion'.[17] For Laplanche the demand to translate this inexhaustible fund of material is a fundamental drive: a pressure that is both somatic and, as Peter Osborne has explained, 'the symptom of a being that is constitutively "with others"'.[18] A condition, then, of the sociality of the human being. The meaning of such a mass of material – verbal and non-verbal – is thus necessarily only established, in translation, in retrospect. Riley's own sense of language working 'across' the writer might be read in relation to this concept of translation.[19] The intense drive to translate is present because of the difference between death and signification: the absolute exteriority and untranslatable otherness of the former, and the possibility of symbolisation. Isn't this part of the dynamic of the lyric? 'I'd thought / to ask around, what's lyric poetry? / Its bee noise starts before I can: / You do that; love me; die alone' (*MM*, 22).

Yet such a model of translation, predicated as it is on an understanding of the unconscious as a fund of enigmatic fragments of communication, does not seem fully to explain the figurative movement of this poetry. It is tempting to read 'A shortened set' as a lyric talking cure, in which psychic damage memorialized at the outset is released in the calm of the final stanzas: 'In a rush / the glide of the heart / out on a flood of ease' (*MM*, 24). This is encouraged perhaps by the intimation of bodily interiority in the opening lines, the depths hinted at beneath the physical scar of memory, which must be revisited if 'right recall' is to be possible. This is too neat, however, for two reasons. Firstly, if the drive of her poetry is to acknowledge 'that I live "outside myself"', it also must be to recognise the part of the 'inside-other' in such exteriority, what Judith Butler has termed 'the verdict of sociality'. In other words, the extent to which that 'I' and the psychic metaphorical landscape that sustains it are the social effects of subjection, such that the reflexivity of the lyric voice becomes 'a recasting of a social "plaint" as psychic self-judgment' (and lingustic guilt?).[20] This would be to suggest that Riley's later work has the lyric take on the scene of subjectification itself. However, and secondly, if the psychoanalytical movement to self-knowledge is plotted here, it is not the only trajectory, as the nomadism of the work might suggest. In 'Is There Linguistic Guilt?' Riley suggests an account of language that is more immediate and that 'cheerfully lacks depths', one which through sound and accident endlessly and anarchically displaces.[21] It is a displacement to be discovered in the affective connections that short through her poetry, caught up in networks and circuits, the contingencies of surfaces, lines and intensities of movement and light. The lyric subject, in the final stanzas of 'A shortened set', becomes connective in this sense. At stake here, perhaps, is a kind of creative agency, in which that psychic landscape is transformed, and it appears possible, despite the risk and fear at such 'impersonal hazard', to affirm new forms of thought and action.

In what senses have the question of women's experience, and the issue of gender, remained 'inseparable' from Denise Riley's work in *Mop Mop Georgette*? Not as tied in any essentialist form to her poetic expression, nor, I think, as holding on to the feminine as other, negativity, body. The shift from 'She' to 'I' in the earlier poetry often concerned ambivalence about the designation of the maternal, and the figure of the mother emerges on a number of occasions in this volume. 'A Shortened Set' begins with what appears to be a mother's body claimed by the 'I', but the 'traveller' of the sequence is stripped of *his* sex. In 'Laibach Lyrik' the lyric 'I' founds its undetermined sex and national identity on a 'settling scar' (*MM*, 9). The 'I' takes on the dispersal of difference, and what might be seen as the ethical field of being 'constitutively "among others"'.[22] Like the conclusion of Julia Kristeva's essay 'Women's Time', Riley's poetry appears to anticipate a movement beyond 'a sexually distinct universe', a radicalism that entails, she explains in *Am I That Name?*, the 'intensifying [of] aesthetic practices which bring out "the relativity of his/her symbolic as well as biological existence"'.[23] Unlike the Kristeva essay, however, in which the maternal is a key and ultimately dehistoricizing (and I would argue, depoliticizing) concept, such a relativizing in Riley's work includes the symbolic figure of the mother.[24] In *Mop Mop Georgette* different temporalities of 'women's time' come into play – teenage, middle-aged, mobile and speeding, mortal, expectant, caught in 'the gleam of a moment's / social rest' (*MM*, 24) – as forms of 'Knowing in the Real World' (*MM*, 33). Life – experience – is something that is liberated from the 'active materiality' of language. Even as they are about the impossibility of escaping the attachments and identifications essential to the social ordering of subjectivity, her poems generate potentialities; not simply prepared to listen to the 'verdict' of sociality, but holding out for intimations of 'ordinary' freedom.

Notes

1. Denise Riley, *Am I That Name? Feminism and the Category of 'Women' in History*, (London: Macmillan, 1988), p. 111.
2. Linda A. Kinnahan, 'Experimental Poetics and the Lyric in British Women's Poetry: Geraldine Monk, Wendy Mulford, and Denise Riley', *Contemporary Literature* 37. 4 (1996), pp. 635, 666.
3. Clair Wills, 'Contemporary Women's Poetry: Experimentalism and the Expressive Voice', *Critical Quarterly* 36. 3 (1994), pp. 41–2, 44, 50.
4. Williams is describing the notion of a modernist 'break'. See his *The Politics of Modernism*, (London: Verso, 1989), p. 43.
5. Denise Riley, *Dry Air* (London: Virago, 1985), p. 10 (hereafter cited in the text as *DA* followed by page number).
6. Alison Mark, 'Reading Between the Lines: Language, Experience and Identity in the Work of Veronica Forrest-Thomson' (PhD thesis, University of London, 1994), p. 284.
7. Denise Riley, 'A Short History of Some Preoccupations', in Judith Butler and Joan W. Scott (eds), *Feminists Theorize the Political* (New York and London: Routledge, 1992), p. 122.
8. Denise Riley, 'Is There Linguistic Guilt?', *Critical Quarterly* 39. 1 (1997), p. 83.
9. Denise Riley, *Mop, Mop Georgette: New and Selected Poems 1986–1993* (Cambridge: Reality Street, 1993), p. 63 (hereafter cited in the text as *MM* followed by page number).
10. Maurice Merleau-Ponty, *The Phenomenology of Perception*, trans. Colin Smith (London: Routledge, 1962), p. 456.
11. Clair Wills rightly argues, following Jacqueline Rose, that an emphasis on

a bodily *écriture* in women's poetry can substitute one form of essentialist expressivity for another. There is however nothing essentialist – or necessarily feminine – about Riley's construction of the embodied lyric subject. See Wills, 'Contemporary Women's Poetry', p. 37.

12. Brian Massumi, 'The Autonomy of Affect', in Paul Patton (ed.), *Deleuze: A Critical Reader*, (Oxford: Blackwell, 1996), p. 226; Massumi distinguishes between affect and emotion, which is the result of assimilation of affective material into consciousness, where it is rendered meaningful.

13. Gilles Deleuze and Félix Guattari, *What Is Philosophy?*, trans. Graham Burchell and Hugh Tomlinson (London and New York: Verso, 1994), p. 177.

14. The 'inside-other' is Jean Laplanche's translation of Freud's *das Andere* ('the other-thing in us'); he also uses the term 'outside-other' for Freud's *der Andere* ('the other person of our personal pre-history'). I will return to Laplanche's notion of the unconscious shortly. See his 'Psychoanalysis, Time and Translation', in *Jean Laplanche: Seduction, Translation, Drives*, ed. John Fletcher and Martin Stanton (London: ICA, 1992), p. 174.

15. Riley, 'Is There Linguistic Guilt?', pp. 84–5.

16. Jean Laplanche, *New Foundations for Psychoanalysis*, trans. David Macey, (Oxford: Blackwell, 1989), p. 45.

17. Laplanche, 'Psychoanalysis, Time and Translation', p. 174.

18. Peter Osborne, *The Politics of Time* (London: Verso, 1995), p. 107.

19. Riley, 'Is There Linguistic Guilt?', p. 85.

20. Judith Butler, *The Psychic Life of Power: Theories in Subjection* (Stanford, CA: Stanford University Press, 1997), p. 198.

21. Riley, 'Is There Linguistic Guilt?', p. 107.

22. Osborne, *The Politics of Time* p. 107.

23. Riley, *Am I That Name?*, p. 110. The quote within quotes is from Julia Kristeva, 'Women's Time', in Toril Moi (ed.), *The Kristeva Reader* (Oxford: Blackwell, 1986), p. 210.

24. I have developed this critique of the Kristeva essay in 'Time and the Working Mother: Kristeva's "Women's Time" Revisited', *Radical Philosophy* 91 (1988), pp. 6–17.

17
Personal Politics in the Poetry of Carol Rumens: A Comparison with Denise Levertov

Marion Lomax

Denise Levertov and Carol Rumens never met, nor did they influence each other. A generation and thousands of miles between them, they have each earned the right to be regarded as exceptional poets for their dedication to the art of poetry, their different lyrical skills, and their individual ways of bringing the personal and the political together so powerfully in their work. Levertov's writings have received considerable critical attention and, although Rumens is still in mid-career, her achievements have certainly not been neglected but there is, perhaps, less evidence than there should be that the hopes Peter Forbes expressed in 1993 have been fulfilled in every direction. Reviewing *Thinking of Skins*, her volume of new and selected poems, he commented, 'the book ought to bring her renewed recognition as one of the best poets of our time'.[1] By bringing her work into focus alongside that of Levertov, I hope to encourage this process further, and also to examine the similarities and differences in their attitudes to the personal and political elements of their poetry.

Both poets were born in England: Levertov in Ilford, Essex, and Rumens in Forest Hill, south-east London, but in 1948, following her marriage to the American writer and political activist Mitchell Goodman, Denise Levertov emigrated to the United States. While her style was influenced by her American contemporaries (particularly William Carlos Williams, Wallace Stevens, and the Black Mountain poets), and she never turned her back entirely on her British literary heritage, her interests always ranged further than Britain and America. As a child she had been made aware of Nazism and Fascism through her parents' involvement with German Jewish refugees: in 1977, she told Sybil Estess, 'I surely knew what Hitler represented, because I had grown up with refugees right in my home. I knew what went on in concentration camps more than most people did until the war was over.'[2] Her father, Philip Levertoff, was a Russian Jew who converted and became an Anglican minister: both he and her Welsh mother nurtured a sense of pride in their children's Jewish heritage as well as a strong social concern. Although Levertov never experienced discrimination herself, she was sensitive to anti-Semitic feeling towards others from an early age.[3]

In America, Levertov's passionate political commitment eventually led to protests and poems about the Vietnam war, Chile, El Salvador, and the Gulf war. She campaigned about anti-nuclear issues and for human rights globally – whether it be those of a people, such as in Vietnam or South Africa – or of an individual, as in the case of the South Korean writer Kim Chi Ha, whose imprisonment and torture she fought against. Actively involved in the causes she embraced, Levertov travelled to Vietnam in 1972, and to Seoul in 1975 in a bid for the release of Kim Chi Ha. From the early sixties, poetry and politics had started to come together in her life as she responded to the Eichmann trial in *The Jacob's Ladder* (1961) and worked towards her Vietnam protests in *The Sorrow Dance* (1967). For the next thirty years she lived up to the title of one of her most popular prose works, *The Poet in the World*.[4]

In her essay 'On the Edge of Darkness: What Is Political Poetry?' Levertov cited Pablo Neruda's view that political poetry 'is more deeply emotional than any other except love poetry' and expressed her own desire to perfect the fusion of didactic and lyrical elements in her poems.[5] For the most influential part of her career, she bravely attempted to write poetry which would be 'strong enough to handle history and not stay cowed within the halting world of self', to borrow a phrase from Terence Des Pres,[6] yet as soon as she considered herself to be 'technically and emotionally capable of doing so', she drew her poetry directly out of her own experiences.[7] When she died, aged 74, in December 1997, Cynthia Fuller wrote:

> She moved effortlessly between spiritual tussles, reflections upon ageing, relationships, places, and world peace, always with the same precision, the same steady gaze.[8]

On this side of the Atlantic, Carol Rumens is also renowned for her broader vision, usually in relation to the history and politics of Eastern Europe, Russia and, latterly, Northern Ireland. Like Levertov (who, in addition to her international reading, translated the poetry of Guillevic, Joubert, and Rilke in an individual fashion), Carol Rumens has reached beyond the narrow confines of British literature and politics. She has translated a number of Russian poets, and her reading of Pushkin, Pasternak, Havel, Rein, Slutsky, Akhmadulina, and others is apparent in her poetry. Her interest in Russian literature, which began in her teens, eventually led her to her Russian-born partner. Despite their origins, neither poet is usually regarded as primarily 'English' by her critics: Levertov has been described as 'America's foremost contemporary woman poet' and Rumens as, 'a European poet whose imagination goes beyond the confines of Europe, a poet of borders and transit and of the movement across frontiers which makes both the experience of alienation and that of "home" a relative matter'.[9]

Ironically, these last ideas are, perhaps, most powerfully expressed in 'Letter from South London', an evocative poem which not only takes its momentum from the rootlessness with which Rumens is so often associated ('Tonight I have no fixed abode, and write to you / sadly from the bus number 159'), but juxtaposes it with her sense of being 'local' and her own intimate knowledge of the capital, as seen from the bus:

> where I brim my head like a child's sea-dipped bucket,
> with swarmings of the city that I call mine.[10]

Elsewhere, she has observed, 'I wish I felt distinctly English or peculiarly at home in England, but I don't'.[11] This seems partly due to the way in which, viewed in relation to other European countries (and those further afield), England lacks 'an acceptable nationalism', and partly because, as she writes in the poem:

> A sense of belonging is something deep and private.
> It flows with language, custom, habit – or
> it can be acquired in twenty seconds flat.

Feelings of alienation can occur in the midst of the familiar if there is a sense of losing faith in guiding principles ('The slender candle-light of democracy / has flickered out in a gloom of broken doorways / where the winos study meths-economy') or simply when you are separated from the one person who is able to provide you with a sense of belonging:

> So it was that I, transported carelessly,
> woke to your smile and thought it must be home.
> This ...
> simply means that there's nowhere else to be
>
> right now. And it's not unbearable, all the while
> I keep on moving ...

This person, who has had such a profound effect on the speaker's sense of belonging, is from a country outside Britain ('your vivid Eastern darknesses'), yet seems better attuned to the speaker's heritage than she is herself. Her prescription for survival is to keep moving – actually, as well as in the imagination.

The poem has a social and political aspect in the way it reviews South London past and present, and in its philosophical pondering on the nature of 'home', the plights of the jobless and those who are homeless or have their lives 'piled into flats' – yet it is primarily deeply personal and any social or political elements are filtered through the eyes and emotions of the speaker travelling on the bus as it:

> roars like a ghetto-blaster,
> reggae-ing down the dusty old A23.

Having read this poem, a reader returns to its opening lines with the realization that the speaker's having 'no fixed abode' is even more powerful as a metaphor than as reality: it could be read as one or both.

Rumens has asserted that her starting point is always personal rather than political. Speaking of her poems as a whole, in August 1998, she said, 'I can't think of one that I wrote purely, or primarily, to give a political message'.[12] So, while Levertov's political poetry came about 'As a natural process of becoming more politically involved',[13] and is rarely, if ever, accidentally political, the political slants which characterize so many poems by Rumens have emerged through personal connections and often only manifest themselves through a complex process of cross-fertilisation:

> Sometimes I start off writing a poem in a very personal way: it's just about me and my experiences, and I'm looking out to some extent ... so I have images from ... the public or political world and, in the end, some weird process seems to turn it into a poem in which, instead of the metaphor being the public thing for my personal

experience... my personal experience seems to have been the metaphor for some public thing, but I'm not doing that on purpose.

A recent poem, 'Thirst for Green',[14] illustrates this. Using lines from Larkin's 'The Trees' to set the scene, and pondering on his use of the rhyme 'grief' to establish the mood, it is, on one level, concerned with the yearning to see signs of life in trees which are, it is later revealed, dying from Dutch elm disease. However, the second stanza, where windows are 'arched like prayers round the heavily pencilled / Shamrock and tudor-rose', takes the reader back to the early conflicts of its Northern Irish setting and the waiting (and praying), which has gone on since, for a rebirth or new spring which will mean peace and healthy growth for all. The title puts the trees' new leaves to the fore, which encourages a reading of 'green' in relation to a thirst for all healthy, hopeful life – and not in the narrow, political sense of Republicanism: the poem does not take sides. 'Thirst' is a desperate, basic need, and the initial quote from Larkin is carefully chosen, as the poem uses his original sense and then augments it by suggesting a new context where 'something is almost being said' by both sides in rela- tion to the Northern Irish peace agreement. At the end of the poem the 'clamped buds' with their 'dream of making light' lead the reader to imagine all the individuals who hope for peace, but are denied growth in that direction because, like the elms, they are in the grip of 'an old disease' which they seem unable to defeat – the memory, imposed on them, of old feuds which, like the elm disease, have a Dutch origin (this time through William III and the Battle of the Boyne). A distance is placed between the Irish political context and the elms by the end of the poem in that the trees are doomed and, although a similar threat hangs over Northern Ireland, the analogy is not exact. The minds of people can be changed: old feuds are not genetically inher- ited; they can be settled and, if they are not, there is no glory and no healthy future growth ('no leaf-heraldries') – the disease will kill the trees. Rumens has explained that the poem came, initially,

> out of a really deep depression, and I'm actually the elm ... that can't flourish. It really is a personal poem, and yet, as I was looking around at my images I had a very strong sense of where that poem was set ... so ... I'm seeing things that do have a public resonance, like the shamrock and the tudor-rose ... I did it knowingly, but I was initially looking for a description of the shapes in a stained- glass window and that's what they often resemble ... then it

occurred to me that I could make some kind of statement ... but that wasn't the prime intention of the poem ... and then I thought about the title and wondered, would that look as if I was taking one particular side and I'm saying I want a united Ireland ..? I just wanted unity full-stop – rather than a particular political version of it.

Just as she does not consider herself to be as overtly political as her critics and reviewers find her, nor does Carol Rumens share their sense of her as firmly European. In 1993 she wrote,

I consider myself to be English first (but Celtic English rather than Saxon), then British, then European. The last two concepts are more or less abstract. When I think of *British* I think of brass-hatted Britannia, ruling the waves from a coin. When I think of *European* I think of former Yugoslavia, and feel sick. When I think of *English* I think of chalk downs, lager louts ... and cardboard cities under wet bridges where the hopeless young say over and over, hopelessly polite: could you spare us a bit of change, please. And I want to kick someone – but I don't know who.[15]

Put this with her acknowledgement that, 'A disinclination to stay any length of time in one place, mixed up with a peculiar disturbing hunger to do so, is one of the energy sources of my poems', and a reluctant sense of imposed rootlessness follows. This may also provide a useful sense of distance to balance any personal connections. Like Levertov, Rumens has criticized the policies of particular governments both directly and obliquely, but the ways in which she scrutinizes sections of a populace are particularly striking in poems such as 'St Petersburg, Reclaimed by Merchants', 'A Lawn for the English Family', or 'The Skin Politic'.[16]

The latter, an early poem, was written at a time when she used to walk down Brick Lane with her children, aware of the history of the multi-ethnic street, and of the fact that the National Front was, then, a prominent presence in London's East End. The speaker's circumstances do not feature in the poem as the emphasis is on the past and present inhabitants of Brick Lane and the attitudes of their neighbours ('Airmail for memories / Shudders for dark nights / Swastikas for bus shelters / White skins for England'), but Rumens believes that her personal connection with the place was responsible for the poem's existence and that she could not have written it without this. She said recently,

Nobody can chronicle all suffering and you can only really be selected by experiences. I don't think you can select them cold-bloodedly either ... and if somebody says to me, 'Have you got a poem about Bosnia?' or 'Could you contribute to an anthology on the Gulf War?', I can't do that. It's not because I don't care ... as a human being, but ... they're not involved with me in that deep, imaginative way ... For me, there would absolutely have to be a personal link.

For Rumens, politics without personal engagement does not produce poetry, though she does not, and never has seen herself as an activist, except in 'a literary way'. Thinking of her work for the Palach Press (which involved helping to produce samizdat literature – a bulletin on human rights abuses in Czechoslovakia), the campaigning she did for International PEN (for the release of political prisoners such as the Russian writer, Ratushinskaya), her work for the Jan Hus Educational Foundation (which took her to Czechoslovakia in the late eighties when, as she recalls, 'Things had lightened up a bit but it was still before the really big changes'), and the trip she made to Czechoslovakia as a messenger for the Palach Press in 1983, not every-one would agree. She wrote about the last event very indirectly in 'A Prague Dusk, August 21st 1983' (*ToS*, 90), focusing, as she later related, on the sense of

complete stasis and a real feeling of oppression, a heavy weight that really seemed to hang over the streets ... People looked thoroughly miserable, looked threatened, looked at me suspiciously because I was obviously a foreigner.

She had gone 'to take material in that couldn't have been sent safely through the post', but the trip became potentially 'disastrous' when she realised that communications had broken down and one of the people she was supposed to call on, did not answer his door:

I had to keep going back to this flat and I was absolutely terrified of alerting the police and being trailed ... I took some other things in ... money and books, and gave them to people, but it was a very frightening trip. It was OK for me; I might have been questioned and that would have been it, but for these people who were actually involved in politics, if I'd alerted any authorities' interest in them they could have been in labour camps ... I'm glad I did it ... You were expected to go as a messenger – and I got material for poems as well, but that was not why I did it.

Reading 'A Prague Dusk', it is clear that this is true because Rumens does not exploit the situation in which she found herself, nor the people with whom she was briefly involved, beyond creating some powerful evocations – from the atmosphere on the Czechoslovakian streets where, when a young soldier leaves a bar,

> Eyes follow him out,
> each glint of hate a coin
> with its own private value.

– to the oppression that closes in on a young mother as she returns from a picnic with her children, in the country which

> never changed,
> monotonous and tender
> as the afternoons of motherhood;

and where, for a short time, she had been able to feel free. While, like most writers, reserving the right to fictionalize and enter into any imagined experience, Rumens has always been uneasy about seeming to be presumptuous. She has revised her poem 'Outside Osweicim'[17] three times for this reason, concerned that 'somebody who'd experienced a concentration camp might feel it was offensive'. During this process it became 'a poem for voices' to signify 'that I'm not pretending to the experience: I'm just, in a way, writing a play' but, by the time she was preparing her second volume of selected poems in 1993, she became self-critical once more, this time at the thought of 'milking it for pathos' through the final stanza in the voice of an eighteen year old female victim: the stanza was removed. She acknowledges that her queries about this poem have always been moral rather than poetic. It is possible that the piece may change form yet again: 'I wonder if it might be a play, perhaps a radio play'. In its present version the reader is more distanced from the victims' voices, which sound across the years less assertively than before. It is still a poem of powerful emotion: several stanzas are more moving because of certain changes ('No, come away, bury yourself in the pit / of tears, be ash and stone, your stare / like his, a star'), others, less so, but perhaps there could be a justification for keeping the earlier, moving ending.

Born in 1944, Rumens does not consider the holocaust to be a distant event on the fringes of her own life. As a young teenager she was so strongly affected by seeing the concentration camp liberations on newsreels, and so appalled at this evidence of what human beings could do to each other that she lost her religious faith, which had been very strong up to that time: it has never returned. So, although she has no Jewish ancestors to her knowledge (*ToS*, 111–12), she has always been deeply impressed by the courage of the Jewish people and has empathized with them. In its motivation to commemorate those who died in Auschwitz, her poem and its ability to move the reader, for many, will transcend concerns about exploitation.

'The Hebrew Class' (*ToS*, 71), set in the early 1980s, when Rumens had started to learn Hebrew, was inspired by the courage of Kitty Hart, a woman who survived Auschwitz. She is not mentioned in the poem but her defiant act, as a teenage schoolgirl in Germany, of pushing her arm through a window rather than make the required Nazi salute, provided Rumens with an example of 'that kind of courage to say "No", that I was thinking about when I wrote the poem'. Opening with an icy, porcelain-like pavement that brings in a reference to Dresden, a reader's associations shift from ice to china to Germany, and the distantly, yet still painfully remembered events of the Second World War (the ice is 'smoking still'), while 'and in lands more deeply frozen, / the savage thaw of tanks' also takes in the present with the martial law that was imposed on Poland at the time and the tanks which, Rumens recalls, 'were actually brought into Gdansk at one particularly bad point of the Solidarity protests'.

Although it begins on a strong, international, political note, out in the cold, the second stanza, inside the warm classroom, suggests a personal recollection of childhood. The speaker, sitting in a largely, but not entirely, Jewish class of adults, rediscovers the powerful desire to please and recognizes its dangers in other, less benign circumstances. As an adult, temporarily reliving a past childhood, the speaker makes an impassioned address to the children of the present or the future and the main thrust of the poem lies in its symmetry:

> Consider your sweet compliance
>
> in the light of that day when the book
> is torn from your hand;
> when, to answer correctly the teacher's command,
> you must speak for this ice, this dark.

'The Hebrew Class' and 'Outside Oswiecim' are examples of the way in which I believe Carol Rumens fulfils Denise Levertov's belief that the writer has an obligation to be responsible for her words and must 'acknowledge their potential influence on the lives of others'.[18]

In 1983 Rumens was quoted as saying, 'My poems are one-sided conversations, they are usually written to people'.[19] The intimacy this implies, between poet and imagined reader, is also strongly present in much of Levertov's work [20] and indicates one way in which these poets coincide in their methods to bring the personal and the political together. The title of Levertov's 'Perhaps no poem but all I can say and I cannot be silent',[21] stresses the very personal nature of the piece and the compulsion she felt to express her feelings. Initially descriptive, it introduces the reader to her mixed Jewish and Christian heritage, then moves into a political mode when it focuses attention on the combined guilt of Jews and Christians in the Shatila massacre in Lebanon (also bringing in the fact that Levertov is writing a libretto about the suffering and deaths in El Salvador when she learns of this). Its biggest impact is achieved through the personal sadness expressed in relation to her parents, who are directly addressed at the close. That nothing has been learnt from so many, previous tragedies, and the grief this would have caused her parents had they lived, creates a powerful and moving final image of bones, too weary from earlier burdens to take on new ones, thankfully relieved of this through death. In her essay, 'Poetry, Prophecy, Survival', Levertov reflected:

> It has been said that the personal is political. I'm not always sure what that means, but I know that to me the obverse is often true, and it is when I feel the political/social issues personally that I'm moved to write of them, in just the same spirit of quest, of talking to myself in quest of revelation or illumination, that is a motivating force for more obviously 'personal poems'.[22]

In 'Thinking about El Salvador'[23] with its imagery of severed heads and silenced tongues, Levertov's own anguish that such things are happening drives her to declare her own sense of speechlessness, which reflects the silence of the murdered. Paradoxically, in expressing their silence, she manages to give the mute dead a powerful channel of communication with her readers. The personal element in this poem comes through in the speaker's empathy with and attempts to individualize the victims – and a poignant, personal footnote which alerts the reader to the role of the United States government in continuing slaughter, indicates that the political element is also educational. Both Levertov and Rumens are concerned with what the living can learn by acknowledging the dead – not just in terms of recognizing the suffering, innocence, and courage which the latter frequently displayed, though that is often the case ('Advent 1966', 'Thinking about El Salvador', and 'Outside Osweicim') – but also in the sense of recognizing the need to mark their very existence. In 'Vocation',[24] Levertov asserts that our entitlement to call ourselves 'human' is solely due to heroic past lives and in a late, remarkable poem, 'The Change',[25] she shows how the dead can be a necessary burden which, once accepted as such, allows the speaker in the poem to share their vision and recognize her affinity with them.

In 'Until We Could Hardly See Them' (*ToS*, 14), Carol Rumens expresses a related idea poignantly. Even though she has said that living in Belfast was not its inspiration, it is possible to view the poem as a justification of reaching back to remember the dead of all present and past political struggles, to the holocaust and beyond. At the end readers become directly involved, not just in the act of remembering and commemorating past victims, but also as potential victims themselves. On a less political level, it can be read as a justification to remember the dead, whoever they are and however they died, because without this they disappear without trace – as we will, ourselves, if we are not remembered in turn:

> They say we take after them.
> They say we're their living image
> And indeed we will be, that day
> We ask nothing more of the future,
> Only not to be left like shadows on the road
> Where so many became no one.

The poem was written after Rumens had seen a television programme about a man who formed a Christian organisation in Poland to help Jews, who had lost relatives in the concentration camps, trace them and find out what had happened. Many, who had lost their families, spoke with gratitude on the programme and Rumens tried to imagine what it might feel like to be in their situation. The need to understand what had been endured, and to remember those who had died, impressed her. The poem was also, in part, a response to criticism that experiences should not be assumed by those who have not lived them. In relation to this poem she has said, 'I was thinking: people take offence, the living take offence, but I'm sure the dead wouldn't – and it was almost as if I had this vision of these old people who were saying, 'Look, you don't really know, but say what you do know; it's better than nothing.' She stands by the statement she gave to the Poetry Book Society in 1983, when her volume *Star Whisper* was its summer choice:

> I do not belong to that school of thought which says that in the face of extreme horror, suffered by others, one should be silent. On the contrary, I believe that all the forces of the imagination should be employed to speak of their suffering. In the same way I believe that, as a feminist, I must still look through other windows than those granted to me purely by virtue of my gender. Like geography, like race, gender is not enough.[26]

Those final words focus on her increasingly off-centre relationship with feminist politics – an approach which resembles, to some degree, that of Levertov.

As Sandra M. Gilbert has observed, Denise Levertov 'is not an aggressively feminist poet',[27] but is a poet conscious of her female experience and how to express it in relation to the world at large. Like Rumens, she has written of the split female self in 'The Earthwoman and the Waterwoman'[28] but, unlike the latter's 'Two Women' (*ToS*, 103), the relationship portrayed between the split selves is not painful, and even Levertov's later poems, 'In Mind' and 'The Woman',[29] can be read as expressions of female complexity which, however problematic, women need and men must accept. In 'The Task'[30] she could seem deliberately feminist in the way she replaces an image of a male God with one of unspecified gender by omitting pronouns in the main body of the poem – but, as she explained to Lorrie Smith, while not finding the idea inappropriate, she did not want 'to lend lip service' to the concept of a female God and was concerned to avoid alienating any of her readers.[31] Levertov may express a different kind of feminism to Adrienne Rich, with whom she has been compared, but critics have recognised that their approaches are not uncomplimentary.

Carol Rumens, on the other hand, despite deservedly receiving credit for many powerfully feminist poems, has also been criticized by Lyn Pykett, for 'attempting to distance herself and … everyone else, from feminism by proclaiming a "post-feminist" era of poetry in her Chatto anthology'[32] and, to some degree, also in her own poems.

Pykett's main criticism of Rumens concerns her perceived refusal to acknowledge a debt to and membership of the feminist movement:

> these 'non-feminist' writers intervene in the discourses of femi-
> nism, and appropriate feminist perspectives and debates as a means
> of addressing their own concerns. Moreover, when they write on
> women's concerns or of their own, specifically female experience,
> they do so with a confidence and authority borrowed from the
> women's movement.[33]

Attempting to demonstrate a separation from the feminist movement in this way seems problematic where Rumens is concerned.

In relation to the much debated term 'post-feminist poetry', Pykett does not mention the new introduction to *Making for the Open*, which Rumens published in the revised edition of her anthology in 1987, and in which she addresses many of the points Pykett raises. Acknowledging that 'post-feminist' was 'commonly misconstrued as "anti-feminist"' in 1985, Rumens expresses her bemusement that it was

> refused the dispensation granted to a similar term, 'post-modernist',
> which is commonly allowed to mean 'modernist – and more'.

In her new introduction she accepts that 'some of the criticism seemed justified' on the grounds that she may not have defined her terms 'with sufficient clarity' and the carefully reasoned explanation which follows makes it quite clear that '*Making for the Open* is not a work of opposition to feminism but it undeniably opposes the feminist aesthetic in its extremer forms': Rumens goes on to justify her decisions effectively. Like Levertov, she argues for poetry's 'integrity as art' above all and, in attempting to represent the, hitherto, neglected 'woman poet who felt herself primarily to be a poet',[34] it could be argued that she was advancing the feminist cause, rather than hindering it.

Rumens may, as Pykett suggests, be ambivalent about some aspects of feminism (as was Levertov), but she is quite unequivocal in her assertion:

> I don't see how any intelligent woman could not be a feminist. I
> would consider myself a feminist, but I don't know whether I would
> say I was a feminist poet because I wouldn't put the politics ahead
> of everything else.

She does not refuse to acknowledge a debt to the feminist movement:

> I would say that my poems had drawn strength from that [the woman's movement], but ... I began as a poet long before I'd even heard of the word feminism ... before I was a woman ... I was just a child who loved poetry and read poets. I didn't care who'd written the poem if I liked it, and by the time I was aware of feminism, I'd written a lot. If the woman's movement hadn't happened it wouldn't have stopped me writing, but because it did happen, it was another resource – so I do owe something to it, but I don't owe everything to it.

She excluded most of her first volume, *A Strange Girl in Bright Colours*, from her latest selected poems, for aesthetic reasons: 'I'm not suppressing it because it's feminist; I'm suppressing it because I don't feel it's good technically.' Readers of poems like 'Houses by Day', 'Menopause', and the Plathian, 'A Death', may not accept this, but can gain comfort from the evidence they will find, in *Thinking of Skins* and the intervening volumes, that Rumens has 'gone on writing feminist poems, perhaps with a small f' – and some of her latest efforts are the most effective. Behind 'Stealing the Genre' (*ToS*, 36) is a deliberate attempt by a non-Irish, female poet to stake her claim in the traditionally Irish, male, Aisling genre of 'the cloud woman; she was Mother Ireland and she was poetic inspiration'. Rarely are such poems set in a public bar, but Rumens does not break all the rules; the Irish muse remains female and the tender encounter (not without wry humour) which results between two women creates the poem to which the speaker felt, at first, she had no right to aspire. That she dared at all, emphasizes the importance of the artistic quest to Carol Rumens, and draws her closer to Denise Levertov who, however secure her personal circumstances became, considered herself, 'as an artist, forever a stranger and pilgrim'.[35]

Notes

1. Peter Forbes, 'Out of Line', *New Statesman and Society*, 26 Nov. 1993, p. 43.
2. Denise Levertov interviewed by Sybil Estess, in *American Poetry Observed: Poets on their Work*, ed. Joe David Bellamy (Urbana and Chicago: University of Illinois Press, 1984), p. 157.
3. Ibid., p. 158.

4. All Denise Levertov's poetry and prose volumes referred to were published in the USA by New Directions and, since 1986, Bloodaxe Books have also published her poetry in the UK, as well as her prose collection, *Tesserae* (1997).
5. Denise Levertov, *Light up the Cave* (New York: New Directions, 1981), pp. 127–8.
6. Terence Des Pres, 'Poetry and Politics', *Tri Quarterly* 65 (1986), p. 17.
7. Lorrie Smith, 'An Interview with Denise Levertov', *Michigan Quarterly Review* 24 (1985), p. 597.
8. Cynthia Fuller, 'Denise Levertov', *Independent*, 27 Dec. 1997.
9. Isobel Armstrong, 'The Matter of Home', *Times Literary Supplement*, 11 Mar. 1994.
10. Carol Rumens, *Selected Poems* (London: Chatto & Windus, 1987), p. 110.
11. Carol Rumens, 'A Railway Child', *The Bloodaxe Catalogue* (1993), p. 17.
12. Carol Rumens interviewed by Marion Lomax, 21 Aug. 1998. Extracts from this interview are published in *Poetry Review*, ed. Peter Forbes, 89. 1 (1999). Unless otherwise noted, all quotations by Carol Rumens are taken from this source.
13. Smith, p. 596.
14. *Poetry Review*, ed. Peter Forbes, 88. 2 (1998), p. 48.
15. *The Bloodaxe Catalogue*, pp. 16–17.
16. Carol Rumens, *Thinking of Skins: New and Selected Poems* (Newcastle: Bloodaxe, 1993) pp. 15, 147, 58. Future references in the text will be to *ToS*.
17. The versions appear in *Direct Dialling, Selected Poems* (1987), and *Thinking of Skins*.
18. Denise Levertov, *New and Selected Essays* (New York: New Directions, 1992), pp. 135–6.
19. Hugh Herbert, 'The Way to Turn the Whisper into a Shout', *Guardian*, 17 June 1983, p. 12.
20. See Lorrie Smith, 'Dialogue and the Political Imagination in Denise Levertov and Adrienne Rich' in *World, Self, Poem*, ed. Leonard M. Trawick (Kent, OH: Kent State University Press, 1990).
21. Denise Levertov, *Oblique Prayers* (Newcastle: Bloodaxe, 1986), p. 33.
22. Levertov, *New and Selected Essays*, p. 150.
23. Levertov, *Oblique Prayers*, p. 32.
24. Ibid., p. 31.
25. Denise Levertov, *Sands of the Well* (Newcastle: Bloodaxe, 1997), p. 62.
26. *Poetry Book Society Bulletin* 117 (Summer 1983).
27. Sandra M. Gilbert, 'Revolutionary Love: Denise Levertov and the Poetics of Politics', in *Conversant Essays: Contemporary Poets on Poetry*, ed. James McCorkle (Detroit: Wayne State University Press, 1990), p. 270.
28. Denise Levertov, *Selected Poems* (Newcastle: Bloodaxe, 1986), p. 12.
29. Ibid., pp. 57, 115.
30. Levertov, *Oblique Prayers*, p. 72.
31. Smith 'Interview', pp. 602–3.
32. Lyn Pykett, 'Women Poets and "Women's Poetry": Fleur Adcock, Gillian Clarke and Carol Rumens', in *British Poetry from the 1950s to the 1990s: Politics and Art*, ed. Gary Day and Brian Docherty (Basingstoke: Macmillan, 1997), p. 255.

33. Ibid., p. 262.
34. *Making for the Open: Post-Feminist Poetry*, ed. Carol Rumens (London: Chatto and Windus, 1987), pp. xiv–xviii.
35. Levertov, *New and Selected Essays*, p. 245.

18

'The Stain of Absolute Possession': The Postcolonial in the Work of Eavan Boland

Rose Atfield

'I am an Irish poet and a woman poet. In the first category I enter the tradition of the English language at an angle. In the second, I enter my own tradition at an even more oblique angle.'[1] Boland's awareness of a dual colonialism is established in the Ronald Duncan lecture for the Poetry Book Society where she refers to 'two identities' which 'shape and reshape what I have to say'.[2] Postcolonialism in the work of Eavan Boland is the result of a process of recognition and exposure of colonialism in its denial and repression of identity and the restoration and reconstruction of that identity in terms of place, history and literary tradition.

Boland employs a traditional representation of colonialism of place as physical location in the reading of maps, in her poem 'In Which the Ancient History I Learn Is Not My Own'.[3] Here Boland recalls the 'linen map' on which

> The colours
> were faded out
> so the red of Empire –
> the stain of absolute possession –
> ... was
> underwater coral.

The bloody implication of a forcible 'possession' the red stain of empire on the map produces is echoed in the third verse of a more recent poem, 'The Harbour',[4] where the word possession is conspicuous by its absence:

Officers and their wives promenaded
on this spot once and saw with their own eyes
the opulent horizon and obedient skies
which nine tenths of the law provided.

Later verses of 'In Which the Ancient History I Learn Is Not My Own', explore, through a wry irony, the associated sense of displacement and loss of identity that the experience of 'exile' created in Boland, who, although born in Dublin, lived with her parents in London as a child:

Ireland was far away
and farther away
every year.
I was nearly an English child.
I could list the English kings.
I could name the famous battles.
I was learning to recognise
God's grace in history.

Boland suggests in an essay on 'The Woman, The Place, The Poet' that 'what we call place is really only that detail of it which we understand to be ourselves', and continues 'I learned quickly, by inference at school and reference at home, that the Irish were unwelcome in London ... All I knew, all I needed to know, was that none of this was mine' (RD). This reaction and the teacher's insensitivity to it is dramatised in the poetic recreation of the lesson:

The teacher's voice had a London accent.
This was London. 1952.
It was Ancient History class ...

Remember this, children,

The Roman Empire was
the greatest empire
ever known –
until our time of course –

Later in the poem Boland's represents the memory of repression of identity and its attempted restoration and reconstruction in terms of place:

… Suddenly
I wanted
to stand in front of it.
I wanted to trace over
and over the weave of my own country.
To read out names
I was close to forgetting.
Wicklow. Kilruddery. Dublin.

The sense of being one of the colonised, despite her father's diplo-
matic status as a Southern Ireland representative in London and living
in the Irish embassy, is further underlined in another recollection of
this time, 'I made a distinction between a city one loved and a city one
submitted to. I had not loved London, for instance, where I had spent
the greater part of my childhood. The iron and gutted stone of its
postwar prospect had seemed to me merely hostile'.[5] The terms
'submitted' and 'hostile' give this personal reminiscence a wider political significance and extend it into an examination of the effect of
such displacement on Boland's creative identity, as implied in another
essay, 'A Kind of Scar' : 'My image-makers as a child, therefore, were
refractions of my exile … For me, as for many another exile, Ireland
was my nation long before it was once again my country' (KS, 75).
     In the poem 'Anna Liffey' (*ITV*, 41–6) she continues the endeavour
to restore and reconstruct identity in terms of place, through her
exploration of the legend of the naming of Dublin's River Liffey:

> *Life,* the story goes,
> Was the daughter of Cannan,
> And came to the plain of Kildare …
>
> The river took its name from the land.
> The land took its name from a woman …
>
>   Maker of
> Places, remembrances,
> Narrate such fragments for me :
>
> One body. One Spirit.
> One place. One name.
> The city where I was born.
> The river that runs through it.

The nation which eludes me.

Fractions of a life
It has taken me a lifetime
To claim.

The personal and national claims are integrated in the poem which directly reflects a further expression of the underlying concern in a later part of the essay: 'Who the poet is, what she or he nominates as a proper theme for poetry, what self they discover and confirm through this subject matter – all of this involves an ethical choice. Poetic ethics are evident and urgent in any culture where tensions between a poet and her or his birthplace are inherited and established' (KS, 80).

This 'ethical choice' and the 'inherited tensions' are particularly evident in the exploration of the 'second category' of identity established by Boland in my opening quotation, 'a woman poet'. In Irish cultural convention, woman's place has been colonised, subjected to restricted and marginalised interpretation and representation. Nationalism has led to placing of an idealised, simplified, passive image of woman on a pedestal. Boland has examined this aspect of colonialism in a number of essays, explaining in 'A Kind of Scar':

When a people have been so dispossessed by events as the Irish in the 18th and 19th centuries an extra burden falls on the very idea of a nation ... The majority of Irish male poets depended on women as motifs in their poetry ... images of women in which I did not believe and of which I could not approve ... these passive and simplified women seemed a corruption ... a species of human insult that ... they should become elements of style rather than aspects of truth ... Once the idea of a nation influences the perception of a woman ... She becomes the passive projection of a national idea. (KS, 81)

In the poem 'Time and Violence' (*ITV*, 49–50), Boland dramatises an imaginative confrontation with such 'passive projections', in the form of typically idealised motifs, 'a shepherdess ... her arm injured from ... the pastorals where she posed ... Cassiopeia trapped ... a mermaid with invented tresses ...'. Having recognised and exposed such colonialism, Boland begins the restoration and reconstruction of female identity in terms of an alternative concept of woman's place. In traditional forms, as she suggested in her essay 'Outside History', 'the real woman behind the image was not only not explored, she was never even seen'.[6]

The challenge the poet imagines issued from the embodiments of the idealised national icons is a desperate plea for release, into what Boland clearly regards as true identity, humanity rather than the fallacious immortality of artifice :

> We cannot sweat here. Our skin is icy.
> We cannot breed here. Our wombs are empty.
> Help us to escape youth and beauty.
>
> Write us out of the poem. Make us human
> in cadences of change and mortal pain
> and words we can grow old and die in.

Boland recognised the challenge in comments published in 1989: 'I could not as a woman accept the nation formulated for me by Irish poetry and its traditions ... it seemed to me that I was likely to remain an outsider in my own national literature, cut off from its archive, at a distance from its energy. Unless, that is, I could repossess it.'[7] At that time, however, the poetic strategies necessary to achieve this repossession had not been realised; a year later Edna Longley suggested that the postcolonial restoration and reconstruction of identity had not been achieved : 'By not questioning the nation, Boland recycles the literary cliché from which she desires to escape ... without considering how that construct itself, both inside and outside poetry, has marginalised and scarred many Irish women and men.'[8] However, in the essay 'Outside History' in 1990, Boland had established the approach of the sequence of poems of the same name published in 1994: 'my own discourse must be subversive ... I must be vigilant to write of my own womanhood... in such a way that I never colluded with the simplified images of women in Irish poetry.'[9]

By 1994 the 'subversive discourse' had been explored in a number of poems described in an interview as 'Writing about the lost, the voiceless, the silent ... exploring my relation to them ... more dangerous still – feeling my ways into the powerlessness of an experience through the power of expressing it'.[10] In 'Story' (*ITV*, 47–8), the powerlessness of the experience into which she feels her way is that of the traditional legend of threatened lovers. She imaginatively enters the restrictive and prescriptive idealised representation of the character of the woman and the powerlessness of her colonised place:

> They do not know. They have no idea
> how much of this : the ocean-coloured peace
>
> of the dusk, and the way legend stresses it,
> depend on her to be young and beautiful.

As the poem progresses Boland moves with it, into the world of a specific woman, not colluding 'with the simplified images' but representing a restoration of female identity in the everyday details of a lived domestic life :

> ... suddenly what is happening is not
> what happens to the lovers in the wood
>
> ... But what is whispering out of sycamores ...
>
> ... And is travelling to enter a suburb
> at the foothills of the mountains in Dublin.
>
> And a garden with jasmine and poplars. And
> a table at which I am writing. I am writing
>
> a woman out of legend. I am thinking
> how new it is – this story. How hard it will be to tell.

The 'new story' which is so hard to tell is not only that of 'real women' but of the woman poet telling the story. In 'Formal Feeling' (*LL*, 56), she describes a similar progression in her re-telling of the Eros and Psyche story, from the traditional presentation of the myth to a modern reassessment. Boland challenges the conventional assumption, of a poet's gender as masculine and of women poets covertly doing what is considered man's work, which she suggests is still evident :

> ... a woman still
> addresses the work of a man in the dark of the night ...

The potential subversiveness of this is celebrated in the final lines of the poem, in a dramatic confrontation of poet with her subject as she calls on the mythic character to consider the contemporary woman poet's activity :

Eros look down.

> ... And see the difference.
> This time – and this you did not ordain –
> I am changing the story.

Thus another kind of colonialism exposed by Boland is that of the literary and cultural establishment in Ireland and the consequent denial of the female voice: colonialism can generally be defined as establishment of ruling power systems by imposition, and Boland remarks that 'power has just as much to do with a poetic sphere of operation as any other...power has operated in the making of canons, the making of taste, the nominating of what poems should represent the age and so on.'[11]

She talks in an interview in 1991 of the difficulty of establishing any place for women writers in the cultural milieu :

> the ugly part is the intimidation for a woman to write a poem, get a book together, wonder where it's going to be published, how it will be received. In other words, the ugly part in every single minority in a writing culture is, 'Where does the power lie? Who has the power?... the contemporary poetry course in Trinity this year carried not one woman poet!... The male Irish poets have treated exclusion as invention but there is absolutely no doubt that that exists. There is no give on this issue. It is a matter of fact ... If you look back at *Eire Ireland* for example, there are almost no references to women's writing.'[12]

This denial of female identity has been counteracted to some extent by Boland's own provision of poetry workshops for women writers, but the cultural imposition, or what she has called 'the weight of the feminine convention on the individual woman',[13] has exacerbated this colonial exclusivity. As she recalls:

> there is not an equal societal commission here for people to explore their individuality in an expressive way – for a woman to cross the distance in writing poetry to becoming a poet. 'If I called myself a poet,' a young woman in one of my workshops told me, 'people would think I didn't wash my windows' ... this community nominates women as the receptors of other people's creativity and not as the initiators of their own.'[14]

In 'Bright Cut Irish Silver',[15] Boland resists the concept of poetic art as a male birthright; she uses the correlative of silver mining, restoring female identity in terms of women's place in creative artistry by advocating the usurpation of poetic tradition:

> This gift for wounding an artery of rock
> was passed on from father to son, to the father
> of the next son;
>
> is an aptitude
> for injuring earth while inferring it in curves and surfaces;
>
> is this cold potency which has come,
> by time and chance,
>
> into my hands.

The postcolonial stance is emphasised by the references to previous 'wounding … injuring … cold potency', implying the aggressive imposition of creative skill which will now be transformed to a more positive collaboration.

In 1991 Boland commented: 'the critique in this country remains obdurately male and patriarchal … Although a great deal of vital work by women has been done, the critique is really sitting on top of it. It's made up of an older writing culture which is predominantly male.'[16] In 1994 she still emphasised the colonialism of the literary-critical establishment in Ireland: 'there won't be good or valuable criticism of this whole area until it's understood that the issues raised by the woman poet are the issues central to poetry now … questions about voice and the self … not to mention the crucial relation of the poet to the act of power …'.[17] However she has opened the way for other women poets to move in from the outskirts and find their place, as she asserts, 'Poetry is not a fiefdom or a private domain. It is a city whose gates stand wide' (RD).

A colonised people's identity is often denied in the suppression of its history. Where Irish experience has been marginalised, Boland restores significance; as she said in an interview, 'you can accept the history on face value and write out of that but I don't want to. I feel a great need to somehow get behind that history as a woman and as a poet, to the great source out of which the history comes and of which it is only a fragment.'[18] One of the most appalling eras of loss in Irish history, notoriously mismanaged by the governmental relief organisation, was the famine, evidence of which still scars the landscape although it is literally obliterated in terms of cartographical record. In the poem 'That the Science of Cartography Is Limited' (*ITV*, 5), Boland reclaims the human aspect of the basic facts of dates and death :

> ... this was once a famine road.
>
> 1847, when the crop had failed twice,
> Relief Committees gave
> the starving Irish such roads to build.
>
> Where they died, there the road ended ...
>
> and ends still and when I take down
> the map of this island, it is ...
>
> ... to tell myself again that
>
> the line which says woodland and cries hunger
> and gives out among sweet pine and cypress,
> and finds no horizon
>
> will not be there.

The poet's imaginative empathy crosses the generations and breaks through the barrier of signs and symbols to individual suffering. The starkness of the final line exposes and challenges the colonial perspective of denial, which is satirically exposed in another poem, the title of which relates the personae directly to the same historical moment, 'March 1 1847. By the First Post' (*ITV*, 7). Here the insensitive arrogance of the colonial presence in Ireland is also individualised in the self-centred concerns of society ladies; the imaginative recreation of the circumstances in epistolary form effectively dramatises the contrasting perspective. The English woman denies any sense of identity to the Irish by concentrating only on her inconvenience, ignoring the desperate plight of another woman who, but for an accident of history, might have been in her place :

> ... A woman lying
> across the Kells Road with her baby –

in full view. We had to go
out of our way
to get home & we were late
& poor Mama was not herself all day.

It is the personalisation of history which brings it to life and restores
the identity of those whose past has shaped the Irish present; this is
demonstrated in Boland's awareness of its repression in official record
in which previously she has colluded, unwittingly, as she suggests in
'Inscriptions' (*ITV*, 11–12) where her frame of reference is particu-
larised by focusing her imaginative attention on a specific item, a
child's cot painted with his name, Peter:

Someone knew
the importance of giving him a name.

For years I have known
how important it is
not to name
the coffins, the murdered in them,
the deaths in alleyways and on doorsteps –

in case they rise out of their names
and I recognise

the child who slept peacefully
and the girl who guessed at her future ...

It is the recognition of her own denial which endorses Boland's
exposure of the colonial repression of Irish identity in the nation's
history; naming individuals evokes a more uncomfortable reality
which cannot so easily be ignored. This colonialism imbued the literature Boland studied and thus influenced her own early work, as she
acknowledges in the poem 'The Necessity for Irony' (*LL*, 54–5)

When I was young
I studied styles ...

... and was always drawn
to a lyric speech, a civil tone.
But never thought

> I would have the need,
> as I do now, for a darker one ...

This 'darker' tone is that of irony, a powerful element in her later poetic practice, described later in the poem as 'my caustic author / of the past, of memory'. She confirms her earlier absorption of colonial influence in a lecture, 'The poem I wrote was nominally called Irish, yet it was blemished by the music of drawing rooms and light tenor voices ... it averted its eyes from the harsh facts of the loss of a language and the abandonment of history ... A darker 19th century, a more bitter 18th century demanded to be acknowledged' (RD).

The self-recognition of unwitting implication is also recognised and examined in 'The Mother Tongue' (*LL*, 30–1), in which Boland admits, 'I speak with the forked tongue of colony.' Later, however, the poem expands into a vision of reconciliation and resistance to the divisions which have for so long separated peoples, poets and genders; a yearning for language which will express harmony rather than dissonance, as the poet imagines

> my pure sound, my undivided speech
> travelling to the edge of this silence.
> As if to find me.

Characteristically, Boland acknowledges the ambiguity of this state, should it ever be reached; the loss as well as the gain: 'I listen: I hear ... what I am safe from. What I have lost.' In her most recent collection, there is more of this fragmented form, the short, sharp phrases balanced with more fluid, meditative expression, perhaps underlining in form the recognition and identification of and with both colonised and colonisers, expressed in 'Daughters of Colony' (*LL*, 16): 'I also am a daughter of the colony. / I share their broken speech, their otherwhereness.' The suggestion is that although the speaker feels more at one with those indigenous Irish women whose 'flat landscape' the colonisers 'Would never enter', all are colonised in terms of the repression of their history,

> No testament or craft of mine can hide
> our presence
> on the distaff side of history.

The same 'abandonment of history' is recognised in another

example of the poet's particular facility for imaginative empathy and developed as a postcolonial strategy counteracting earlier denial, in the poem 'In a Bad Light' (*ITV*, 8). In this poem she moves from the contemplation of a doll clothed in period costume, to identification with the colonised peoples who would have sewn the fabric for the woman who had the resources and influence to travel to the New World of St Louis in 1860.

From her privileged position of distance in her own time, 'I stand in a room in the museum', Boland reads: 'A notice says no comforts / were spared. The silk is French. The seamstresses are Irish.' She then becomes one with those whose history has been abandoned, restoring their identity in reclaiming their part in this history :

> I am in the gas-lit backrooms.
> ... We are sewing
> coffin ships, and the salt of exile. And our own death in it. For
> history's abandonment we are doing this ...

The ironic contrast of the seamstresses' suffering with the ignorant pleasure of the woman is underlined in the presentation of the dress as a symbol of exploitation:

> We dream a woman on a steamboat parading in sunshine in a dress
> we know we made. She laughs off rumours of war. She turns and
> traps light on the skirt. It is, for that moment, beautiful.

In this recreation of women's experience, both colonisers and colonised, Boland again confirms the second of her declared identities, which she also emphasises in interview: 'I think it's important that Irish poets have a discourse with the idea of Irishness and I think it's probably very important that an Irish woman poet doesn't shirk that discourse because there have been gaps, vacancies or silences in the literature.'[19] In 'Daughters of Colony' (*LL*, 16), she describes this aspect of her poetic practice :

> I put my words between them
> and the silence
> the failing light has consigned them to ...

In her recognition and exposure of a dual colonialism Boland vocalises such silences, embodies the gaps and vacancies by reconstructing *her* story in history, restoring the identity of women in the Irish past. In an introduction to her collection *Outside History* for the Poetry Book Society she comments:

> I think a good few poems in the book are anchored in the conflict between the received version and the unofficial one ... So much that matters, so much that is powerful and frail in human affairs seems to me, increasingly, to happen outside history: away from the texts and symmetries of an accepted expression ... for that very reason, at risk of being edited out of the final account.[20]

As Margaret Ward suggested in 'The Missing Sex: Putting Women into Irish History', 'despite all our efforts, our foremothers remain in the margins, unknown to most'.[21] Eavan Boland went on a personal pilgrimage to recover one of hers, as she records in 'The Woman, The Place, The Poet'. She bears witness to the identity denied one of the typical inmates of the workhouse her great-grandfather ran:

> I refused to imagine him – my ancestor ... Instead, I imagined a woman...There were several reasons why she might have been there. The most obvious – unmarried motherhood – remains the most likely. She could as easily have been a survivor of an eviction – hundreds of them, complete with bailiff and battering ram, took place in Ireland every year ... was this where my great-grandfather had lived? At least, by these visible survivals, I could guess at his existence. There was no trace of hers ... She is part of all our histories ... (*WPP*, 102–3)

Boland inscribes the woman's identity through imaginative recreation; a similar witness is made to her grandmother, for whom she also creates a story and thus reconstructs a silent history. She defends this imaginative process as a validation of the life lived but only remembered through 'something thrown out once in a random conversation; / a hint merely.'; the history is derived from the 'Lava Cameo' (*ITV*, 35) of the poem's title, the static artefact which has been handed down and must be used as the catalyst for the revitalisation:

> ... there is a way of making free with the past,
> a pastiche of what is
> real and what is
> not, which can only be

justified if you think of it

not as sculpture but syntax:

a structure extrinsic to meaning which uncovers
the inner secret of it.

By 'making free' with the past, rather than being casually irresponsible
to the facts of the lives lived, Boland releases them from the restrictions, simplifications and marginalisation of colonialism; the static
'sculpture' gives way to the fluid 'syntax', the dead stone to the living
word.

Boland exposes the disregard of women's contribution to Irish
history, such as the suffrage movement, noted by Margaret Ward as
being reduced to marginalia in even fairly recent standard textbooks:
'The professional historian's level of awareness concerning women's
contribution to politics and society can only be described as abysmal
... the effects of this blinkered vision are not confined within the walls
of academia.'[22]

Boland recognises this ubiquitous 'blinkered vision', referring to
Irish popular culture and literary expression reflecting an internal
colonialism, '... it has never admitted of women. Its flags and songs
and battle-cries, even its poetry ... make use of feminine imagery ...
the true voice and vision of women are routinely excluded.'[23] This
remark is made in the essay 'Outside History' and in the poem of the
same title Boland offers a way forward, exposing the idealised mythical
representation of women and reconstructing a more realistic identity :

I have chosen:

out of myth into history I move to be
part of that ordeal ...

How slowly they die
as we kneel beside them, whisper in their ear.
And we are too late. We are always too late.

Boland rejects the traditional concept of women as merely carers, the
comforters after the battle, at the edges, on the periphery of history,
'too late' to have any significant effect. She challenges the sanitisation
of women in myth, the decorative adjuncts of the real action in the

male world, in another remark in the essay, 'in using and re-using women as icons and figments, Irish poets were not just dealing with emblems. They were also evading the real women of an actual past: women whose silence their poetry should have broken.'[24]

The postcolonial response to this challenge comes in restoration of these women's identities through reclaiming the history previously unrecognised and unregarded. It has been the journey of Boland's professional writing life to do this, a counterpart to the physical pilgrimage she made to the site of her ancestor's workhouse. At first she despaired the lack of matrilineal poetic foremothers, commenting: 'I did not feel in possession of a tradition. I simply felt that I could not record the life I lived in the poem I wrote, unless I could find my name in the poetic past ... when I turned to the tradition to find support for that visionary claim, I could not find it. The name of my life was missing in the history of my form' (RD).

In 'The Achill Woman',[25] she records a confrontation with a real woman who she could not write into her poem without betraying the history the woman represented; the poem is a searingly honest indict-ment of her failure yet in itself it establishes a great distance travelled from the position described:

> She came up the hill carrying water...
>
> ... I was all talk, raw from college –
> week-ending at a friend's cottage
> with one suitcase and the set text
> of the court poets of the Silver Age.
>
> We stayed putting down time until
> the evening turned cold without warning.
>
> ... but nothing now can change the way I went
> indoors ...
>
> ... took down my book
> and opened it and failed to comprehend
>
> the harmonies of servitude ...
>
> ...

In a prose version of this incident, from her essay 'A Kind of Scar', Boland again castigates herself but also recognises the responsibility of the colonised literary-historical tradition in which she was brought up:

> I knew, without having words for it, that she came from a past which affected me ... I went in, lit a fire, took out my book of English court poetry and memorised all over again – with no sense of irony or omission – the cadences of power and despair ... nothing that I understood about poetry enabled me to understand her better ... I turned my back on her in that cold twilight and went to commit to memory the songs and artifices of the very power systems which had made her own memory such an archive of loss. (KS, 74, 77–8)

She exposes the falsification of the record produced by such 'songs and artifices', 'How had the women of our past ... suffered Irish history and inscribed themselves in the speech and memory of the Achill woman, only to re-emerge in the Irish poetry as fictive queens and national sibyls?' (KS, 81). Her answer is to produce a postcolonial history through an alternative poetic representation, as she described in interviews, 'For a poet like myself, who comes into the tradition at an oblique angle, experiments of usurpation can be ... exciting and rewarding. Turning the poem inside out. Taking the nature poem, the dream-poem, the love poem and subverting them ... I don't have a desire to separate myself from the body politic of poetry. I have a great desire to subvert what is there. In this sense, the invention of a male muse would have been a separatist initiative, the holding to a female one would be a subversive one.'[26] In the poem 'Time and Violence' (*ITV*, 49–50), Boland exposes colonialism in the literary tradition of 'fictive queens and national sybils'; its denial and repression of what she sees as the true identity of Irish women, by subverting the aisling or vision-poem and offering a postcolonial representation of the female muse:

> ... a voice was saying:
>
> This is what language did to us. Here
> is the wound, the silence, the wretchedness
> of tides and hillsides and stars where
>
> we languish in a grammar of sighs,

in the high-minded search for euphony,
in the midnight rhetoric of poesie.

In this poem, published in 1994, Boland offers an answer to the question with which she challenged herself in her 1989 essay, 'A Kind of Scar', 'Why do you ... write in forms explored and sealed by English men hundreds of years ago? You are Irish. You are a woman. Why do you keep these things at the periphery of the poem? Why do you not move them to the centre, where they belong?' (KS, 79)

By the time she came through to the elegant simplicity of the poem 'Anna Liffey' (*ITV*, 41–6) the confidence of having found that authority and claimed it for herself and others is celebrated :

> Make of a nation what you will
> Make of the past
> What you can –
> There is now
> A woman in a doorway.
>
> It has taken me
> All my strength to do this.
>
> Becoming a figure in a poem.
>
> Usurping a name and a theme

The same confidence in this postcolonial restoration of her woman's identity in literary tradition underlies her comment on her own work, 'I knew this world was worthy of poetry. I knew it deserved the visionary claim I wished to make on its behalf. I knew that I was Irish; I knew I was a woman; that these categories of identity made a duality of reference' (*ITV*, 41–6).

To return to the image of map-making at the beginning of this essay, Boland's final words in an interview after the publication of *In a Time of Violence* sum up her achievement and the concept of postcolonialism in her work: 'When the history of poetry in our time is written – I have no doubt about this – women poets will be seen to have re-written not just the poem, not just the image. They won't just have re-balanced elements within the poem. They will have altered the cartography of the poem. The map will look different' (RD). The postcolonial space mapped in this way is already occupied; Eavan Boland can take credit for contributing to the wider cultural encouragement of the Irish woman's voice through her poetic practice and to the continuing vocal presence, throughout the nineties, of those whom Mary Robinson (to whom Boland's most recent volume is dedicated) thanked in her victory speech at the beginning of the decade: 'the women of Ireland, *mna na hEireann*, who instead of rocking the cradle, rocked the system and who came out massively to make their mark on the ballot paper and on a new Ireland.'

Notes

1. Eavan Boland, 'Gods Make Their Own Importance: On the Authority of the Poet in Our Time', notes taken by the author at the Ronald Duncan Lecture, Southbank Centre, London, Oct. 1994; hereafter cited as RD.
2. Eavan Boland, *In a Time of Violence* (Manchester: Carcanet 1994), pp. 28–30; hereafter cited as *ITV*.
3. Eavan Boland, *The Lost Land* (Manchester: Carcanet 1998), p. 14; hereafter cited as *LL*.
4. Eavan Boland, 'The Woman, The Place, The Poet', *Georgia Review* 44.1/2 (1990), p. 100; hereafter cited as WPP.
5. Eavan Boland, 'A Kind of Scar: The Woman Poet in a National Tradition', in *Twelve Lips* (Dublin: Attic Press, 1989), p. 76; hereafter cited as KS.
6. Eavan Boland, 'Outside History', *American Poetry Review*, 19.2 (1990), pp. 32–8, repr. in *P.N. Review*, 17.1 (1990), p. 35.
7. Marilyn Reizbaum, 'An Interview with Eavan Boland', *Contemporary Literature*, 30.4 (1989), p. 476.
8. Edna Longley, 'From Cathleen to Anorexia : The Breakdown of Irelands', in *Twelve Lips* (Dublin: Attic Press 1990), p. 178.
9. Boland, 'Outside History', p. 36.
10. J. Allen-Randolph, 'An Interview with Eavan Boland', *Irish University Review*, 23.1 (1993), p. 129.
11. N. Means Wright and D.J. Hannan, 'Q&A with Eavan Boland', *ILS* 10.1 (1991), p. 10.
12. Ibid.
13. Adrian Frazier, interview with Eavan Boland, 'Nationalism and Obsession in Irish Poetry', *Literary Review* 22 (Winter 1979), p. 240.
14. Means Wright and Hannan, 'Q&A with Eavan Boland', p. 10.
15. Eavan Boland, *Outside History* (Manchester: Carcanet, 1990), p. 22.
16. Means Wright and Hannan, 'Q&A with Eavan Boland', p. 10.
17. Allen-Randolph, 'Interview', p. 130.
18. Deborah Tall, 'Q&A with Eavan Boland', *ILS* 7.3 (1988), p. 39.
19. Ibid., p.40.
20. Eavan Boland, *Poetry Book Society Bulletin* (London: Poetry Book Society, 1990).

21. Margaret Ward, 'The Missing Sex : Putting Women into Irish History', in *Twelve Lips* (Dublin: Attic Press 1991), p. 205.
22. Ward, 'The Missing Sex', p. 212.
23. Boland, 'Outside History', p. 45.
24. Ibid., p. 36.
25. Ibid., p. 27.
26. Allen-Randolph, 'Interview', p. 129.

19
'Now I Am *Alien*': Immigration and the Discourse of Nation in the Poetry of Carol Ann Duffy

Linda A. Kinnahan

For Carol Ann Duffy, the decade of the 1980s seems to have been disheartening. In a poem written on the cusp of the nineties, she lists in serial form items that 'may be prosecuted for appalling the Imagination', including quick jabs at emblems of right-wing ascendency in Western capitalism: 'President Quayle', 'British Rail', 'The Repatriation Charter', 'A Hubby', 'Bedtime with Nancy and Ron', 'Eating the Weakest Survivor', 'Homeless and Down to a Fiver'.[1] Signifying the shift in Britain from a post-war collectivism to a free-market economy (including the deregulation of the British Rail, a celebration of market individualism, and a retreat from social forms of responsibility), concurrent with a call to traditional family values (the heterosexual family as the primary unit of both society and the market) and a renewed nationalism (eliciting arguments over immigration and repatriation), the poem's juxtaposed soundbites position issues of economic policy, social control, and national identity in close relationship to one another. The poem, like others of Duffy's, suggests the intertwined rhetoric arising around these issues both during and prior to the years of Thatcher's three governments. Culminating the rise of the New Right in Britain, Thatcher's election in 1979 set in motion strategies of economic renewal that 'entailed a moral revolution: a return to individual responsibility, free market entrepreneurialism and British nationalism'.[2]

Accompanying this 'revolution', a rhetoric of British nationalism sought to redefine British identity and state as ethnic rather than empire; in effect, the language of populist discourse and of legal policy articulated new national boundaries to exclude previous subjects of the empire, often on the basis of their ethnic difference and in response to new immigration patterns.[3]

Part of a larger crisis of national identity brought on by the de-colonization process following the second world war, debates over immigration both cloaked and revealed questions of race, national identity, and social order. In post-empire Britain, the developing discourse of the New Right and of its most important variant, Thatcherism, increasingly associated nation with ethnicity, shaping a nostalgia for a 'true' Britain in danger of being completely 'swamped by an alien culture', effectively casting (non-white) immigration as an economic, cultural, and even moral obstacle to free-market prosperity.[4]

Carol Ann Duffy's poetry explores the discursive constructions surrounding the issues of immigration, ethnicity, and nationalism. A Scots-born poet who attended Liverpool University in the seventies before moving to London and then to Manchester, Duffy draws upon these urban, industrial environs to reflect the impact of changes in fiscal policy that lessened support for public programmes and by the increase in racial, ethnic, and class tensions attending debates over immigration. Moreover, Duffy's poetry – often in the form of dramatic monologues, including a number spoken in the voices of both immi-grants and nationalists – traverses ideological and discursive constructions of nationalism. Duffy's attention to the shaping power of words draws in many ways upon a feminist politics inflected by post-structural interrogations of language; moreover, her poetry's concern with the voices and positions of 'outsiders' – what Ian Gregson calls 'the desire to give a voice to those who are habitually spoken *for*' – may be motivated, in part, by her own experiences of marginality as both lesbian and Scottish.[5] However, the voices that speak in her poetry, rather than assuming a true or unified self capable of transparent expression through language, are inevitably intersected by discourses of national and cultural identity as they shape concepts of self and other, of affinity and difference, of belonging and exclu-sion. Drawing upon poems included in the four books Duffy published during or just after the Thatcher years – *Standing Female Nude* (1985), *Selling Manhattan* (1987), *The Other Country* (1990), and *Mean Time* (1993) – this essay will examine Duffy's treatment of national identity as a strategically constructed and disseminated rhetoric, situated within ideological contexts and material conditions developing in Britain in recent decades.[6]

The policies developed in response to post-colonial patterns of immigration in England legislated increasingly restrictive definitions of citizenship. Duffy's poetry not only is interested in the impact of these policies upon the material lives of the subjects they affect but also, through her formal manoeuvres, intervenes in the process by which language of identity becomes stabilized and naturalized to support an exclusionary nationalist agenda. Terms central to a discourse of ethnic nationalism, such as 'alien', 'British', 'family', or 'home', appeal to a stable, common sense notion of British identity from the perspective of the Anglo-ethnic subject; in Duffy's poetry, the meaning of these terms (and others like them) is contingent upon social position, revealing an instability of word arranged, by nationalist rhetoric, to seem stable in the face of the intersecting and unsettling complications of race, class, ethnicity, and gender. A word like 'family', transparently employed in discourses of British nationalism to signify the core of the nation, simultaneouly signifies a threat to that core when the family is immigrants. Duffy's poetry often plays upon the dissonance of such rhetorical shiftiness within a discourse claiming a natural authority, a true language. Before turning to Duffy's poems, the context of recent immigration policies and their attendant discourse will be briefly sketched.

The 1914 British Nationality and Status of Aliens Act conferred British subject status on all the inhabitants of the British Empire, although prior to 1948, the numbers of immigrants of color to arrive in England was slight. However, attracted by relative prosperity in Britain, and enabled by the 1948 British Nationality Act and its open-door policy towards immigration from British Commonwealth countries, unprecedented numbers of West Indian and Asian newcomers entered the country as British subjects or their descendants. To supply the needs of Britain's post-war boom, immigrant workers were often recruited in this decade to fill low-end labour needs; however, amidst slogans of 'Keep Britain White', racial conflict had developed by 1958, when an estimated 210,000 immigrants of colour were living in Britain. The violence perpetrated against blacks in Nottingham and Notting Hill by a group of 'teddy boys' (who called themselves 'nigger hunters') in this year marked the growing intolerance of racial and ethnic difference within which 'issues of racial discrimination, immigration control, and police conduct' would be debated for the next thirty years.[7]

By the early sixties, restrictions on immigration aimed at Commonwealth citizens began to alter the concept of British subjecthood. The 1962 Commonwealth Immigrants Act set up an entry system based on work vouchers and effectively restricted the flow of immigrants from the Caribbean and Indian sub-continent. Moving toward a 'process of racial categorization [that] lay at the heart of these measures' and those to follow, a second Commonwealth Immigrants Act in 1968 act limited the entry of Commonwealth citizens to individuals who could demonstrate a close ancestral relationship with the United Kingdom and thus, a predominantly white heritage.[8] Under the terms of the 1971 Immigration Act, any applicant for immigration was required to furnish evidence of 'patriality', that at least one grandparent had been born in the United Kingdom, thus relating 'citizenship and immigration in a manner that had not hitherto been done' and denying automatic entry even to people outside the UK who held British passports by virtue of Commonwealth citizenship. These acts targeted non-white Commonwealth countries, which came to be referred to as the 'new Commonwealth', despite the fact that many of these countries had been settled by Britain as early as the sixteenth century.[9] The state's powers of expulsion were also strengthened in ways that made possible and permissible the division of families through deportation.

These policies interacted with public rhetoric on race and nationality. The National Front, a nationalist organization formed as a populist pressure group in 1967, urged the need 'to preserve "our British Native stock" by "terminating non-white immigration"'.[10] The rhetoric of Powellism during the sixties, a phenomenon spurred by the public prominence of Enoch Powell and his speeches on immigration, combined concepts of race and nation through focusing upon the 'alien' and culturally incompatible nature of ethnic and racial minorities (even those British-born), spreading restrictionist sentiment and urging repatriation policies. As the anti-immigration movement took hold in the sixties, its discourse was often overtly racist and apolcalyptic, inciting fears of racial violence (such as Powell's famous prophecy of 'rivers of blood' or common references to a 'black invasion')[11] and of racial mixing, disseminated not only through populist vehicles like the National Front but also by the words of conservative politicians: Sir Cyril Osborne, for example, warned that 'the English people have started to commit race suicide'.[12] At the same time that images of miscegenation evoked the demise of racial purity, the enforced or self-imposed segregation of immigrants was perceived as evidence of their inabililty to assimilate, a condition threatening the 'plain fact that the English are a white nation', as Powell (speaking here in 1970) continually claimed.[13] The immigrant family was perceived as a particular problem, an entity preserving the 'alien' culture.

This period, numerous cultural critics argue, evidences a movement from empire to nationalism driven by the need to define and limit

who is 'British'; moreover, the racial and ethnic implications of immigration policy culminate in Thatcherisms's development of an *ethnic
understanding* of the British nation.[14] By the 1970s, Conservative
opinion displayed a 'growing interest ... in defining a coherent
nationalism which often associated nation with race', a nationalism
'discursively theorized by right-wing intellectuals and think tanks
while popularly expressed through the issue of immigration'.[15]
Thatcher appealed in 1979 to the popular vote on this issue as a way
of discrediting Labour, and in part, her promise to further restrict
immigration aided the Conservative rise to power.

Upon Labour's defeat in 1979, issues of racial and ethnic difference
became further focused upon questions of national identity and the
possibilities for free-market prosperity for a 'true' Britain, principally
through Thatcher's passage of a new British Nationality Act in 1981.
Fully in effect by 1987, it nullified the open-door policy of the 1948
British Nationality Act, already disabled through legislation of the
sixties and seventies. Restricting immigration finally meant redefining
British nationality to exclude the 'new Commonwealth' through
replacing a single citizenship of the United Kingdom and Colonies by
three separate citizenships, only one of which maintains the right of
entry and settlement. Displacing the long-standing bestowal of
subjecthood to those born on British soil or in territorial waters, British
citizenship now required the ancestry of a parent or grandparent born
or naturalized in Britain.[16] Hence, the 'alien' born in Britain remains
alien, as does the Commonwealth citizen (most often non-white)
without ancestral links to the UK.[17]

Within these discourses, the words 'home' and 'alien', 'origin' and
'identity' become charged as and by identifiable markers of belonging
or exclusion, further attenuated by the position from which they are
spoken. A cluster of Duffy's dramatic monologues, spoken in the
voices of immigrants, explores the relationship between positionality
in discourse, meaning in language, and constitution of self. Included
in volumes published toward the end of the 1980s, 'Originally',
'Foreign', and 'Deportation' take on public issues of immigration as
their subject-matter while enacting, linguistically, a questioning of
ideologies underlying these issues. 'Originally' opens *The Other Country*
with the voice of a child who has immigrated from 'our own country'
– a longed-for 'Home, Home' – to a city where 'Your accent wrong'
(p. 7). Longing for that home country seems to diminish as the child
identifies with the new culture: 'But then you forget, or don't recall, or
change, / and, seeing your brother swallow a slug, feel only / a skelf of

shame. I remember my tongue / shedding its skin like a snake, my voice / in the classroom sounding just like the rest.' Within a British identity predicated upon 'native stock', however, even the speaker's conformity of tongue will not dissuade the cultural identification of him / her as alien, prompting the question, 'Do I only think / I lost a river, culture, speech, sense of first space / and the right place? Now, *Where do you come from?* / strangers ask. *Originally?* And I hesitate' (*OC*, 7). In part, this hesitation suggests the varying cultural resonances with which the phrase 'our own country' becomes invested in post-colonial Britain. While the claim to 'my country' echoes through the mainstream discourse as a way of identifying a British identity that is 'native', the immigrant's attachment to his/her country of origin is perceived as a threat to successful assimilation. Advancing a popular argument against immigration in the 1960s, Enoch Powell warned that non-white immigrants 'still look to the countries whence they came as home', a cultural allegiance that, he argued, would inhibit their ability to assimilate as British.[18] Thus, for the immigrant to speak of 'our own country' threatens the idea of 'my country' preferred by Anglo-ethnic nationalism. The concept of 'nation' or a 'we' that draws upon a shared 'continuity with its past' and 'rootedness in its homeland'[19] is a 'very particular and characteristic focus of the British New Right's ideological and discursive function' that enacts an 'elision of nation, culture and race, and the emphasis upon "rootedness"'.[20] Discursively, the claim to 'our country' circulates simultaneously as a sign of British nationalism, when spoken from the position of the native, and a sign of unassimilable ethnicity, when spoken from the position of the immigrant. Registering these dual significations, Duffy's poem ends by suggesting the difficulty of answering the question of national origin ('*Where do you come from ... Originally?*') without entering the vocabulary of ethnic nationalism.

The material stress of operating within this discourse, of perceiving oneself through the 'word' offered as 'alien,' surfaces in the tellingly-titled 'Foreign'.[21] The reader is asked to imagine inhabiting dual languages even after 'living in a strange, dark city for twenty years', segregated into 'dismal dwellings on the east side'.[22] Segregation resulting from discriminatory housing practices in Britain extends to language: 'On the landing, you hear / your foreign accent echo down the stairs. You think / in a language of your own and talk in theirs.' To hear oneself as foreign accompanies the apprehension of the self through words naming it as other, alien, undesirable:

> Imagine one night
> you saw a name for yourself sprayed in red
> against a brick wall. A hate name. Red like blood.
> It is snowing on the streets, under the neon lights,
> as if this place were coming to bits before your eyes.

Recalling the rise in white violence in the late 1950s and re-intensify-
ing in the 1970s – commonly accompanied by graffiti by such groups
as the White Defence League in the Notting Hill area – the poem
underscores the violent potential of language denoting otherness and
alienness, whether as sprayed on a wall or spoken in Parliament. To
exist in otherness is to 'not translate' except within the language
constructed to identify that otherness, to be 'inarticulate' within the
dominant articulations of selfhood: 'And in the delicatessen, from
time to time, the coins / in your palm will not translate. Inarticulate,
/ because this is not home, you point at fruit.'

   Learning 'their' language does not gain one entry into the discursive
constitution of selfhood: in 'Deportation,' for example, the speaker
notes 'Now I must leave, / the words I've learned for supplication, /
gratitude, will go unused ... Now I am *Alien*' (*SM*, 59).[23] The word
'alien', in this poem, reveals the recategorization of national subjecthood and its impact on a sense of self. The poem's 'I' speaks from the
position of the New Commonwealth subject, whose status is changed
by the series of immigration restrictions and laws that redefined the
British citizen to exclude many prior subjects.

> I used to think the world was where we lived
> in space, one country shining in big dark.
> I saw a photograph when I was small.
>
> Now I am *Alien*. Where I come from there are few jobs,
> the young are sullen and do not dream.

As Smith emphasizes, 'the status of entire black populations was
abruptly changed precisely at the time of de-colonization. Although
they had been British passport-holders with full legal rights to settle in
the United Kingdom, they became foreign immigrants who were
subjected to extensive immigation controls'. As the colonized became
immigrants and outsiders, the history of their contribution to the
making of Britain was denied: the '"known" colonized became
"unknown" "strangers" in the land of their own making'.[24] Not only

had the formerly colonized contributed to the wealth of the nation, and hence been a part of the economic system for hundreds of years, but they often had been acculturated to think of England as the 'mother country' and of themselves as belonging to her: 'After all, a disproportionate large part of their schooling had been dedicated to nurturing an understanding of the glory that was England's' and to the notion of a 'common British enclosure',[25] or, in the poem's terms, 'one country shining in big dark'. From the perspective of many immigrants who first arrived in the 1950s and 1960s, 'We came to share the wealth that we ourselves had created, claiming what was legitimately ours.'[26] Nevertheless, the 'wealth' was not about to be shared; the need of the poem's speaker to learn words for 'supplication, / gratitude' suggests the prevalence of low-paying service and non-skilled labour positions available to immigrants who met with intense job discrimination upon entry to Britain.

The poem suggests the erasure of the immigrant's perspective, of his or her account of Britishness, as opposed to the dominant discourse aimed at containing Britishness within particular boundaries. Such language of containment sustains the 'Building of Exile', where the speaker must go to register: 'They are polite, recite official jargon endlessly. / Form F. Room 12. Box 6.' Categorized as '*Alien*' within the 'official jargon,' the speaker is denied his family and faces deportation, pointing to the doubled meaning of 'family' within the rhetoric of ethnic nationalism. The speaker clearly imagined that this family would join him to make a home: 'My lover / bears our child and I was to work here, find / a home. In twenty years we would say This is you / when you were a baby' (*SM*, 59).[27] However, the issue of immigrant families became charged once the initial groups of primarily male immigrants (such as this poem's imagined speaker) were joined, by the late fifties, by wives and families, leading to Enoch Powell's denunciation of the immigrant family in 1968 as (re)generating cultural difference, a problem in need of containment. Indeed, by the late 1960s, the attention of the anti-immigration lobby focused particularly upon the entry of dependants of immigrants already settled in England, fueling allegations that false claims to family relations were common, particularly among individuals from the Indian subcontinent, and leading to the introduction of 'entry clearance' for dependants, a long and complicated process making it 'increasingly difficult' for dependants to join a family member.[28] The state's expanded power over the expulsion of immigrants after 1971 and the redefinition of British citizenship in 1981 attenuate this poem's consideration of 'family' in relation to its rhetorical configuration in public discourse during the Thatcher years; while family and family values are being newly celebrated by the Conservative right, the ethnically or racially marked family is a site of cultural difficulty in reproducing cultural difference from 'Britain', and in bringing more 'aliens' (now legally so even if born in Britain) into the country.[29] As in 'Foreign' or 'Originally', being at 'home' or within the familial boundaries of the post-imperial nation cannot happen within discursive and material realities labeling one as alien.

The idea of the British nation as 'home' to a 'native stock' found expression in the cross-class appeals to nationalism that enabled the rise of the Conservative Party and its reign in the eighties. The migration of members from Labour's traditional social base (unionists, workers) to Conservative support marked the success of Thatcher's populist appeal to the interests of the industrial classes, articulated in terms of the 'immigrant problem'. This appeal effected what Stuart Hall terms a reconstruction of the 'social order' through ideologically empowering the 'discursive space' created by Thatcherism's endorsement of free-market economics, possessive individualism, and competition as opposed to social need.[30] Within this discursive space, traditional class lines are rhetorically manipulated through invoking images of an England that purportedly existed before population diversity and a collectivist economy altered the country's 'essence'. The cross-class power of this ideal, stipulating Britain as white, Christian, and civilized, helped Thatcher to gain support in the 1979 election. In the midst of political rhetoric that referred to immigration as a kind of 'flood' or 'swamping', many working-class individuals felt their job security and way of life threatened by the influx of non-white immigrants. As urban neighbourhoods changed rapidly in combination with growing economic hardship for the working and poor classes, the immigrant became a target of blame.[31] In public rhetoric during the 1960s, associations developed between what Powell called 'excessive' numbers of immigrants of color and 'undesirable social problems'; in reality, while these immigrant communities 'had to bear the brunt of socio-economic hardships themselves,' they were 'defined in racist discourse as the most potent signifier of the post-colonial national decline'.[32]

Duffy's poem 'Mrs. Skinner, North Street' (*OC*, 12) directly engages this process of signification, particularly in recalling and dismantling a populist strategy employed by Enoch Powell. In speeches of the late 1960s, Powell would often read from letters that he claimed to voice the *true* (i.e.natural and transparently expressed) experience of his white constituents, who feared what he called the social disorder of immigrant 'strangers.'[33] In Duffy's poem, the voice of an older woman, poor and bitter, speaks in halting, broken lines about her life in an urban neighborhood altered by social neglect and ethnic diversity. Isolated, she feels she lives among a 'terrace of *strangers*':

> Scrounger. Workshy. Cat, where is the world
> she married, was carried into up a scrubbed stone step?
> The young louts roam the neighbourhood.
> Breaking of glass. Chants. Sour abuse of aerosols.
> That social worker called her *xenophobic*. When he left
> she looked the word up. Fear, morbid dislike, of strangers.
> Outside, the rain pours down relentlessly.

Recalling Powell's designation of immigrants as strangers, the poem further reconfigures one of Powell's most notorious representations of populist sentiment – a letter quoted in his famous 'rivers of blood' speech, which told a supposedly true story of an elderly white woman whose neighborhood transforms until she is the last white person on a street devolving into 'noise and confusion', populated by sinister outsiders. The woman recounts how she must retreat into her home, fearful of the 'wide-grinning piccaninnies' outside her door.[34] As Smith analyses this speech, the woman's 'retreat dramatically symbolizes white Britons as a besieged minority,' threatened by the 'black [immigrant of color] invader,' a truth naturalized by the use of the letter form in a political speech.[35]

The woman in the poem, like the woman in Powell's letter, fears 'young louts' as disorderly invaders; however, unlike the femininized victim Powell represented as the epitome of Britain's vulnerability, Mrs. Skinner is shone less as a victim than as an unaware participant in discursive constructions of the immigrant that work to conceal the economic forces materially affecting her life. Powell, and others prior to Thatcher's success, linked anti-immigration issues to free market advocacy through the image of a restored Britain; in effect, they paved the ideological way for the massive changes in economic policy enacted under Thatcherism. Rather than restoration, by the mid-1980s, a recession brought on by government cutbacks, declines in heavy industry, and economic reform, had resulted in inflation and high unemployment, especially among the minority populations in low-skilled and low-wage jobs to which they had been restricted. As

market forces distanced the poor from the rich and the state elimi-
nated forms of social welfare, living conditions deteriorated for the
poor – both black and white – and their environs. In an extreme image
of urban isolation perpetuated by these economic forces, Mrs. Skinner
imagines that no one will look in upon her until 'the day the smell is
noticed / ... the day you're starving, Cat, and begin / to lick at the
corpse'. However, for Mrs. Skinner, whose retreat echoes that of
Powell's pensioner, the change in her neighborhood and 'the world /
she married' cannot be seen except through the metonymic significance of 'the Asian man next door'. The representation of her
xenophobia, particularly in its engagement with Powell's discursive
framing of immigrant invaders and their victims, exposes the ethnic
nationalism shaping her perspective. Just as 'xenophobia' is a word she
does not know, the concept of 'foreign' is shaped from within the
discourse she encounters most prominantly, encouraging the perception that the 'foreign' is not British and not of her world. Indeed, the
'Asian' may well be a British citizen but cannot be incorporated into
the frame or discourse of British identity within which Mrs. Skinner
has been shaped. Such was the situation facing many East African
Asians, in particular, following the decolonization of African colonies.
Descendants of Asians brought by the British to help build the African
colonies, these individuals were offered the choice of British citizenship when individual colonies began declaring independence, and
approximately 7,000 Asians a year immigrated to England under these
conditions throughout the 1960s. Represented as a 'national emergency' resulting from a 'flood' of 'foreigners', their entry – even as legal
citizens whose numbers were slight in comparision to net emigration
from Britain – helped stimulate the immigration restrictions of the
sixties while enabling Powell's emergence as an anti-immigration
spokesperson. The specific reference to an 'Asian' in Duffy's poem illuminates the historical complexities threatening the unitary sense of
British identity urged by Powell and others; moreover, it interwines
the woman's bigotry with the colonial transactions of the empire's
past and an antipathy toward its consequences .[36]

Such complexities of the post-colonial state suffer elision within a
nationalistic discourse appealing to both nature and common sense as
arbitrators of a native British essence. While a rhetoric of identity and
nation is most effective when presented as seamless, Duffy's poems
formally enact identity as a collision of words and discourses. Duffy's
dramatic monologues, so often composed of catalogued fragments and
soundbites that are harshly enjambed and juxtaposed, belie the

'natural' or unitary self outside of language. Often, as in 'Translating the English, 1989' (*OC*, 11), a claim to selfhood is revealed as an effort to elide (or refuse to articulate) what cannot be contained within the terms of self-naming. That which cannot be contained keeps breaking in on the official narrative of the British, in effect 'translating' the narrative of national selfhood:

> Lloyd-Webber. Jeffrey Archer. Plenty culture you will be agreeing.
> Also history and buildings. The Houses of Lords. Docklands.
> Many thrills and high interest rates for own good. Muggers.
> Much lead in petrol. Filth. Rule Britannia and child abuse.
> Electronic tagging, Boss, ten pints and plenty rape. Queen Mum.
> Channel Tunnel. You get here fast no problem to my country
> my country my country welcome welcome welcome

This process of 'translation' suggests, through the juxtaposed frag-ments, that a discourse or narrative interweaves with and depends upon the discourse it purports to oppose or erase. For example, the ideology of domination underlies both 'Rule Britannia' and 'child abuse', although the former cannot recognize the latter and remain an idealized narrative of nation and history. Moreover, paratactic posi-tioning calls attention to the codedness of naturalized phrases (like 'Rule Britannia') and the claim to common sense assumed through such coding. The economic medicine of 'high interest rates' cannot be separated from the rise in crime, the poem suggests, nor significantly, can the dominant representations of either 'muggers' or market forces be disentangled. Attributing high interest rates, unemployment, and other economic downturns to a need to discipline the economy, and particularly the working class (and unions),[37] Thatcherism cast its economic policies of enterprise as supplying the corrective to a sick national economy, recoding economic deprivation as medicine for a wayward patient.

Duffy's insertion of this rhetoric into the poem calls up a series of socio-economic changes brought on by Thatcher's government as well as the rhethoric of Thatcherism that justified them. As David Edgar argues, 'the crucial role of the free market' within Thatcherism 'is not to emancipate the entrepreneur but to chastise the feckless, an instru-ment not of liberation but of discipline'.[38] Similarly manifesting a concern with disciplining an unruly element, the word 'Muggers' hangs in overly determined fashion at the end of the line, just as it hangs within the public consciousness as a nexus of race, immigration, crime, and nationalism. What Paul Gilroy first argued was a 'policing of blackness,' the linking of blackness (and hence, immigration) with criminality developed as a 'policing discourse' in the 1970s that accompanied repressive law and order practices targeting the non-white communities.[39] 'Mugging', used to refer to types of crime associated with America but unexperienced in Britain on any scale until the 1970s, began to appear within the popular media, who 'conjured up images of black "crime waves"' that resonated through the term 'mugger'.[40] Although the 1970s and 1980s brought an increase in racial attacks and breakdowns in police / community relations, blackness is aggressively 'policed' through discourse situating blackness as 'outside' the boundaries of nation, thus omitting the abuse suffered by minorities while furthering the construction of the foreign invader, the dangerous excess of British colonization, the mugger.[41] In Duffy's denaturalization of these various narratives, the disciplining of the economy and the immigrant each depend upon a rhetoric of nationalism supporting the directives of Thatcherism.

Like 'Translating the English, 1989', 'Comprehensive' offers an interweaving of discourses within a nationalistic capitalism.[42] The poem breaks into distinct stanzas spoken from ethnically marked positions that, to varying degrees, reveal the tension between assimilation and cultural plurality underlying debates over Britain's changing demographics. There is the African immigrant who claims, 'I like Africa better than England', to be told by her / his mother that home ownership will bring a sense of belonging; the 14-year-old Wayne who supports the National Front, enjoys 'Paki-bashing', and asserts, 'I don't suppose I'll get a job. It's all them / coming over here to work. Arsenal'; the young Muslim who almost eats pork until another stops him and they become friends; the boy whose 'sister went out with one. There was murder. / I'd like to be mates, but they're different from us'; and the teenager from Jhelum whose family members bear the name of Moghul emperors but who can't get milk in school because 'I didn't understand' the teacher's words. This final stanza, situated in the British classroom, connects multiple issues organized around language and identity that emerged in discussions over education in the 1980s. While the children of immigrants in the 1950s and 1960s met with an educational system unprepared for and often hostile to their presence, by the late 1970s debates over multi-ethnic education developed in response to demands by immigrant and minority groups for equatible education for their children. In reaction, the notion of a natural and right British education, what Seidel calls 'an organic view of education within a larger, untroubled, white vision of culture and tradition', was harnessed to argue against the use of 'mother-tongue teaching' (or instruction in the native languages of the students) and other multi-cultural initiatives. In effect, these debates promoted the ideology of the unassimilable immigrant through claiming that an expression of (non-white) ethnic identity was essentially non-British. In public forums, conservative educators like Ray Honeyford criticized multi-cultural projects in the name of preserving an authentic and natural British education.[43] A rhetoric of authenticity disguising an institutional racism within a concept of Britishness would instruct its white children that the non-white is 'different' and to be avoided; that 'all them' must be defended against. It teaches its non-white children to remember a homeland and a sense of home in stark contrast to the conditions in Britain and to the promises that 'everything was easy here'.

Complex things happen in this poem – almost each stanza deserves close attention – but I will conclude by pointing to the tension between diversity and seperation that the polyvocal poem sets up, a tension reflecting a duality of ethnic consciousness and communalism. Harry Goulbourne, analysing the development of ethnic nationalism around the issue of immigration in Britain, recently voiced concern that the varied peoples of Britain enjoy 'only a market relationship' resulting from the pressure of concurrent emphasis upon cultural pluralism and cultural conservatism.[44] Similarly interested in the dynamics of a 'communal model' in which elements remain separate except in a market relation,[45] the poem gathers multiple voices that remain distinctly identifiable within ethnic parameters (and class and gender to an extent). At the same time, the interplay of the voices – how one offers an alternative discourse to the other, how one seems tied to another, how one seems dependant upon but blind to another – suggests the 'comprehensive' plurality of space that is shared but not acknowledged. For Duffy, the discursive space of a British identity constructed partially in reaction to growing diversity and nurtured by Thatcherism's linking of race, family, free market, and nationalism in both policy and public utterance, slices up the 'comprehensive' possibilities of a plural nation, threatening to insert spaces of silence between the voices making up this poem and, by extension, remaking Britain.

Notes

1. Carol Ann Duffy,'The Act of Imagination', in *The Other Country* (London: Anvil Press, 1990), p. 25.
2. Anna Marie Smith, *New Right Discourse on Race and Sexuality* (Cambridge: Cambridge University Press, 1994), p. 3.
3. This essay uses the term 'New Right' to refer to a cultural, political, and intellectual shift in British conservatism toward a laissez-faire concept of market freedom and a stress on social morality. For analysis of the term's varied nuances, see Smith, *New Right Discourse*; also see Ruth Levitas (ed.), *The Ideology of the New Right* (Cambridge: Polity Press, 1986). The argument of this essay is situated within recent discussions of New Right ideology and discourse in relation to post-empire immigration issues.
4. This quote is from a 1979 Thatcher campaign speech, pivotal in that her anti-immigration remarks greatly increased her popularity.
5. Ian Gregson, *Contemporary Poetry and Postmodernism: Dialogue and Estrangement* (New York: St. Martin's Press, 1996), p. 99. A number of critics have usefully explored Duffy's discursive and feminist strategies. See Gregson's Bakhtinian discussion of discursive intersections in Duffy's poetry; for a discussion of problems of representation regarding gender, see Danette Dimarco, 'Exposing Nude Art: Carol Ann Duffy's Response to Robert Browning', *Mosaic: A Journal for the Interdisciplinary Study of Literature* 31.3 (Sept. 1998); for an analysis of post-structuralist elements, see Jane E. Thomas, '"The Intolerable Wrestle With Words": The Poetry of Carol Ann Duffy', *Bete Noire* 6 (1989): pp. 78–88; and for a discussion of gender, language, and poetic form, see Linda A. Kinnahan, '"Look for the Doing Words": Carol Ann Duffy and Questions of Convention', in *Contemporary British Poetry: Essays in Criticism and Theory*, ed. James Acheson and Romana Huk (New York: SUNY Press, 1996), pp. 245–68.
6. Carol Anne Duffy, *Mean Time* (London: Anvil Press, 1993); *The Other Country* (London: Anvil Press, 1990), hereafter cited as *OC*; *Selling Manhattan* (London: Anvil Press, 1987), hereafter cited as *SM*; and *Standing Female Nude* (London: Anvil Press, 1985), hereafter cited as *SFN*.
7. Asa Briggs, *A Social History of England* (New York: Penguin, 1983), p. 310. Foundational studies of these interrelated issues of race and law and order include Paul Gilroy, *There Ain't No Black in the Union Jack* (London: Hutchinson, 1987); Stuart Hall, Chas Critcher, Tony Jefferson, John Clarke, and Brian Roberts, *Policing the Crisis: Mugging, the State, and Law and Order* (New York: Holmes and Meier, 1978); Harry Goulbourne (ed.), *Black Politics in Britain* (Aldershot: Avebury, 1990); and most recently, Smith, *New Right Discourse*.
8. Colin Holmes, *A Tolerant Country?* (London: Faber and Faber, 1991), p. 61.
9. Harry Goulbourne, *Ethnicity and Nationalism in Post-Imperial Britain* (New York: CUP, 1991), p. 115.
10. Holmes, *A Tolerant Country?*, p. 57, quoting Clause 8 of the NF's programme.
11. Powell used this first metaphor in a speech in Birmingham, 20 Apr. 1968. See Smith, *New Right Discourse*, p. 23 for discussion of the terms 'black invasion' and 'black invader.'

12. Hall et al., *Policing the Crisis*, p. 240. Hall includes numerous similar quotes from Conservative members of Parliament opposed to immigration. As Gill Seidel persuasively demonstrates in 'Culture, Nation and "Race" in the British and French New Right' (in Levitas, *The Ideology of the New Right*), it is not necessary to 'allege an *organizational connection*' between populist groups and conservative leaders, the latter of whom protested any association with such groups as the facist National Front (my emphasis, p. 114). More significant is to 'illustrate the *discursive continuities and overlaps*' among 'a whole range of xenophobic, racist and sexist discourses', whether framed in populist or academic language (my emphasis, pp. 114, 113).

13. Smith, *New Right Discourse*, p. 166.

14. The phrase and concept of ethnic nationalism is taken from Goulbourne, *Ethnicity and Nationalism* (1991). I am greatly indebted to him for his analysis of immigration in Britain.

15. Holmes, *A Tolerant Country?*, p. 63. See also the essays in Levitas, *The Ideology of the New Right* for analysis of the language and concepts of intellectuals and economists influencing New Right politics. Particularly useful in this regard are Andrew Belsey, 'The New Right, Social Order, and Civil Liberties'; David Miriam, 'Moral and Maternal: The Family in the Right'; Andrew Gamble, 'The Political Economy of Freedom'; Ruth Levitas, 'Competition and Compliance: The Utopias of the New Right'; David Edgar,'The Free or the Good'; and Seidel, 'Culture, Nation and "Race"'.

16. The 1981 Nationality Act created three categories: the British citizen, whose parent or grandparent is born or naturalized in the UK; the British Dependent Territories citizen, who is born or naturalized, or whose parent was born or naturalized, in a British colony, and who possesses rights only in that colony; and the British Overseas citizen, who is granted UK citizenship by virtue of living in colonies that become independent but may nevertheless suffer entry restrictions. For an excellent discussion of this legislation in regard to race and gender, see Jacqueline Bhabha, Francesca Klug, and Sue Shutter (eds), *Worlds Apart: Women Under Immigration and Nationality Law* (London: Pluto Press, 1985).

17. Exceptions to the patriality rules include the granting of citizenship to inhabitants of the Falkland Islands following Britain's conflict with Argentina and to the financial and cultural elite of Hong Kong.

18. Quoted in 'After Powell', *The Economist*, (14–20 Feb. 1998, p. 56). This 1998 essay focuses on the Muslim Pakistani population in Bradford and the patterns of 'separateness' in education, marriage, and family maintained by this group, demonstrating a continuing anxiety over these issues.

19. Powell, quoted in Seidel, 'Culture, Nation and "Race"', p. 110.

20. Ibid. See this essay for an excellent analysis of the New Right theory of race and nation, as exemplified by the Conservative group associated with the *Salisbury Review* but overlapping with other Conservative discourses in the 1980s.

21. *SM*, p. 47.

22. The 'extensive discrimination' confronting non-white immigrants included housing discrimination by 'the majority of white landlords, estate agents and building societies', forcing them 'to rent the worst types of local government housing or to finance their own mortgages with groups of

friends, often for the purchase of condemned housing' (Smith, *New Right Discourse*, p. 141).

23. See Bhabha et al., *Worlds Apart* for useful information on deportation patterns.

24. Smith, *New Right Discourse*, p. 130.

25. Goulbourn, *Black Politics in Britain*, p. 107.

26. Margaret Prescod-Roberts and Norma Steel, as quoted in Lauretta Ngcobo (ed.), *Let It Be Told: Essays By Black Women Writers in Britain* (London: Virago, 1988), pp. 14–15.

27. Gender discrimination in immigration laws is extensively documented in Bhabha et al., *Worlds Apart* The gendering of the immigrant in immigration discourse and policy, and Duffy's engagement with aspects of gender, receive further consideration in a book on women poets and economics I am currently completing.

28. Bhabha et al., *Worlds Apart*, p. 48.

29. The counter-discourse produced by immigrant and minority populations in Britain is important to note here, although beyond the scope of this essay. For fuller accounts of the prominence of minority activism and voices in relation to mainstream and community politics since the 1970s, see Beverley Bryan, Stella Dadzie, and Suzanne Scafe, *The Heart of the Race: Black Women's Lives in Britain* (London: Virago Press, 1985); Goulbourne, *Black Politics in Britain*; and Bhabha et al, *Worlds Apart*.

30. Stuart Hall, 'The Toad in the Garden: Thatcherism Among the Theorists', in *Marxism and the Interpretation of Culture*, ed. Cary Nelson and Lawrence Grossberg (Urbana: University of Illinois Press, 1988), p. 42.

31. During these years, 'pressures on the British economy accelerated the disruption of white workers' positions in the manufacturing sector and the disintegration of white working-class neighbourhoods. At the same time, the majority of black workers were locked into the lowest-paid occupational positions, such as unskilled manufacturing and service sector positions. The low incomes of the black workers and the racist exclusionary practices [in housing] ... led to the concentration of the black communities in the most run-down and overcrowded inner-city areas' (Smith, *New Right Discourse*, p. 146).

32. Ibid., pp. 139, 146–7.

33. Enoch Powell, speech at the London Rotary Club, Eastbourne, 16 Nov. 1968, in *Freedom and Reality*, ed. John Wood (Kingswood: Paperfront, 1969), pp. 217–18; quoted by Smith, *New Right Discourse*, pp. 154–5.

34. Ibid.

35. Ibid., pp. 155–6.

36. The patriality laws of the 1968 Commonwealth Immigrants Act and the 1971 Immigration Act were stimulated by this 'national emergency' and severely restricted the right of entry of non-white colonials and former colonials; as Smith argues, 'the boundaries of the nation became officially conceptualized in terms of familial blood ties', so that descendants of many white Britons in Australia, Canada or New Zealand whose parents or grandparents had emigrated from England could resettle in the UK, while individuals of the New Commonwealth countries, even though descended from British subjects in colonies, usually lacked the ancestral tie to England

that would allow free entry and citizenship (ibid., p. 181).

37. Hall et al., *Policing the Crisis*, p. 264.
38. David Edgar, 'The Free or the Good', in Levitas, *The Ideology of the New Right*, p. 75.
39. Smith, *New Right Discourse*, pp. 123, 98.
40. Ibid., p. 98.
41. For discussions of discursive developments around the issue of 'mugging' and the campaign for a law and order state, see Gilroy, *Ain't No Black*; Hall et al., *Policing the Crisis*; and Smith, *New Right Discourse*.
42. *Nude*, pp. 8–9.
43. Honeyford was a headmaster in Bradford, running a school with a 90% population of Asian-British children. He was fired following published critiques, in the *Times Educational Supplement* and the *Salisbury Review* in 1984, of multi-ethnic education, and went on to become a leading spokesperson for Conservative opposition to multiculturalism. See Seidel, 'Culture, Nation and "Race"', pp. 116–17, and Smith, *New Right Discourse*, pp. 115–16.
44. Goulbourne, *Ethnicity and Nationalism*, p. 231.
45. Ibid.

20
Curious Rarities? The Work of Kathleen Jamie and Jackie Kay

Joanne Winning

> The question is:
> Is there another road,
> fresh pasture,
> unattested,
> sweet meadow-grass
> on that endless skinned moor,
> and end to that pasture/deceit
> which has been there so long,
> for two hundred and seventy-two years?[1]

It may well be that Scotland has finally found the answer to the bleak and plaintive question posed by Derick Thomson in his poetic response to the outcome of the 1979 Devolution referendum. The 1980s and 1990s have witnessed an upward trajectory in Scotland's sense of autonomy, culminating most significantly in the successful referendum on May 1st 1998, and perhaps more symbolically in the opening of the long-promised Museum of Scotland on St Andrew's Day (30 November). Both events, one might say, signify the awakening of a Scotland poised now at the edge of a new, stronger sense of selfhood and identity; looking for its coordinates both backwards into the past, and forwards into the future, for the next millennium. This is surely one of the most exciting periods in Scottish history, time in which Scotland is being returned to itself. Amidst the euphoria and the forward planning, however, let us hope that questions of 'difference', gender, race, class, sexuality, do not sink miserably out of sight. As Christopher Whyte notes, in his book *Gendering the Nation*: 'If we want to bring back a Scotland that once was, what place will there be in it for blacks or lesbians or the children of Pakistani immigrants?'[2]

So far at least, the avowed aims of both new institutions would seem to be structured on principles of accessibility and inclusiveness. The Scottish Parliament, we are told, will mark a departure from the way of political life conducted in the 'mother of all parliaments' in London. It will be more accessible, less 'stuffy', younger, *more female*. Its hours and its holidays will reflect the needs of working parents and not the lifestyles of the macho residents in the boys' club at Westminster. The new Museum of Scotland was built expressly to offer the full, unedited story of the Scots. The Scots here represent a culture fully aware of difference, placing themselves squarely in a European context. Between its cylindrical, sandstone walls its visitors ascend through a series of displays which begin in the Celtic basement, rise up through the Enlightenment and arrive in the Twentieth Century on the top floor. History, in the Museum of Scotland, is told through objects and artefacts: Pictish stones, Roman gold and Celtic relics, in addition to more codedly female artefacts, which also got to make up a nation's sense of identity, its clothes, teapots, games, jewellery. Its range of exhibits demonstrates a laudable eclecticism which privileges neither public nor private spheres. Yet as an instructive little quote from Hugh MacDiarmid proves, the relations between Scottish politics, history and women have always been, to say the very least, troubled:

> Scottish women of any historical interest are curiously rare ... our leading Scotswomen have been ... almost entirely destitute of exceptional endowments of any sort.[3]

The masculinist bias in Scottish culture and nationalism, what Liz Lochhead describes as its 'macho flowering', has been well documented.[4] Undoubtedly this bias may be read through larger questions of nationalism and the exclusions of women; as Joanne P. Sharp argues, 'Women are not equal to the nation but symbolic of it'.[5] Nevertheless, this need not necessarily be the face of nationalism, indeed at moments of transition, national identities can acknowledge their pluralities. As Whyte notes, 'in small, emergent cultures, national identity can never been taken as a given'.[6] In fact, it may well be that it is the intersections of gender, race, and Scottishness (not forgetting class and sexuality, but not having the space to explore either here) may become the loci of richest dialogue and instruction. Such productive intersections can be found within the burgeoning body of Scottish women's poetry, which as Dorothy McMillan notes is 'having a better time of it now' than it ever had.[7] Cairns Craig, writing on twentieth-century Scottish literature, has argued that Scotland's sense of independence has always been strongest in the written word. Scottish literature, he argues, has 'retained and indeed asserted its independence in a context where the Scottish people – unlike the Irish, for example – have seemed deeply resistant or apathetic about other forms of independence'.[8] True to Craig's location of writing as the index of Scottish national identity, the recent collection of Scottish poetry *Dream State*, edited by Daniel O'Rourke, announces the arrival of 'the new Scottish poets'. The poets, all under the age of 40, have been collected by O'Rourke to represent the new range of 'Scotlands' being created in verse, and the new definitions of an autonomous Scottishness. Looking at two women poets from this collection, Kathleen Jamie and Jackie Kay, this article seeks to trouble the terms of this project to some degree, and explore ways in which contemporary definitions of Scottishness are set to fail unless they acknowledge the range of 'difference' within that identity.

Whae dae ye think ye ur? Kathleen Jamie

As readings in dominant Scottish male texts, such as MacDiarmid's *Drunk Man*, proves, 'Woman' as cultural signifier has always unsettled the 'certainties' of Scottish national identity and its history. Indeed, the project of the new Museum of Scotland may be playfully undercut by a reading of the poem 'Arraheids' from Kathleen Jamie's 1994 collection *The Queen of Sheba*:

> See thon raws o flint arraheids
> in oor gret museums o antiquities
> awful grand in Embro –
> Dae'ye near'n daur wunner at wur histrie?
> Weel then, Bewaur!
> The museums of Scotland are wrang.
> They urnae arraheids
> but a show o grannies' tongues,
> the hard tongues o grannies
> aa died an gaun
> back to thur peat and burns,
> but for thur sherp
> chert tongues, that lee
> fur generations in the land
> like wicked cherms, that lee
> aa douce in the glessy cases in the gloom

o oor museums, an
they arenae lettin oan. But if you daur
sorn aboot and fancy
the vanished hunter, the wise deer runnin on;
wheesht ... an you'll hear them,
fur they cannae keep fae muttering
ye arenae here tae wonder,
whae dae ye think ye ur?[9]

First and foremost, the tongues multiply on the page since the poem
is written in Scots. Yet this poem isn't just about registering a Scottish
voice, or the bizarre edges of a Scottish sense of humour. Amidst its
wryness, it makes the serious point that in fact we may well get history
wrong, and that the constructions and interpretations of nationhood
may overlook other narratives of identity. Here traditional readings of
Scottish prehistory are deconstructed by the revelation that the objects
that have been collected and interpreted by archaeologists as arrow-
heads are, in fact, the hardest-wearing and most indestructible
body-parts of irascible old grandmothers – their tongues. The poem
constructs a version of ancient Scottish womanhood which is in
keeping with popularised images of harridans, formidable in both
physical and verbal battle. Yet it also embues this womanhood with
the ability to deceive the unwitting historian. The tongues themselves
play tricks on historians and curators alike by withholding their real
identity. Femininity exists sleekitly beneath the master narratives of
prehistory: 'they arnae lettin oan.' Well, nearly. The desire for
constructing such historical narratives at all is called into question by
the grannies' ultimate inability to hold their tongues and their judgement of the day-dreaming museum-goer who 'fancies' the
romanticised prehistoric scene of deer and hunter: *'ye arenae here tae*
wonder, / whae dae ye think ye ur?' The ludic deconstruction of traditional historical narratives within the poem is matched by a
significant recasting of history and identity which locates this hector-
ing, verbose femininity as an indelible part of Scottishness.

'Arraheids' centralises a vision of womanhood within Scotland's
prehistoric past which might well be said to be at odds with the dominant constructions of Scottish identity, *à la* MacDiarmid. Suzanne
Hagemann, in her discussion of the relation between women and
nation in Scotland, alights on Hugh MacDiarmid's *A Drunk Man Looks*
at the Thistle (1926) to exemplify a dominant trope in Scottish literature which insistently positions womanhood outside Scottish identity.

MacDiarmid's treatise on national identity, in which the drunken protagonist philosophises about the condition of both himself and Scotland in his contemplation of the emblematic thistle on a moonlit night, offers two opposing configurations of the feminine. The thistle itself represents the Drunk Man himself and the larger sphere of Scottish life and culture. By contrast, the moon is by turns associated symbolically with the divine Goddess Sophia and the version of femininity he finds somewhat closer to home, his wife Jean. Its light confers upon the Drunk Man his sense of identity: 'Be thou the licht in which I stand/ Entire, in thistle-shape, as planned ...'[10] Reading the shifting relations between the moon and the thistle, Hagemann argues, reveals the time-honoured binary between nature/culture, in which the feminine is 'assign[ed] a position beyond the realities of Scottish life, beyond nationhood'.[11] Something of this positionality 'outside' culture is imaged in another of Kathleen Jamie's poems, 'Bairns of Suxie: A Hex'. In this poem, Jamie fashions another figuration of womanhood which again draws on older, this time pagan, images of disruptive femininity. Here the witch Suzie bears wild, unkempt children who run amok across the countryside of the Tay valley, communing in an ecstatic, orgiastic dance with each other and with nature:

> Children of Suzie come out to play
> on the stone nipple
> of the Black Craig
>   open-leggèd, chuckling
> as Vorlich and Shiehallion
> snow-rise across the wide Tay,

Suzie's bairns are borne and nourished out of the rugged Scottish landscape, suggesting again a primal relation between femininity and Scottishness which precedes current social organisation. Again, like the 'chert' tongues of grannies, they trick and defy. The serious element of their play is to disrupt the patriarchal custodians of society, hexing 'invisible arrows' which fly into the 'too-hot / todd-reeking rooms' of the men who make laws and would 'take this hill, / shake in the people's faces keys / to courtrooms and gates'. Their sneaky, persistent persecution makes these men 'whey-faced and desperate', and sends them out on to the 'dour pavements' they'd have people walk 'nose to tail', to try and find their persecutors. And where do they look first?

> among the wifies in scarfs,
> the prams at the Co-op door the old boys'
> grey-muzzled dogs
> by the sunny bench at the mill.[12]

Suzie and her wild children exist beyond the rigid patriarchal control of Scotland and possess a constant and timeless potential to erupt and disrupt: 'And the Bairns of the witch of this hill / run on, loose limbed & laughing.' The danger might be that the wee women in headscarves, doing their shopping in the Co-op, might well be hiding their affiliations to a dangerous, disaster-reeking femininity. The ability of women to shake up dominant social structures is represented also in Jamie's 'Queen of Sheba' in which the exotic, bespangled Queen, whose 'gorgeous breasts' outdo even those of 'Vi-next door', arrives in the 'dump' of Scotland to ask 'some Difficult Questions'. Riding her camel straight over the 'fit-ba pitch', reeking of spice and musk, the Queen of Sheba proclaims her desire for 'the keys to the National Library' and the unwavering attention of 'the lasses in the awestruck crowd'. Most importantly, the Queen of Sheba convinces the ecstatic, breathless girls that there is another way to be, and something else beyond the limited horizons which insistently restrict the lives of Scottish women:

> Stick in
> with the homework and you'll be
> cliver like yer faither.
> but no too cliver,
> no *above yersel*.[13]

As Raymond Friel has argued, one of the consistent themes which emerges in this collection is the way in which women's lives can be, and often are, dictated by 'biological and cultural forces'.[14] The psychic effects of these limiting discourses, which at times have as much to do with class as with gender, are explored in the haunting and moving 'Child with Pillar Box and Bin Bags'. Here Jamie explores the specific psychic effects upon working-class Scottish womanhood which result from the straitjacketing of social and cultural parameters. In the actions of the mother in the poem, we witness the way in which these very real restrictions become completely internalised into a woman's sense of self and worth:

> But it was the shadowed street-side she chose
> while Victor Gold the bookies basked
> in conquered sunlight, and though
> Dalry Road Licensed Grocer gloried and cast
> fascinating shadows she chose
> the side dark in the shade of tenements;
> that corner where Universal Stores' (closed
> for modernisation) blank hoarding blocked
> her view as if that process were illegal;
> she chose to photograph her baby here,
> the corner with the pillar box.

The opening 'But' suggests the other, alternative ways in which this photograph could have been taken. And yet, the photograph gets taken in a certain way *because* of the identifiable landscape (the Dalry Road) in which it is taken, and the only tools available (a cheap camera). We witness this impoverished celebration of maternity as it is constrained both by economic and social circumstances in working-class Edinburgh, but also, and more importantly, by the mother's own internalised sense of her belittled self, its unimportance, its secondariness:

> The traffic ground, the buildings shook, the baby breathed
> and maybe gurgled at his mother as she
> smiled to make him smile in his picture;
> which she took on the kerb in the shadowed corner,
> beside the post-box, under tenements, before
> the bin-bags hot in the sun that shone
> on them, on dogs, on people on the other side
> the other side of the street to that she'd chosen,
> if she'd chosen or thought it possible to choose.[15]

Being denied choices leads to denying yourself choices, setting yourself apart unthinkingly from even the dogs on the 'other side' of the street, believing, in fact, that you deserve no more. The seemingly small, insignificant vignette, caught by Jamie's flâneur-like gaze, in fact reveals a disturbing truth about both female and Scottish identity. Explorations such as these have lead Sean O'Brien to argue that Jamie's work is becoming 'a poetry of the Condition of Scotland', yet ironically this is probably a mantle which Jamie herself would rather not wear.[16] Interviewed in 1990, and responding to the question 'What does it mean to be a Scottish poet?', Jamie offers the following observation: 'I suppose you're inevitably Scottish, like you're inevitably female, but there are other things more essential.'[17] Interviewed again in 1994, introducing her poems in *Dream State*, Jamie explains that attempts to construct herself as either 'woman writer' or 'Scottish writer' in the past have resulted in feelings of irritation and confinement.[18] Why might it be that such poetic identities begin to feel like shackles?

The dedication in Jamie's *The Queen of Sheba* reads 'this one's for the folks at home'. Working out where 'home' is and what it looks like, is, Robert Crawford argues, perhaps the 'major' preoccupation of twentieth-century poetry:

'Where do you come from?' is one of the most important questions in contemporary poetry – where's home? Answering the pulls and torsions of that question certainly produces much of the verse of Heaney, Harrison, Murray and Dunn.[19]

Exploring this recurring theme in these and other male poets, Crawford constructs the notion of 'identifying poet'; one who creates a poetic identity through which to locate themselves within certain territory regarded as home. Crawford draws most centrally on the work of Mikhail Bahktin in his thinking through these issues, particularly his critical pronouncements on 'culture' and 'outsideness' in his essay 'Response to a Question from the *Novy Mir* Editorial Staff'. Crawford uses Bakhtin's argument that: '[i]n the realm of culture, outsideness is a most powerful factor in understanding. It is only in the eyes of *another culture* that foreign culture reveals itself fully and profoundly …'[20] to give him critical leverage on the experience of exile and the writing of identity in poets such as Robert Frost. Sorley MacLean, Les Murray and Hugh MacDiarmid. Crawford argues that the Bakhtinian notion of 'another culture' might be extended to include the past of your own culture, or might mean the sense of otherness brought about in a geographical remove such as travelling, such as the sojourn in Scotland which allows Les Murray to give poetic voice to his Australianness. A possibility which Crawford does not explore is that it is possible, particularly if one is a woman, or black, to be 'outside' even when one is within one's own culture. In this case perhaps 'home' becomes a somewhat more difficult terrain to claim. Crawford notes, but does not ponder, the following observation: 'The poetic celebrants of home at the moment tend not to be women'.[21]

As other critics have noted, Jamie writes her 'Scottish book', with its dedication to her ain folks, after several years of travel in North

Pakistan, China and Tibet.[22] This travel, Raymond Friel argues, allows her to complete the 'complex task of conjuring the lives and the culture she left behind'.[23] Jamie's travels allow her to reach back to Scotland in a way which might well be read alongside the exile in the North African desert in the Second World War which allowed Sorley Maclean to create that definitive, and crucially-important Gaelic voice on his return to Scotland. Yet what differences might this elide? As the poems explored in this article suggest, Scottishness for Jamie is a complex, often oblique identity. She can, and she does, ponder the 'state' of Scotland and questions of Scottish national identity. Thinking through the evolution of Scotland as a nation in 'Mr & Mrs Scotland Are Dead', Jamie asks: 'Do we save this toolbox, these old-fashioned views / addressed, after all, to Mr and Mrs Scotland?' The answer she finds is that any images of the past we salvage will only disappear when the next generation comes to perform 'the sweeping up' it will want to do.[24] Such a cyclical purging suggests that national identity never remains static. Her thoughts on Scottish identity are always clearly inflected by questions of gender and race. In 'The Republic of Fife', the future strength of Scotland lies in 'citizenship', in the recognition of 'difference', be it of gender, class, race, mental health, species and respect, both symbolic and political, for that difference:

Citizens:

our spires and doocots
institutes and tinkies' benders,
old Scots kings and dancing fairies
give strength to my house

on whose roof we can balance,
carefully stand and see
clear to the far off mountains,
cities, rigs and gardens,

Europe, Africa, the Forth and Tay bridges,
even dare let go, lift our hands
and wave to the waving citizens
of all those other countries.[25]

This assertion that Scotland needs to attend democratically to 'difference' both within and outwith its borders, and indeed writes its best material when it does so, is echoed in Jamie's introduction to the recent issue of *New Writing Scotland*, edited with James McGonigal. Here their selection of recent Scottish writing praises it because '[f]ar from being inward-looking, a sharp attention is turned firth of these shores. The "Scottish" vision and voice extends to Iceland, Africa, America, Italy – though we carry our cultural baggage with us on the journey.'[26]

Writing about Irish and Scottish women's writing, and its relationship with national identity, Marilyn Reizbaum has problematised the pursuit of nationalism for women, arguing that the 'patriarchal dimension' of nationalist movements makes them unlikely political ports of call for women.[27] Already battling to crack open one essentialist identity, ie gender, women are uneasy to collude in the delineation and political fashioning of another, ie. nationality. What emerges from this seemingly unresolvable tension, she argues, is the attempt in both Irish and Scottish women's writing to define 'the relationship between their national and sexual identities.[28] Thus writing about 'home', for women, becomes a problematic project; one which institutes as many exclusions, shuts out just as many people out as it keeps in the warm. As Helen Kidd notes, in her perceptive overview of Scottish women's poetry, there is a resistance throughout women's writing as a whole, to taking up the authority of enunciating an identity for everyone:

> it is more noticeable among women poets that the urge to express and encompass the whole is predominantly absent. The recognition that differences are not to be elided but celebrated is what distinguishes the range of women poets in Scotland.[29]

'Ah, but you're not pure': Jackie Kay

In addition to the inflections of gender, the question: 'Where do you come from? Where's home?' also needs to be pried open further to acknowledge the inflections of race. 'Home' is sometimes a place refused you categorically because you don't 'belong'. Scotland is still swithering about taking the long and painful journey of exploring its own whiteness. The question 'Where do you come from?' opens one of Jackie Kay's early poems, 'So You Think I'm a Mule?', but here prompts even more complicated answers than those located in Jamie's work. Written after an actual experience, the poem records a conversation which takes place between an unwittingly racist white Scotswoman, and Kay. The interlocutor's inability to accept that Blackness and Scottishness are not mutually exclusive identities and the subsequent observation: 'Ah, but you're not pure' occasions Kay's articulate and feisty refusal to accept the terms 'mulatto', 'hybrid', 'half-caste':

> If you Dare mutter mulatto
> hover around hybrid
> hobble on half-caste
> and intellectualize on the
> 'mixed race problem',
> I have to tell you:
> take your beady eyes offa my skin
> don't concern yourself with
> the 'dialectics of mixtures';
> don't pull that strange blood crap
> on me Great White Mother.[30]

Taking the terms of the conversation, staunching the flow of the woman's refusal to accept her allows Kay to carve out a space for her identity and to make the following assertion:

> There's a lot of us
> Black women struggling to define
> just who we are
> where we belong
> and if we know no home
> we know one thing:
> we are Black
> we're at home with that.[31]

Here Kay rewrites the word 'home' in order to transform and multiply its meanings. Thus home might well mean 'place', or 'country', both of which are denied Black women within dominant white culture; but it also describes an emotional state, being 'at home', inscribing the feelings of ease and security which comes with the sense of community with other black women. The question materialises again in a later poem, 'In My Country':

walking by the waters
down where an honest river
shakes hands with the sea,
a woman passed round me
in a slow watchful circle,
as if I were a superstition;

or the worst dregs of her imagination,
so when she finally spoke
her words spliced into bars
of an old wheel. A segment of air.
Where do you come from?
'Here,' I said, 'Here. These parts.'[32]

The question here has an inevitability about it. The woman's words, when they come, traverse the same age-old, terrain, like 'an old wheel'. As Kay notes elsewhere: 'the question ... is one that probably every Black person in this country is asked too many times for comfort. And the question always implies "You don't belong here."'[33] In contrast to 'So You Think I'm a Mule', the tone of the poem is less conversational, more sinister. The woman circles Kay, viewing her as 'a superstition'. The woman's 'imagination' symbolises the cultural consciousness of white Scots, carrying within it age-old narratives about race and possession. Yet in the face of this performative ownership and aggressive interrogation, Kay here asserts her right to exist on Scottish soil succinctly, claiming her place within 'parts' of the country.

In contrast to Kathleen Jamie, Kay's exploration of Scottish identity and its exclusions occupies a large part of her poetic oeuvre from its very beginnings. Here we must extend the Bakhtinian notion of 'another culture' further; for Kay the realities of being 'outside' are powerfully inflected by issues of gender, race (and indeed sexuality). 'Another culture' becomes literally written both on and through her body, and becomes an internalised sense of continual otherness. Her subjectivity becomes forcibly split between blackness and Scottishness. Kay's first collection of poems, *The Adoption Papers* (1991), won the Saltire First Book of the Year award, a Forward Prize and was awarded a Scottish Arts Council Book and situated her, as Fred D'Aguiar has argued, as 'a new and distinctive voice on the British literary scene'.[34] The newness of the now familiar story of a black child's adoption by white Communist parents in Glasgow importantly registered the politics of race upon the map of Scottish national identity. Yet the question remains quite it is that Scotland has done with this politics since.

Kay is rightly included in *Dream State: The New Scottish Poets* as one of the 'major' voices at the cutting-edge of Scottish poetry. Her work is represented by several poems from *The Adoption Papers*. In his Introduction, Daniel O'Rourke characterises the poetic voice of *The Adoption Papers* by its 'openness and amiability'. Despite her threefold 'status as an outsider' (being black, lesbian and Scottish), O'Rourke is impressed that Kay manages to produce 'the friendliest and most "upbeat" poetry' in his collection. Her poetic voice, he argues, is at all times '[f]resh, chatty, funny, yet capable of great depth and serious-ness'.[35] Yet the question must surely remain just how 'upbeat' an 'outsider' can continue to be when faced with these exclusions and their impact upon his/her sense of selfhood. *The Adoption Papers* sequence within the larger collection is rendered in three 'voices': adoptive mother, birth mother and daughter. There is certainly humour, particularly in the voice of the white, Glaswegian woman who hitches her hopes onto the wee sick black baby in the Edinburgh hospital. There is also incredible energy in the rough and ready Scots of the feisty black kid facing up to those who call her 'Sambo' in the playground. Yet registered also throughout is the sharp-edged, broken pain of giving a child up for adoption, and the painful recognition of separation and otherness from a birth mother: emotions to be worked through in writing and relationships for years to come. In the voice of the daughter:

> One dream cuts another open like a gutted fish
> nothing is what it was;
> she is too many imaginings to be flesh and blood.
> There is nothing left to say.
> Neither of us mentions meeting again.[36]

O'Rourke's appraisal of Kay's work might be taken to signify a larger refusal on the part of the white, male Scottish literary mainstream to work through questions of race and Scottish national identity. Kay's poetry, within *The Adoption Papers* itself, and in the two collections which have followed it, extends the poetics of identity in complex, often very painful ways. The range of her poetic voices is, in fact, incredibly broad and represents, amongst other things, a journey towards a unified sense of self which deserves serious critical consideration.[37] Faced with the 'impossibility' of being Black and Scottish, Kay found her coordinates by looking beyond its shores, searching out an iconic blackness which transcended national boundaries:

> I did not think that Bessie Smith only belonged to African Americans or that Nelson Mandela belonged to South Africans. I could not think like that because I knew then of no black Scottish heroes that I could claim for my own. I reached out and claimed Bessie.[38]

Kay's work after *The Adoption Papers* plots the map with which she learned to negotiate the often impassable landscape of growing up black in Glasgow, despite loving and devoted parents. The blues singer Bessie Smith in particular features as one of the key figures in Kay's early imaginary. Kay writes a sequence of seven poems in her second collection *Other Lovers* which eulogise Smith, and explore the terms of her influence on Kay. It is a sustaining love affair which begins early, when Kay is a young child. Her first encounter with Smith is related movingly in 'In the Red Graveyard':

> I am coming down the stairs in my father's house.
> I am five or six or seven. There is fat thick wallpaper
> I always caress, bumping flower into flower.
> She is singing. (Did they play anyone else ever?)
> My father's feet tap a shiny beat on the floor.
>
> Christ, my father says, that's some voice she's got.
> I pick up the record cover. And now. This is slow motion.
> My hand swoops, glides, swoops again.
> I pick up the cover and my fingers are all over her face.
> Her black face. Her magnificent black face.
> That's some voice. His shoes dancing on the floor.[39]

The child's first encounter with Smith's blackness is her 'voice'. A voice she has already been taught to love because of her parents' awe of it. This voice 'claims the rooms' of her childhood house. It changes 'the shape of [her] silence'. It teaches her that she is neither alone nor the only one. The movement of the poem slows right down, creating cine-footage of the epiphanic moment in which the young child picks up the record cover and recognises something like herself in Smith's 'magnificent black face'. Focusing in with a close-up of this wonderful instance of first identification with a black face, the father figure recedes into the background, still dancing; Kay, we understand, is off on her own journey now. Taking Smith as a role-model allows Kay to access a cultural heritage which has previously been denied her as an anomalous black, adopted, Scots kid. Coming to writing as an adult, she explores the terms of the release this gave. In the Bessie Smith sequence, Kay literally joins Smith on the 'blues trail' across America, 'from Chattanooga to Chicago'.[40] As Paraskevi Papaleonida notes, 'Kay uses the Blues Tour, the wandering Pullman as a memory of her own, and at the same time a kind of collective memory of which she partakes.'[41] Taking these imaginary trips with Smith, across alternative landscapes and national identities, 'halves' Kay's 'heartbreak':

> We got so much heartbreak, we can't divide it easily.
> I take one piece, she takes another, we both drive
> And our sadness drives further,
> It's way up ahead, ahead of Bessie and me.[42]

Such imaginary leavings must finally and inevitably be made real and indeed Kay's development, in terms of both her identity and her writing, meant quitting Glasgow for the cultural diversity and political flashpoint of London in the summer of 1981. Living in a squat in Vauxhall, close enough to feel involved in the events in Brixton and joining her first black women's writing group, Kay discovered emotional support, political language and a tradition of black women's writing through Toni Morrison and Audre Lorde. Lorde in particular, as a black lesbian, gave her 'a name. In print'.[43] Accessing this black culture, however, created a kind of split subjectivity in which Kay felt she had to deny her Scottishness in order to acknowledge her black-ness. In an interview in 1994, Kay explains: 'At first when I really began to acknowledge my blackness, I wanted to deny my Scottishness, because I felt ashamed at being so old without knowing any black culture.' Such a split says much, in the first instance, about the refusal of dominant Scottish culture to find any way of accommodating blackness, and something very profound too about the pressure and necessity of living in 'one' national identity in modern culture. Yet writing poetry became a way for Kay to knit these two identities back together, of reaching backwards to her Scottishness: 'This, to me, is [what] writing is all about, being able to embrace contradictions, acknowledge them.'[44] Such a restitution of multiple selfhood can be found in the poem 'Kail and Callaloo', in which Kay explores the complexities of what it might mean to be Afro Scot:

> I'm eating callaloo and kail now
> tattie scones and pumpkin pie
> so many foods I never tasted
> mango before I was nineteen
> or yam or cocoa root or sugar cane
> like I never read Ngugi or Bessie Head
> only Hugh MacDiarmid and Liz Lochead
> (and they werenie even taught in school)
> Liz was my teenage hero
> OCH MEN and her stop and start rhythm
> I'd never heard of Audre Lorde then.[45]

Paraskevi Papaleonida argues that Kay's poetry (in addition to the poetry of Grace Nichols) displays a syncretism common to most post-colonial literatures, in which seemingly irreconcilable elements are brought together 'as harmoniously as possible'.[46] Certainly, in 'Kail and Callaloo' we witness a compelling and powerful fusion of cultural difference: words, food, writers, history. The poem opens with Kay's disgust at the 'origin' question in passports and job applications. To be Celtic-Afro-Caribbean is a 'contradiction' and, these official documents imply, an impossibility: 'how kin ye be both?' Yet the speaker of the poem insists that she does exist and she is both. Exploring the terms of this identity then occupies the body of the poem. Most importantly, this poem allows Kay to *inscribe* this identity, literally *writing* it into existence. Here she insistently bringing the previously polarised parts of her black Scottish identity together. One of the ways in which this is done is through history; colonialism and marginalisation are mapped across both blackness and Scottishness. Ngugi and Bessie Head may have been unavailable to the teenage Kay but so, it transpires, were MacDiarmid and Lochhead, displaced from the Scottish curriculum by the colonisations of *English* literature. Embracing both facets of her blackness and her Scottishness, allowing the fluid boundaries of these identities to meld, Kay begins to make connections between her two cultural inheritances. Reading about the successful slave revolt on the Caribbean island of San Domingo in 1791, in C.L.R. James's *The Black Jacobins*, Kay can suddenly see similarities between Caribbean and Scottish history:

> I'm learning about the Black Jacobins
> from CLR James and the memories of the
> Cheviot the stag and the Highlanders

being forced oot of their crofts
came flooding back[47]

There are after all, this poem suggests, ways of bringing blackness and Scottishness together, not least, to some degree, by a shared experience of colonial oppression. Brutal moments within Scottish history, such as the Highland Clearances, mirror and overlap the history of black slavery in the West Indies. Plotting these parallels, both of which become kinds of historical memory-traces in her consciousness, allows Kay to make the powerful political statement: 'Clearances is a common word'.[48] Thus the intimate, domestic realities of being an Afro-Scot, eating both kail and callaloo, celebrating both Halloween and Hogmanay are braced within a larger, overarching political frame in which the fact that passports and job applications refuse to accord a place to Celtic-Afro-Caribbeans can be understood.

'And I found my feet': in conclusion

As Scotland constructs itself, at the edge of a new millennium, the narratives of identity found in Scottish women writers and poets, with their insistence on a pluralistic, complicated version of Scottishness that recognises 'difference', are surely of the greatest importance. Now, as always, Scotland's writing remains its greatest asset. As Jackie Kay argues: 'writing [is] a sort of up-to-date history – a writing of the present that in the future will stand as a document for the past'.[49]

Not least the poetry of contemporary Scottish women poets such as Jamie and Kay reveals to us that notions of identity and 'home' are never stable or static, but always evolving and transforming. To be a woman, to be black, to be lesbian, to be young, to be Scots (male or female) means that the search for 'home' is an unending quest without closure – a journey which inevitably involves both the past and the future. Perhaps instead it is 'homing' that is the on-going and perpetual psychic state. In two recent poems, this sense is evoked by both Jamie and Kay. In 'Forget It', Jamie articulates her difference from her parents, who opt for a kind of forgetting of the pain of Scottish history. For Jamie, however, looking to that history is a principal part of her selfhood:

We done the slums today!
I bawled from the glass
front door she'd long desired.

> *What for?* bangs the oven shut.
> *Some history's better forgot.*[50]

But for Jamie, 'stories are balm, / ease their own pain, contain / a beginning, a middle –', but no end? The 'end' remains to be seen because: '... this is a past / not yet done ...'[51] Jackie Kay's search for selfhood continues to grapple with the complexities of 'dual citizenship'. To be white and Scottish still seems like a tighter narrative, a surer thing. In the poem 'Pride', Kay enters into a conversation with a black man on the overnight train back to Glasgow. As they 'journey' back to Scotland, this man tells Kay that he can tell the Nigerian village to which she belongs – she is an Ibo. He can read it in her face. If she were to go back, he assures her, they would throw 'massive celebrations'. His insistence, his pride, his rootedness remind Kay of strains of Scottish nationalism:

> His face had a look
> I've seen on a MacLachlan, a MacDonnell, a Macleod,
> the most startling thing, pride,
> a quality of being certain.[52]

This 'certainty' is appealing to Kay. It sends her on an imaginary journey back, beneath and over this train-ride to Scotland. The man's stories of the Ibos imbue her fantasy of return with an appealing and seductive sense of authenticity, closure, belonging. Some older, deeply hidden part of her emerges as she dreams this homecoming:

> And I found my feet.
> I started to dance.
> I danced a dance I never knew I knew.
> Words and sounds fell out of my mouth like seeds.
> I astonished myself.
> My grandmother was like me exactly, only darker.

It is an evocative, powerful dream, densely riven with the pain of previous exclusions and losses. It tells of the joy of being returned to oneself after years of isolation, contradictions, refusals. But it dies, as quickly as it was born, when Kay comes back to the present: 'When I looked up, the black man had gone. / Only my own face startled me in the dark train window.'[53] The 'quality of being certain' about oneself is a desirable, but unattainable thing. All that remains is her own face, the embodiment of all the complexities and apparent contradictions of her identity. The face caught in the movement of the train-window at some indiscriminate point between London and Scotland, between the past and the future: a fitting metaphor for Kay as she continues to write herself into existence, and for Scotland.

Notes

1. Derick Thomson, '1707–1979', *Creachadh Na Clarsaich (Plundering the Harp): Collected Poems 1940–1980* (Edinburgh: Macdonald, 1982), p. 261.
2. Christopher Whyte, 'Introduction', in *Gendering the Nation: Studies in Modern Scottish Literature*, ed. Whyte (Edinburgh: Edinburgh University Press, 1995), p. xii.
3. Hugh MacDiarmid, cited in Margaret Bain, 'Scottish Women in Politics', *CHAPMAN* 6. 3–4 (Summer 1980), p. 7.
4. Liz Lochhead, interviewed in *Poem, Purpose and Place: Shaping Identity in Contemporary Scottish Verse*, ed. Colin Nicholson (Edinburgh: Polygon, 1992), p. 204.
5. Joanne P. Sharp, 'Gendering Nationhood: A Feminist Engagement with National Identity', in *Bodyspace: Destabilising Geographies of Gender and Sexuality*, ed. Nancy Duncan (London: Routledge, 1996), p. 99.
6. Whyte, *Gendering the Nation*, p. xvi.
7. Dorothy McMillan, 'Twentieth-century Poetry II: The Last Twenty-five Years', in *A History of Scottish Women's Writing*, ed Douglas Gifford and Dorothy McMillan (Edinburgh: Edinburgh University Press, 1997), p. 549.
8. Cairns Craig, 'Twentieth Century Scottish Literature: An Introduction', in *The History of Scottish Literature*, vol. I; *Twentieth Century* (Aberdeen: Aberdeen University Press), p. 3.
9. Kathleen Jamie, 'Arraheids', *The Queen of Sheba* (Newcastle: Bloodaxe, 1994), p. 40.
10. Hugh MacDiarmid, *A Drunk Man Looks at the Thistle* (Edinburgh: Scottish Academic Press, 1987), p. 148.
11. Suzanne Hagemann, 'Women and Nation', in Gifford and McMillan, *A History of Scottish Women's Writing*, p. 319.
12. Jamie, 'Bairns of Suzie: A Hex', in *The Queen of Sheba*, pp. 25–6.
13. Jamie, 'The Queen of Sheba', in *The Queen of Sheba*, pp. 9–11.
14. Raymond Friel, 'Women Beware Gravity', in *Southfields: Criticism and Celebration* (London: Southfields Press, 1995), p. 31.
15. Jamie, 'Child with Pillar Box and Bin Bags', in *The Queen of Sheba*, p. 15.
16. Sean O'Brien, *The Deregulated Muse: Essays on Contemporary British and Irish Poetry* (Newcastle: Bloodaxe, 1998), p. 266.
17. Kathleen Jamie, interviewed in *Sleeping with Monsters: Conversations with Scottish and Irish Women Poets*, ed. Gillian Somerville-Arjat and Rebecca E. Wilson (Edinburgh: Polygon, 1990), p. 94.

18. Kathleen Jamie, in *Dream State: The New Scottish Poets*, ed. Daniel O'Rourke (Edinburgh: Polygon, 1994), p. 156.

19. Robert Crawford, *Identifying Poets: Self and Territory in Twentieth-Century Poetry* (Edinburgh: Edinburgh University Press, 1993), p. 144.

20. Mikhail Bakhtin, 'Response to a Question from the *Novy Mir* Editorial Staff', quoted in Crawford, *Identifying Poets*, p. 12.

21. Ibid., p. 144.

22. These travels are recounted through various poetic selves. See Kathleen Jamie, 'Karakoram Highway', in *The Way We Live* (Newcastle: Bloodaxe, 1987) and *The Autonomous Region*, with Sean Mayne Smith, (Newcastle: Bloodaxe, 1993).

23. Friel, 'Women Beware Gravity', p. 29.

24. Jamie, 'Mr and Mrs Scotland Are Dead', in *The Queen of Sheba*, p. 37.

25. Jamie, 'The Republic of Fife', in *The Queen of Sheba*, pp. 50–1.

26. Kathleen Jamie and James McGonigal (with Meg Bateman), 'Introduction', in *Full-Strength Angels: New Writing Scotland* 14, 1996.

27. Marilyn Reizbaum, 'Canonical Double Cross: Scottish and Irish Women's Writing', in *Decolonizing Tradition: New Views of Twentieth-Century 'British' Literary Canons*, ed. Karen Lawrence (Urbana: University of Illinois Press, 1992), pp. 165–90.

28. Here Reizbaum uses the undoubtedly central example of Eavan Boland, who for reasons of space I do not explore in more depth. Boland finds a way back to Irishness, despite the exclusions of Irish nationalism, by beginning to understand both Ireland's 'otherness' and her own as being cognates of the same system. From this position she can begin to write about Ireland in her poetry. See Eavan Boland. 'The Woman Poet in a National Tradition', *Studies* 76. 302 (Summer 1987).

29. Helen Kidd, 'Writing Near the Fault Line: Scottish Women Poets and the Topography of Tongues', in *Kicking Daffodils: Twentieth-Century Women Poets*, ed. Vicki Bertram (Edinburgh: Edinburgh University Press, 1997), p. 99.

30. Jackie Kay, 'So You Think I'm a Mule', in Somerville-Arjat and Wilson, *Sleeping with Monsters*, p. 128.

31. Ibid.

32. Jackie Kay, 'In My Country', in *Other Lovers* (Newcastle: Bloodaxe, 1993), p. 24.

33. Jackie Kay, interviewed by Rebecca E. Wilson in Somerville-Arjat and Wilson, *Sleeping with Monsters*, p. 121.

34. Fred D'Aguiar, 'Have You Been Here Long? Black Poetry in Britain', in *New British Poetries: The Scope of the Possible*, ed. Robert Hampson and Peter Barry (Manchester: Manchester University Press, 1993), p. 66.

35. Daniel O'Rourke, 'Introduction', in *Dream State: The New Scottish Poets*, ed. O'Rourke (Edinburgh, Polygon Press, 1994), pp. xxxiv–xxxv.

36. Jackie Kay, 'The Meeting Dream', in *The Adoption Papers* (Newcastle: Bloodaxe, 1991), p. 33.

37. These poetic voices are now supplemented by her 'arrival' on the prose scene with her first novel *Trumpet*, winner of the Guardian Fiction prize in 1998. Continuing to explore the boundaries of identity, *Trumpet* tells the story of Joss Moody, a celebrated trumpeter who 'passes' throughout his

jazz career, until posthumously outed as a woman. See Jackie Kay, *Trumpet* (London: Picador, 1998).

38. Jackie Kay, *Bessie Smith* (Bath: Absolute Press, 1997), p. 15.
39. Kay, 'In the Red Graveyard', in *Other Lovers*, p. 13.
40. Kay, 'The Right Season', in *Other Lovers*, p. 11.
41. Paraskevi Papaleonida, 'Holding My Beads in My Hand: Dialogue, Synthesis and Power in the Poetry of Jackie Kay and Grace Nicols', in Bertram, *Kicking Daffodils*, pp. 133–4.
42. Kay, 'In the Pullman', in *Other Lovers*, p. 10.
43. Jackie Kay, interviewed in *Into the Nineties: Postcolonial Women's Writing*, ed. Anna Rutherford, Lars Jensen and Shirley Crew (Armidale, NSW: Dangeroo Press, 1994), p. 534.
44. Ibid., p. 535.
45. Jackie Kay, 'Kail and Callaloo', in *Charting the Journey: Writings by Black and Third World Women*, ed. Shabnam Grewal, Jackie Kay, Liliane Landor, Gail Lewis and Pratibha Parmar (London: Sheba, 1988), p. 196.
46. Papaleonida, 'Holding My Beads in My Hand', p. 126.
47. Kay, 'Kail and Callaloo', in Grewal et al., *Charting the Journey*, p. 196.
48. Ibid., p. 197.
49. Kay, in *Into the Nineties*, p. 535.
50. Kathleen Jamie, 'Forget It', *Penguin Modern Poets 9* (Harmondsworth: Penguin), p. 145.
51. Ibid., pp. 146–7.
52. Jackie Kay, 'Pride', in *Off Colour* (Newcastle: Bloodaxe, 1988), p. 63.
53. Ibid., p. 64.

21
'A She Even Smaller Than a Me': Gender Dramas of the Contemporary Avant-Garde

Harriet Tarlo

> Write poetries. Write writings, write readings, write drafts. Write
> several selves to dissolve the bounded idea of the self
>
> who is 'I' who is 'you'
> who is 'he' is 'she'
> fleeting shifts of position, social charges implying a
> millenia [*sic*] of practice. To disturb the practice
>
> by 'itness' a floating referent, a bounding alone the
> multiplex borders of marginality. An avoidance of
> transcendence everywhere, including in the idea of the artist –
> – no genius. no god. no prophet, no priest.[1]

This extract from *The Pink Guitar,* Rachel Blau DuPlessis's book of
experimental essays on writing as feminist practice, shows critical
writing at the intersection of poststructuralist theory, feminist liguis-
tics, and experimental writing, an intersection which this essay will
explore. In this piece DuPlessis is thinking, feeling and writing her way
out of a specifically female 'prison house' of language and subjectivity.
She attempts to break down the notion of the self as singular and
whole in structure and in gender, whilst also tackling the idea of the
poet as the transcendent masculine conveyer of truth and beauty.
DuPlessis favours instead the model of a dialogical and disrupted
poet/self, a model which we shall see later in action in her poetry.

The aspect of this quotation I want to draw attention to here is
DuPlessis's unusual use of pronouns. The placing of inverted commas
around 'I', 'you', 'he' and 'she' draws attention to, and yet questions,
the essentialism of pronouns. The elision of the expected second 'who'

in the line 'who is "he" is "she"' and the lack of question marks throughout these lines seems to blur the pronoun's definitive referential status, bringing into question both the whole notion of individual subjectivity, and of gender difference. Yet the fundamentally mysterious nature of the pronoun without referent remains in the alternative reading of these polysemous lines as a series of questions leading to one major question: who *is* I/you/he/she? What is the pronoun?

Here I explore the role of the pronoun, in particular its gender significance, in contemporary women's poetry. I shall show that the questioning, the disruption, of the pronoun in writing often considered 'avant-garde', 'experimental' or 'linguistically innovative' forms a significant part of the gender and language politics of this writing, and forms interesting parallels with the feminist linguistic critique of androcentric language and prescriptive grammar.[2] At times, these poetries go so far as to achieve such a shift in pronominal and hence gender consciousness as feminist linguists have proposed. The poets have an advantage that the linguists do not. As Susan Ehrlich and Ruth King point out in their essay on 'Gender-Based Language Reform and the Social Construction of Meaning' the difficulty in reforming language is that the socio-political context must be ready to receive such reform or it will simply be re-assimilated and re-signified into the sexist status quo.[3] Avant-garde poetry, though it may have difficulty in achieving a wide socio-political forum, has at its basis a defamiliarisation of language which cannot be reassimilated. Its challenge remains with the reader or listener.

It is not surprising that the use of pronouns by experimental women writers should be of particular interest, since these poets are deeply concerned with language, language politics and, very often, social change. Whereas more traditional contemporary women writers usually adopt an undisturbed first person singular voice (either in lyric or dramatic monologue mode), experimental writers adopt a plethora of different – usually unattributed – pronouns, thus disturbing the semantics of their work. Contemporary women poets in the innovative tradition often perceive their writing as descending from that of early twentieth-century Modernist women writers like H.D. and Gertrude Stein which also makes great play with the pronoun's powers and ambiguities. To some extent then these poets are part of a tradition for whom playful manipulation of the smaller elements of language has long been significant.

What then are the mysterious powers of the pronoun? It was Roman Jakobsen, in his study of duplex structures, who first referred to pronouns as 'shifters' and Roland Barthes, in his *Elements of Semiology*, who introduced the term to twentieth-century structuralists and post-structuralists. Jakobsen explains how 'shifters' are one of the last structures of language that the child learns to control. Although shifters obey the conventional rules of language, being words used to refer to their objects, he points out that 'I' can only designate the person using it, and 'you' the person spoken to.[4] A shifter then depends absolutely on the context in which it is used and, by its very nature, an unidentified shifter can never be resolved in retrospect: the shifters will again have shifted. Grammatical sense depends on reliably attributed shifters; much contemporary experimental work thrives on grammatical non-sense. One effect of this, of course, is that the reader is forced into active participation in the work. In the poetry I discuss here, the reader must negotiate with mysteriously detached, dispersed or uncertainly attributable shifters. I shall use the term 'shifter' here, since it emphasizes the agile and elusive qualities of the shifting shifters we find in these poetries.

The second important aspect of shifters to stress is their gender-significance. For women writers and linguists concerned with gender issues the pronoun is particularly significant. In English 'I' and 'you' are not of course gender specific, nor are 'me', 'we' or 'they', but 'she' and 'he' are. I should like then to make a distinction here between the gender specific shifter and the gender-mysterious shifter. A further point about the gender politics of shifters, as the feminist critique of androcentric language structures has amply demonstrated, is that the male pronoun always takes precedence. The most notable example of this in English is when the masculine third person singular (he) is used as the referent for a universal generic human being, who could in fact be male or female. As Deborah Cameron points out, with reference to some of the writers featured in her useful reader, *The Feminist Critique of Language*, feminist linguistic analyses of, and responses to, this state of affairs differ:

[According to] Black and Coward ... women are always defined by their gender, whereas men are allowed to pass themselves off as generic human beings with no gender.... Black and Coward suggest that the way to tackle this asymmetry is not to de-gender women but to *engender* men.... Irigaray, like Black and Coward, points to an asymmetry between men and women, but while she would agree that men are represented as the universal human subjects, her argument is not that men have no gender whereas women are defined by it, it is rather that men are the *only* gender that is recognized in language or culture.... The difference that underpins gender distinctions ... is not 'man/woman' but 'man/not-man'.[5]

As I shall show at greater length later, Irigaray's perception of the problem leads her to conclude that it is women who need to be engendered. One of the interesting aspects of tracing the shifts of the shifter in contemporary avant-garde women's poetry is seeing how poets' responses to language – their search for ways out of the female prison house – form intriguing parallels with those of feminist theorists and linguists. We shall find that the distinctions Cameron so clearly points to, between the work of Maria Black and Rosalind Coward, and that of Luce Irigaray, are reflected in the work of the poets discussed here. The other major area of feminist criticism to which the problematisation of pronouns relates closely is the vexed question of subjectivity and gender, which has so exercised poststructuralist feminist thinkers in recent decades. This too forms part of the theoretical framework of my enquiry.

Gender-specific pronouns

Gender dramas

The gender-specific pronoun is often used shiftily in contemporary work to draw attention to the shifter and its sex. In an experimental poetry which is not especially interested in the referential or the narrative, shifters are frequently liberated from reference (to a name) and narrative (the all important context), which would, in common discourse or traditional dialogue, place them. The shifter then loses its referential power but gains as a non-specific gender marker, for the one story that the gender-specific shifter *always* tells is a gender story. The gender story may be more or less evident, more or less encoded or emphasized, more or less intentionally invoked, but can never wholly be eradicated from the form. Here are two poems by the British poet Frances Presley which form clear examples of the gender-specific pronoun in dramatic action:

MIRO

We are sand and oil
on tar paper
we are forms on a black ground

stencils
black lace gloves
light through dark leaves
on a kitchen table
– Those aren't stencils, he said
scintilla
spangles[6]

Purple, White & Green

– A terrible colour combination, he said
                              I'm not sure
I like the clematis drooping on its stem
              as we raise it through the trellis

Did Emily train the reins
              or was she already under turf
                     in her purest thoughts ?[7]

In both these poems we see a gender drama in action. In the first the 'we' is cut across by the definitive denying statement made by the 'he' who speaks himself out of the 'we' set up in the poem thus far. In the second poem the statement made by the 'he' pronoun is again at odds with the private musing 'I', who likes the 'terrible colour combination', at least in part through its identification with the suffragette movement and Emily Pankhurst. In these gender dramas the gendered fragments of casual speech, both masculine, exist as powerful interventions from the outside into a private ungendered inner world, the 'we' and the 'I'. Hence the 'he', as the only gendered pronoun, becomes more significant. The implication could be that, inside oneself, one does not dwell on one's own gender – yet the gender of the outside/other person is always significant, especially if it is not the same as your own. From a more radically feminist viewpoint (and perhaps Emily is the clue here), the implication could be that these poems by a woman writer are making the feminine gender the assumed norm when using the non-gender specific pronoun and the masculine the exception, a reversal then of the cultural status quo: here the 'he' not the 'she' is the other. These poems can therefore be seen to attempt a shift in consciousness in the direction Black and Coward advocate, that of the engendering of the previously universal masculine.

A similar effect occurs in the next poem, from Rosemarie Waldrop's book-length sequence, *Lawn of Excluded Middle*. The book is an investigation into the feminine which both exploits and critiques the laws and language of logical philosophy. Waldrop is particularly, and very wittily, critical of syllogism and binary thinking. As this piece shows, her work examines the relation of the female body to language, time and history, as well as to the 'other' of the masculine:

> The silence, which matted my hair like a room with the windows shut too long, filled with your breath. As if you didn't need the weight of words in your lungs to keep your body from dispersing like so many molecules over an empty field. Being a woman and without history, I wanted to explore how the grain of the world runs, hoping for backward and forward, the way sentences breathe even this side of explanation. But you claimed that words absorb all perspective and blot out the view just as certain parts of the body obscure others on the curve of desire. Or again, as the message gets lost in the long run, while we still see the messenger panting, unflagging, through the centuries. I had thought it went the other way round and was surprised as he came out of my mouth in his toga, without even a raincoat. I had to lean far out the window to follow his now unencumbered course, speeding your theory towards a horizon flat and true as a spirit level.[8]

Here the fractured narrative gives us the silence of a woman 'without history', a silence weighed down by the presence of the unnamed other, but with a desire to explore history and culture ('the grain of the world'). Then a spiralling of simile takes over – language is the metaphor for culture, and the body is the metaphor for language – giving way to the riddle of the messenger, an unnamed 'he' or male other. This messenger metaphor suddenly becomes actualised in the narrative, absurdly, yet grotesquely, emerging from the speaker's mouth in a comic twist. We and she are left with no answers about the 'grain of the world', as she gazes into infinity after the other's 'theory'. We can also read that his 'theory' is spinning out of her belief system, that she rejects here the whole notion of a theoretical, hence logical, explanation. Certainly when we follow the 'logic' of the piece, we find, as we often do in women's experimental writings, that it is thwarted, just as the female speaker is thwarted in her quest here. The speaker becomes entangled in the historic art of metaphor which pulls her further and further away from her desire, until it is finally exposed by the literalising of an absurd metaphor and even dressing it in a Roman toga, suggestive of the Latinate construction of 'our' language. Since the 'he' referring to this messenger is the only gender specific pronoun in the poem 'he' becomes associated with generic masculinity and masculinity becomes associated in turn with the dominant theories mentioned above. Although 'he' is a somewhat ludicrous figure in the poem, nonetheless *his* power to come out of *her* mouth, apparently against her conscious will, is sinister. This, and his joke historical wear, the toga, are clearly a wry dig at the androcentric nature of language and history.

The sequence from which the poem comes can also be read as a love sequence and Waldrop uses the traditional 'I/you' pronominal structure of love poetry throughout. The judicious use Waldrop makes of 'he' and 'she' however, allows her to interrogate the power inequalities and sexual difference of the generic masculine and the generic feminine. In the case of this poem, the final sentence, 'I had to lean far out the window to follow *his* now unencumbered course, speeding *your* theory towards a horizon flat and true as a spirit level [my emphasis]', clearly identifies the 'you' lover with the 'he' messenger. 'He' and 'she' then ruptures the smooth, personal, non-gendered 'I' and 'you' allowing the poet space for subtle gender commentary. This technique of rupture also emphasizes that, in writing love lyric, women are breaking into a masculine genre in which the woman is traditionally the silent 'you', not the 'I'. Note how Waldrop in the words, 'Being a woman', takes care to identify here that the poem's speaker is female.

Another striking example of the use of the shifting shifter by an avant-garde woman poet experimenting with the love lyric is Mei-Mei Berssenbrugge's sequence 'Pack Rat Sieve' from her book *The Heat Bird*.[9] Berssenbrugge shifts the shifters in 'Pack Rat Sieve' between 'he' and 'you'; 'I' and 'you'; 'I' and 'he' and 'she' and 'he'. The effect is to shift the narrative, the extent to which the speaker of the poems becomes lyric subject, the degree of reader-identification, and our gender consciousness. All these elements become destabilised in the sequence to the extent that we are not always sure who is speaking in the poem, especially as other referents enter the poem at times.

When 'I' and 'he' and 'I' and 'you' are the personal pronouns employed, the poems resemble more traditional love lyrics as spoken by the conventional lyric subject:

> ... If I want
> to call you. I could use the radio, still ... (17)

> ... He says it's hard to shut out the world
> with a thought. I shut my eyes. I hear a long branch
> scraping against another, continuously, like a violin
> without breath ... (18)

However when Berssenbrugge uses 'you' and 'he', 'you' is not the addressee, but the generic 'you' who includes the speaker and women in general. This 'you' also implicates us, her readers, who thus become drawn into the sequence:

> Never mind if he calls, the places you get
> through inwardness take time ...
> ... and the horizon is just a change where
> from going deep you go wider, but go. (13)

When 'he' and 'she' are used in the same sequence the poems shift again, and the effect, as in Presley and Waldrop, is to emphasize the gender-specific pronoun. Both speaker and reader become outsiders watching a gender-specific and hence gender-significant exchange:

> ... He told her
> the Chinese put halves of a settee on opposite
> sides of a room, but she preferred a white jar's
> closing arc to the sky, like the arms of two hills
> holding it. He disdained her fear.... (21)

Whereas Presley and Waldrop could be said to universalise the female and engender the male, Bersenbrugge, in engendering both male and female, poses the problem of 'she'.

The problem of 'she'

> *19.54*
>
> She beetles the sheets with screams.
> She puts hair and dying together.
> She keeps washing – combing – drying.
> She is dwarfed and oppressed by reason.
> A she even smaller than a me.
> The child Mary? No. A banshee.[10]

In this poem from her book-length sequence *O'Clock* Fanny Howe plays with simple diction and sentence structure to flummox our linguistic expectations. We expect the word 'dying' for instance to read 'drying' or even 'dyeing', when put with 'hair'. There is wry humour, yet an unease too, when we make the slip. The structure of the piece suggests a riddle but, although the shifter 'she' dominates each line, the question, 'who is "she"?', remains mysterious. 'She' appears to be marginalised in a domestic yet desperate ('sheets with screams') scene. In the context of Howe's sequence, which makes reference to Catholicism, 'Mary' suggests the New Testament Mary, but the word 'banshee' suggests a traditional Irish supernatural female spirit, an alternative 'she' image. Yet could ban/shee also suggest a banned she, even one who is in some sense 'dying'? The most riddling line, 'A she even smaller than a me', draws attention, by its 'ungrammatical' use of the indefinite article, to both 'she' and 'me' and allows us to read them as simultaneously specific and generic. It is the line which most suggests that this possibly worn out, dying 'she' cannot contain 'me', the multitudinous self. Here Howe seems to suggest that the gender-specific feminine pronoun is insufficient or indeed over gender-determined, associated with a series of wornout images.

The gender-specific pronoun 'she' poses an immediate problem of essentialism. I cited a similar problem above when discussing the work of Ehrlich and King. They identify socio-political context as the all-important context for gender-based language reform. A sexist status quo will continue reproducing sexist language. In 'she' we do at least have a sexed pronoun, but that pronoun has existed in a sexist context for generations and is coloured accordingly. With pronouns, of course, context is all; as Fanny Howe writes elsewhere in *O'Clock*, 'No she without a where, no I without a when' (69). In her first poetry book, *Marxism for Infants*, Denise Riley identified the problem and longed for escape or radical revision of 'she' in her poem, 'A note on sex and "the reclaiming of language"':

> The work is
> e.g. to write 'she' and for that to be a statement
> of fact only and not a strong image
> of everything which is not-you, which sees you[11]

How then do women poets deal with this problem of 'she'; how can they deconstruct and/or reconstruct our only direct gendered representation in language? One way is of course to lay emphasis, to shine a light, as Howe does here, on 'she', thus interrogating and defamiliarising the pronoun. Another, as we have seen, is not to allow the reader to forget where 'she' is situated within a pronominal structure which gives precedence to 'he'.

Rachel Blau DuPlessis's poetry is acutely aware of the 'rose-pink/ border'[12] of assimilated femininity constantly constraining women through an intimately bound web of time, place and culture, the 'set of girl hankies, saying Monday, Tuesday'.[13] DuPlessis now calls her poems 'drafts', stressing their provisionality. The drafts form a long series of interrelated poems (thirty-eight as of 1999) stretching across book boundaries. A major linguistic interest for DuPlessis is the pronoun, in particular its relationship to the construction of gendered selfhood. Here is an extract from her very first draft, 'Draft 1: It':

> There's no way to read it?
> One point is to achieve a social momentum of switched
> referrents and (merry coral   white clover
> ding ding ding) commentary in which what   he (you)
> says or does must be read differently from what she
> does or says whether he, you does it to her or them to
> it (of whom?) she to it feels different (nights of Holly-
> wood fascism) in an unsettling but not articulate way.
> power power imbedded in, in its   (days of military realism)
> place on the pronoun grid, cells squeak in protest 'it's
> just language' 'we're just nature'[14]

Here, in a poetics of wit and wordplay, the first line suggests the intangibility of the written pronoun whilst demonstrating the sheer shiftiness of language when the referent is also the referee. DuPlessis goes on to weave some serious nonsense, in part a fantasy of the liberated referent escaping its preset role. Questions of gender and ideology are written in to this dance of shifters as the difference of the male and female pronouns is stressed and the ideological nature of power in language is emphasised by the image of the grid and the amusing protest of the elements of language 'we're just nature'. As feminist linguists have shown, this naturalising of prescriptive grammar is relatively recent. Ann Bodine in her historical study of the generic masculine third person singular proves that pre-nineteenth-century grammarians justified such grammatical rules by citing masculine superiority as the 'natural' fact.[15] Deborah Cameron explains how, in a more gender-conscious world, it is grammar that has become naturalised:

... today, defenders of traditional androcentrism usually protest that it is 'just a fact about grammar' which is not intended to mark women's inferiority in the real world, and is not interpreted by reasonable people as doing so.... Thus a rule that was originally made on overtly ideological grounds (language should express the natural law of male superiority) can now be justified by portraying it as intrinsic to the structure of English and devoid of any ideological significance.[16]

For DuPlessis a major reason for her desire to 'rupture' the text is 'because of the gender contexts in which these words have lived, of which they taste'.[17] We see this in her treatment of 'she':

It is not surprising that	where in the placement of
	saffron this is simple 'you'
It is not surprising,	are listening 'I' am alert
that.	enough 'she' is learning how to
	talk 'we' are reconstituted.[18]

Here DuPlessis brings shifters under pressure, playing on their narrative suggestiveness, weighing the seemingly neutral logical 'it' ('It is not surprising that') against the shifting gender-mysterious 'I', 'you' and 'we'. The 'she' here who is learning how to talk, emphasises the female gendered being as the servant or pupil of language, an idea which recurs in DuPlessis's 'Draft 2 She'. In 'Draft 2 She' DuPlessis continues her investigation into femininity, not replacing or deepening 'It', but inter-weaving or folding (an image she often uses) into 'it'. The poem plays on the association of the feminine with pink which recurs throughout DuPlessis's poetry:

> There is a pink rib goes
> deep, up to the hilt,
>
> rose heart, bound.
> Between me? that?
> heavy-eyed light gazing.[19]

There is a sense of wounding here, via reference to the Adam and Eve myth. This wound has the power to divide the self as DuPlessis's defamiliarative 'Between me?' suggests, but the drafts are not just a lament or a pink plaint. DuPlessis quests for, as well as questions, the feminine gender, in part through her constant interrogation of the female shifter. In 'Draft 2: She', we can see this in action within a part of the poem which explores feminine identity through the mother-daughter relationship:

> That hard to write
> 'the mother'? to get that
> empty for that full
>
> mouth(e)
>
> her(e)
>
> sh(e)?
>
> ...
>
> The time inside, makes tracks, seems a small
> room lurches into the foreground, anger, throwing, some
> dash, power swirls up against MErock, pick it UP,
> Mommy me NEED
> it a push a touch a
> putsch pull a flailing kick a spool
> for her who is and makes thread
> 'I'
> The she that makes her her
> The she that makes me SHE[20]

Here the 'she' is both constant, hard-to-get repletion, likened to the total satisfaction of the mother's breast, but also the liberation of separation of mother and daughter into two separate 'shes'. The affirmation of the capitalised 'SHE' at the end of this extract suggests a unity between pronoun and subject. At the same time, the gendered 'she' seems to be in collision to some extent with 'me' in this piece and in a later draft, 'Me', the gendered distanced 'her memoirs' is flooded out by 'me':

> Lucid cool green twi-day (say) a struggle
> between different
> voices competing   don't use that, meaning
> that model that word to identify

things that this isn't it isn't my   voice

it?

A saturated brush it streaks and blots
a nursery easel struck
with spatter lines – what

speaks?

'me'–

her memoirs?

The big-mouth
bears came chasing me and made me
dash all dark–
far run of little me – and that started
some me screaming *of*
me, a tuneful tidal wave
of much engulfing light.

Do ray me
far so large.[21]

Here 'me' becomes 'far' and 'large' in a singing [fa so la], sweeping
wave of language reminiscent of the Kristevan semiotic.[22] This 'me' is
accessed through a simultaneous polysemous rejection and re-
inscription of alternative voices ('this / isn't it / isn't my / voice /
it?'). These possible 'me's are in turn suggestive of Kristeva's theory of the
'subject-in-process', or series of 'selvings' as DuPlessis herself calls it,
in her essay on 'Language Acquisition'.[23] This pluralised notion of
female selfhood, DuPlessis seems to suggest, might escape encapsula-
tion by perpetually rejecting imposed models of femininity.

In DuPlessis's work then we find a deep ambivalence regarding the
third person singular, 'she', an ambivalence which becomes a part of
her linguistic art of inter-layered deconstruction and recreation. We
see this ambivalence, after the moment of affirmation has passed, in
the ending of 'Draft 2: She':

Hold her unutterable.

And press another quire of girl bound in, bond in, for pink.
Draw drafts of 'milk' these words
are milk the point of this is
drink. (103)

The recurring pink image, the acute consciousness of the culturally constrained feminine, and the sense that the mother's arms are themselves a part of that binding, are all counter-balanced here by the sense of female intimacy within that binding. My final reading of these lines is that DuPlessis's drafts are themselves a way out of the predetermined gender trap; they are a nourishing milk, always exploring new ways to say 'she'.

Gender-mysterious pronouns

The deconstruction of 'I'

The poststructuralist deconstruction of stable accounts of identity and the experimental poets' rejection of the overweening lyric poetic persona form an interesting alliance with the feminist discomfort with the supposedly neutral first person singular. We saw this in the quote from DuPlessis' essay which began this piece and in the attempt of women poets to disrupt the traditional 'I/you' structure of the love lyric discussed earlier. Other women poets have expressed the same discomfort with subjectivity in poetry. This is from an essay by the poet and critic, Helen Kidd, who describes here her uneasy relationship to 'I':

> ... if I were to use the subject position 'I' confidently and authoritatively, my words would always begin to sound hollow to me. The implications of fixed authority and all its attendant rhetoric carried by the assertive 'I', leave me feeling that such an attitude begs the presence of an abyss ... underlying the brittle and temporary subject.[25]

Revealing her own post-structuralist context, Kidd goes on to describe the process of 'exploring the great shifter 'I' (157).

We do not have far to go to find the problematisation of 'I' in avant-garde women's poetry, concerned as it is with subjectivity and gender.

Here are some extracts from Denise Riley's poem, 'Slip', in which selfhood, in particular location in the body, keeps slipping away from the speaker and the reader of the poem:

> I am not my body, as much as I always am: could have stayed on
> that sand, gone coldly
> calm in the stare of the sea, and an opal incision of light where
> water slid under sky
> but could not hold still long enough into that speechlessness, was
> too loud to stay put in such death.
> ...
> I can't get to things there, I'm here, thrashing around in a meadow
> of my own
> that days won't end, that they will. Haul yourself hand over hand,
> along
> the months' strings. Haul yourself in like the washing....[26]

This piece plays on and questions the idea of 'writing the body'. Here Riley's 'I' finds a simultaneous difficulty in grasping hold of the bodily and the linguistic self. Both body and voice elude her yet simultaneously attract her as she attempts to break out of 'speechlessness' and, in an unmistakenly physical image, haul herself in like washing. The linguistic slippage in phrases that play on common cliche, like 'I am not ... as much as I always am' and 'that day's won't end', is characteristic of Riley and mirrors the slippage of self in the poem. Riley's 'I' in this poem is not linguistically gendered, though all signs say that she is feminine, but she must struggle to achieve this against the masculinity of the traditional lyric I or Kidd's 'great shifter "I"'. As Frances Presley points out in her essay '"The Grace of Being Common": The Search for the Implicit Subject in the Work of Denise Riley', Riley's poetry enacts a long struggle with the lyric 'I', striving toward a democratic female vision which ultimately goes beyond 'I' or 'she', in places escaping the pronominal 'grid' altogether.[27]

The association of 'I' with the masculine is one to be found amongst avant-garde women writers throughout the twentieth century. In 1929 in *A Room of One's Own* Virginia Woolf remarks on the shadow of an 'I' that lies across the page of the male novel and obliterates all else, be it landscape, tree or woman: 'Not but what this "I" was a most respectable "I"; honest and logical; as hard as a nut, and polished for centuries by good teaching and good feeding', she acerbically remarks.[28] This well-nourished 'I' of the literary world cannot be, the implication is, the same feminine 'I' which struggles to gain a foothold and to create what Woolf was to call a 'feminine sentence'. One simple formal technique for disturbing this 'I' is the use of the lowercase 'i'. Although this is less common in the nineties than the sixties (when Anglo-American men as well as women employed it), we still find it in the work of some women poets. Nicole Brossard, and Ntozake Shange both use the lowercase 'i' in their work, as I discuss below.

One of the most notable and angry attacks on the androcentric 'I' was made by Monique Wittig in the introduction to *The Lesbian Body* (1973), a text which could be described as prose-poetry.[29] Wittig created her own slashed 'j/e' (translated *I* , *m/e, m/y* in the English edition) in an attempt to distinguish a specifically female 'I':

> 'I' [*Je*] as a generic feminine subject can *only* enter by force into a language which is foreign to it, the human not being feminine grammatically speaking but he [*il*] or they [*ils*] ... 'I' [*Je*] obliterates the fact that *elle* or *elles* are submerged in *il* or *ills....* But the 'I' [*Je*] who writes is driven back to her specific experience as subject. The 'I' [*Je*] who writes is alien to her own writing at every word because this 'I' [*Je*] uses a language alien to her ... *J/e* is the symbol of the lived, rending experience which is m/y writing, of this cutting in two which throughout literature is the exercise of a language which does not constitute m/e as subject. (10–11)

It is this frustration with the masculinity of the supposed non-gender-specific pronoun which fuels the desire for sexed pronouns amongst writers, theorists and linguists, particularly in France where the masculinity of the pronoun structure is of course more marked.

The theoretical argument in favour of the sexed pronoun has recently been made most powerfully in Luce Irigaray's 1993 book *je, tu, nous: Toward a Culture of Difference* (the book to which Cameron refers above).[30] Here Irigaray argues passionately for the need for a 'sexed culture' (15–16). She makes clear that values which are said to be 'universal' in our culture are in fact exclusively masculine, and that in order to recover the feminine we need a 'transformation of language and culture ... the nature of which we can barely conceive' (16, 19, 21). In the section entitled 'How She Became Not-He', Irigaray illustrates the ways in which patriarchal culture is 'marked in the deep economy of language' (20). This of course includes pronouns, along with the gendering of words and division into grammatical classes. Interestingly, Irigaray traces all this back to the male appropriation of the divine and casting of himself as the 'Word made flesh' the new power (20, 67–8). Ultimately Irigaray's point about language is that grammatical gender is never arbitrary. There is no neutral position in language; such a position is always a 'loss of sexed subjective identity' (21). Along with new laws to valorise sexual difference (22), Irigaray argues that we also need new ways to say 'I', 'you' and 'we' and for those words to be gendered feminine:

> It would be better if women, without ceasing to put sexual difference into words, were more able to situate themselves as *I, I-she / they (je-elle[s])*, to represent themselves as subjects, and to talk to other women. (33)

If they do not, Irigaray makes painfully clear, then discourse, conversation, exchange with the other, will always be dominated by the masculine 'norm' (33–4).[31] What the language lacks, she argues, is the ability for the female speaker to move from 'you' to 'she' to 'I' and that this represents a 'loss of sexual identity in the relation to herself and to her gender, especially genealogically' (as the first you, the mother, is erased by this lack of a gendered you) (34). This sense that women need to forge a female genealogy or genre through language is central to Irigaray's argument.[32]

Creating a feminine genre

Elizabeth Hirsh, in a stimulating essay on Irigaray and the poet Adrienne Rich, has linked the Irigarayan forging of a feminine genre with Rich's poetry.[33] Rich is a rather more conventional poet than those discussed here and the examples Hirsh cites are not always *linguistically* interesting, but the following lines from Rich's famous poem 'Diving into the Wreck' are clearly relevant to this discussion of shifters:

> We circle silently
> about the wreck
> we dive into the hold.
> I am she: I am he
>
> . . .
>
> We are, I am, you are
> by cowardice or courage
> the one who finds our way
> back to this scene. . . .[34]

Here it is important to note how Rich shifts and defamiliarises pronouns in order to lead the reader to consider female experience as a common one between us (speaker, other, writer and reader). As Hirsh succinctly notes, '"[t]his scene" is above all the place of meeting between "we," "I," and "you"'.[35] Hirsh, however, keen to build up her picture of Rich as Irigarayan in her creation of a feminine genre, does not quote the first four lines in full. Whilst in general I agree with her view of Rich, the androgynous implications of the first four lines should not be glossed over. They raise the question of the gender exclusivity of gendered pronouns which is surely relevant at a time when gender is increasingly commonly perceived as constructed rather than given.

In some of the most radically feminist poetry of the contemporary scene we do, however, find the unadulterated Irigarayan craving to create a feminine genre. In such poets there is a more sustained consciousness of the need for a shift in linguistics. Nicole Brossard, the French Canadian poet and novelist, writes within a lesbian context, making the sex of usually unsexed pronouns clear by textual references to the feminine, and by manipulating French sex-indeterminate pronouns and references. Brossard's book, *Amantes*, for instance insists on its feminine context by the addition of an 'e'. Her translator, Barbara Godard, has recreated this by the insertion of a feminine pronoun into an ungendered English word, thus creating *Lovhers* as the English title for the book.[36] As the title suggests, Brossard's writing strives continually, consciously and playfully, toward the creation of an exclusively feminine and lesbian genre in writing: what she calls '*my continent woman*' (90). This extract is from *My Continent*:

> my continent of spaces of reason and
> (of love) like a history of space
> where we can speak concretely
> about allegiance and caresses in silence
> a form of reverberation/i cut across
> cities without stimulating *nature* because
> i'm so civilized before the sea
> at flood tide, persistent / i read ... (91)

This characteristically fluid piece employs 'i' and 'we': these shifters, along with 'you' are the most commonly employed by Brossard, who feminises them into her continent or context of the feminine.

The African-American poet, dancer, playwright and novelist Ntozake Shange seems to me, like Brossard, to be engaged in creating a feminine genre. The use of the lowercase 'i' by both writers is clearly significant in their attempt to create a radical female democracy, since it places the 'i' on the same level as the 'we' and 'you'. Shange, when asked why she uses the lowercase, replied that she finds capitalisation 'boring' and that she 'like[s]' the idea that letters dance'.[37] This, too, is important, coming as it does from a writer whose primary concern is to capture the voices and bodies of her own people in word and action.

It is in her choreopoem, *for coloured girls who have considered suicide when the rainbow is enuf*, that Shange is most successful at creating a series of voices to represent the female genre and genealogy called for by Irigaray.[38] Shange's piece is performed by a group of 'ladies' dressed in different colours who speak, dance and act together and apart; she has then set up a female context. Interviews suggest that the imperative for Shange is to draw out a genre of women whose subjectivity as individuals and as a group was in danger, the precise conditions that Irigaray sees affecting the women she writes about. In Shange's case the genre is also cultural; it is the African-American woman whose 'continent' she explores. She writes from a position of responsibility as an older woman to younger girls:

> The reason that *For Coloured Girls* is entitled *For Coloured Girls* is that that's who it was for. I wanted them to have the information that I did not have. I wanted them to know what it was truthfully like to be a grown woman. I didn't know. All I had was a bunch of mythology – tales and outright lies.[39]

It is the cultural element of Shange's work which is usually the focus of critical attention. Yet, as Gabriele Griffin has begun to show in an essay on 'writing the body' which makes reference to Shange, we should not neglect her revolutionary form.[40] The choreopoem begins with seven women on stage but only one speaking, the emblematic 'lady in brown' who begins and ends the piece:

> dark phrases of womanhood
> of never havin been a girl
> half-notes scattered
> without rhythm/ no tune
> distraught laughter fallin
> over a black's girl's shoulder

it's funny/ it's hysterical
the melody-less-ness of her dance
don't tell nobody don't tell a soul
she's dancin on beer cans & shingles

this must be the spook house
another song with no singers
lyrics/ no voices
& interrrupted solos
unseen performances

are we ghouls?
children of horror?
the joke?

don't tell nobody don't tell a soul
are we animals? have we gone crazy?

i can't hear anythin
but maddening screams
& the soft strains of death
& you promised me
you promised me ...
somebody/ anybody
sing a black girl's song
bring her out
to know herself
to know you
but sing her rhythms
carin/ struggle/ hard times
sing her song of life
she's been dead so long
closed in silence so long
she doesn't know the sound
of her own voice
her infinite beauty
she's half-notes scattered
without rhythm/ no tune
sing her sighs
sing the song of her possibilities
sing a righteous gospel

the makin of a melody
let her be born
let her be born
        & handled warmly.[41]

In this piece, a generic hybrid of blues and ritual invocation, Shange explores and enacts loss of identity and birth of identity for the African-American woman. The images she uses, that of the girl as a dancer, a singer, and a song, grow organically out of her form. Her context is made clear by the references to 'womanhood' and 'girl' early on, once again suggesting the genre of woman. The speaker in this poem shifts from the position of observer (using the neutral 'it's' about the image of the dancing girl), to a more involved position as one of the genre of women (using the first person plural, 'we'), to the first person singular, 'i' (but not a capitalised superior 'I'), and then, distancing herself again, to the third person singular, 'she'. The speaker, by her shifting pronominal positions and the ladies' lack of names, emphasizes the generic experience of the African-American woman, yet at the same time allows space for individual experience to be articulated. This continues throughout the choreopoem. After this piece, for instance, the ladies who have remained on stage throughout assert their individuality by declaring their places of origin as in:

> *lady in brown*
> i'm outside chicago
>
> *lady in yellow*
> i'm outside detroit
>
> *lady in purple*
> i'm outside houston (5)

While the different places mentioned here give the ladies specificity, anchoring them in the realism of time and place, the fact that the word 'outside' can be taken non-geographically to suggest their marginal position in society suggests a commonality, which is reinforced by the identical structure of their sentences. Equally, the colours of the ladies suggest difference and yet, at the same time, the image of the rainbow, which recurs throughout the poem, suggests that these colours come together. The rest of *for coloured girls* shifts between: first person singular narratives spoken by one lady; conversations or narratives built up between the ladies; stories about women narrated in the third person singular, and first person plural statements like 'we gotta dance to keep from crying'. In addition, the ladies sing and dance alone and as a group, chanting lines in the first person which clearly refer to all, and enacting scenes described, by one, again for all. The shifting pronouns and speaking positions, taken with the figure of the dance which accentuates one and then becomes all again, create in Shange's choreo-poem a feminine gender and genre through voice and movement.

I have looked at a diverse group of poets here, united only by a degree of formal experimentation, yet all regarding the shifter as an element of language in need of interrogation. In all these poetries, these nominatives without a name, referees without referents, become highly charged. Whether gender-specific or gender-mysterious, their usage by women poets has created a challenge to androcentric language at least as powerful, and often more subtle, than that of linguists. These poets are also united by the push in their work to recreate as well as deconstruct, to seek generic expression for self (both reader and writer) through their playful manipulation of the English language. As Rachel Blau DuPlessis writes:

I am a GEN$\left\{{der \atop re}\right.$ made by the writing; I am a GEN$\left\{{der \atop re}\right.$ read in the writing.[42]

Acknowledgements

Grateful thanks to the poets whose poetry is reproduced here for permission to reprint their work. All rights granted by the authors' permission and all copyright remains with the authors. Rachel Blau DuPlessis's works published by Potes and Poets Press are available from SPD, 1341 Seventh St., Berkeley, CA 94710-1403, USA (spd@igc, apc.org). UK rights to reprint material from Ntozake Shange's *for coloured girls who have considered suicide when the rainbow is enuf* granted by Methuen Publishers and US rights reprinted with the permission of Simon & Schuster from *for coloured girls who have considered suicide when the rainbow is enuf* by Ntozake Shange. Copyright © 1975, 1976, 1977 by Ntozake Shange.

Notes

1. Rachel Blau DuPlessis, 'Otherhow', in *The Pink Guitar: Writing as Feminist Practice* (London and New York: Routledge, 1990), p. 149.
2. 'Prescriptive grammar' defines grammar as taught in schools as opposed to 'descriptive grammar', which defines grammar as used in society and analysed by most linguists (Ann Bodine, 'Androcentrism in Prescriptive Grammar: Singular "They", Sex-Indefinite "He", and "He or She"', in Deborah Cameron, ed., *The Feminist Critique of Language:* A Reader, 2nd edn (London: Routledge, 1998), p. 124. As Black and Coward point out, it is in prescriptive grammar that the problem of androcentricity of language rules is often rooted and it is here that change is needed (Maria Black and Rosalind Coward, 'Linguistic, Social and Sexual Relations: A Review of Dale Spender's *Man Made Language*, in Cameron, *The Feminist Critique of Language*, p. 106). Grammar as used in society is often less sexist. Bodine gives the example of the use of the singular 'they' commonly used instead of the generic 'he' (as in 'Anyone can do it if they try hard enough'), but she points out how the singular 'they' has been persistently attacked by prescriptive grammarians as incorrect (Bodine, pp. 125–8).
3. Susan Ehrlich and Ruth King, 'Gender-Based Language Reform and the Social Construction of Meaning', in Cameron, *The Feminist Critique of Language*, pp. 164–79.
4. Roland Barthes, *Elements of Semiology* (1964), trans. Annette Lavers and Colin Smitt (London: Jonathan Cape, 1967), p. 22–3.
5. Cameron, *The Feminist Critique of Language*, p. 84–5.
6. Frances Presley, *Hula Hoop* (London: The Other Press, 1993), p. 31.
7. Frances Presley, *Linocut* (London: Oasis Books, 1997), p. 38.
8. Rosemarie Waldrop, *Lawn of Excluded Middle* (Providence, RI: Tender Buttons, 1993), p. 48.
9. Mei-Mei Berssenbrugge, *The Heat Bird* (Providence, RI: Burning Deck, 1983).
10. Fanny Howe, *O'Clock* (London and Suffolk: Reality Street Editions, 1995), p. 49.
11. Denise Riley, *Dry Air* (London: Virago Press, 1985), p. 7.
12. Rachel Blau DuPlessis, 'Writing', *Tabula Rosa* (Elmwood, CT: Potes and Poets Press, 1987), p. 62.
13. Rachel Blau DuPlessis, 'Schwa', *Drafts 3–14* (Elmwood, CT: Potes and Poets Press, 1991), p. 65.
14. Rachel Blau DuPlessis, 'Draft 1: It', in *Tabula Rosa*, p. 92.
15. Anne Bodine, 'Androcentrism in Prescriptive Grammar', in Cameron, *The Feminist Critique of Language*, pp. 127–9.
16. Cameron, *The Feminist Critique of Language*, pp. 84–5.
17. Rachel Blau DuPlessis, 'Otherhow', in *The Pink Guitar*, p. 144.
18. Rachel Blau DuPlessis, 'Draft 1: It', p. 88.
19. Rachel Blau DuPlessis, 'Draft 2: She', in *Tabula Rosa*, p. 99.
20. Ibid., pp. 100–2.
21. Rachel Blau DuPlessis, 'Me', in *Drafts 3–14*, pp. 23–4.
22. See Julia Kristeva, *Revolution in Poetic Language*, trans. Margaret Waller (New York: Columbia University Press, 1984).

23. DuPlessis, *The Pink Guitar*, p. 99.
24. 'Draft 2: She', p. 103.
25. Helen Kidd, 'The Paper City: Women Writing and Experience', in *New British Poetries: The Scope of the Possible*, ed. Robert Hampson and Peter Barry (Manchester: Manchester University Press, 1993), p. 157.
26. Maggie O'Sullivan, ed., *Out of Everywhere: Linguistically Innovative Poetry by Women in North America and the UK* (London: Reality Street Editions, 1996) pp. 84–5.
27. Frances Presley, '"The Grace of Being Common": The Search for the Implicit Subject in the Work of Denise Riley', Southfields 5 (1999), pp. 47–54.
28. Virginia Woolf, *A Room of One's Own* (London: Hogarth Press, 1929), p. 150.
29. Monique Wittig, *The Lesbian Body* (1973), trans. David Le Vay (Boston: Beacon Press, 1986).
30. Luce Irigaray, *je, tu, nous: Toward a Culture of Difference*, trans. Alison Martin (New York and London: Routledge, 1993).
31. Irigaray points out that women will have to remain among themselves for the plural to be feminine (*elles*) – an option which does not of course exist in English, where 'they' is 'neutral'.
32. Although not all of Irigaray's examples are fully relevant to the English language, her basic philosophy is easily translatable into that language; we have already seen examples of it discussed by the Anglo-American linguists mentioned above. Indeed, Irigaray herself takes Anglo-Saxon and Gerrmanic feminists to task for thinking that they can be liberated by sexed possession of e.g. '*her (sa)* post' and '*her (sa)* book' – instead of owner-ship, she argues, we should be seeking existence as 'free female *subjects*' (p. 72).
33. Elizabeth Hirsh, 'Another Look at Genre: *Diving into the Wreck* of Ethics with Rich and Irigaray', in *Feminist Measures: Soundings in Poetry and Theory*, ed. Lynn Keller and Cristianne Miller (Ann Arbor: University of Michigan Press, 1994), pp. 117–38.
34. Adrienne Rich, *The Fact of a Doorframe: Poems Selected and New 1950–1984* (New York and London: W.W. Norton, 1984), p. 164.
35. Hirsh, 'Another Look at Genre', p. 134.
36. Nicole Brossard, *Lovhers*, trans. Barbara Godard (Montreal: Guernica, 1987).
37. Claudia Tate, ed., *Black Women Writers at Work* (Harpenden, Herts: Oldcastle Books, 1985), p. 163.
38. Ntozake Shange, *for coloured girls who have considered suicide when the rainbow is enuf* (1977) (London: Methuen, 1985).
39. Tate, *Black Women Writers at Work*, pp. 161–2.
40. Gabriele Griffin, '"Writing the Body": Reading Joan Riley, Grace Nichols and Ntozake Shange', in *Black Women's Writing*, ed. Gina Wisker (London: Macmillan, 1993), pp. 19–42.
41. Shange, *for coloured girls*, pp. 3–5.
42. Rachel Blau DuPlessis, 'Otherhow', p. 156

Index